FRANK WRIGHT

NORTHERN IRELAND

A Comparative Analysis

Gill and Macmillan

Barnes & Noble Books
Totowa, New Jersey

Published in Ireland by
Gill and Macmillan Ltd
Goldenbridge
Dublin 8
with associated companies in
Auckland, Dallas, Delhi, Hong Kong
Johannesburg, Lagos, London, Manzini
Melbourne, Nairobi, New York, Singapore
Tokyo, Washington
© Frank Wright 1987
0 7171 1428 7
Print origination in Ireland by
John Augustine Ltd, Dublin
Printed in Great Britain by
The Camelot Press, Southampton

British Library of Congress Cataloguing in Publication Data
Wright, Frank
　Northern Ireland: a comparative analysis.
　1. Northern Ireland—Social conditions
　I. Title
　941.608　HN398.N6
　ISBN 0-7171-1428-7

First published in the USA 1988 by
Barnes & Noble Books
81 Adams Drive
Totowa, New Jersey 07512
0-389-20769-1

Contents

Maps

1. *Province of Ulster, showing the boundary between Northern Ireland and the Republic and places named in the text. The shaded area indicates where more than one-third of rural adult males were engaged in clothing manufacturing, rather than agriculture, in 1851.*

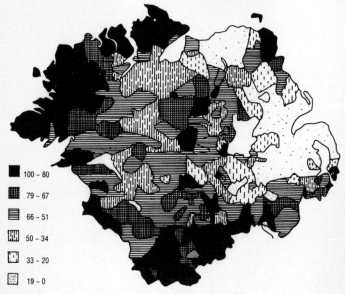

2. *Proportions of Roman Catholics in rural parishes in 1861.*

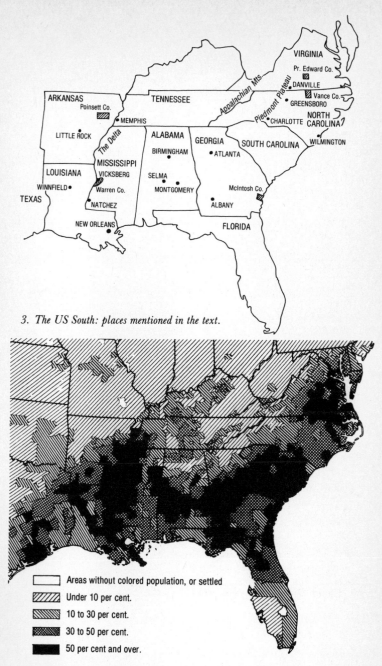

3. *The US South: places mentioned in the text.*

Areas without colored population, or settled

////// Under 10 per cent.

10 to 30 per cent.

30 to 50 per cent.

50 per cent and over.

4. *Proportion of coloured people by county in 1900. (Source: C.O. Paullin,* Atlas of Historical Geography of the United States.*)*

5. Eastern Europe, 1900: places mentioned in the text.

Preface

'Why do you need to teach politics here?' said a friend of mine when he learnt what I do for a living. 'Sure we're all born with that around here.' It's a good question and I am not sure whether I've got a decent answer.

I have met people who have been deeply wounded by things that have happened to them. The conflict in Northern Ireland encourages apathy in many and a grim determination in many others that 'they' must be stopped/defeated. Most people don't seem very 'bigoted' until they are provoked by remarks that are insensitive to the losses of their friends and neighbours—and anyone who wants to call that bigotry had better be careful with 'first stones'.

But if people in Northern Ireland manage to find a way of coexisting together that is qualitatively superior to the order of pre-1968, in spite of the nationality division between them, it will be a major achievement. If they fail it won't be for lack of legions of people trying in inevitably contradictory ways. Most of this book is about the frankly unoptimistic related experiences of other parts of the world—it is political. But the purpose is to focus more sharply on the shafts of light.

Once upon a time Algeria was part of France, much of present day Poland was part of Germany, present day Czechoslovakia was part of Austria, as the southern States are part of the United States of America and Northern Ireland is part of the United Kingdom. These were the largest imperial powers in the process of developing capitalism and democracy. There are many places that a comparative study of Northern Ireland might include, but these cases have one important feature in common. Being parts of the proclaimed territories of big powers has shaped the relationships between French and Moslems (Algeria), whites and blacks (USA), Germans and Polish nationalists (Poznan, West Prussia), German Austrians and Czech nationalists (Bohemia), Ulster unionists and Irish nationalists (North of Ireland) in somewhat similar ways. Within Northern Ireland today it is very easy to feel that what is happening inside it is quite unique—which in one sense it is, as all societies are unique—and even amongst students of politics and history it is not uncommon to find the world 'outside' looked to as an anchor of sanity. Yet talking with visiting groups, discussions about Northern Ireland seem to strike home when they take root also in their experience; then all of us begin to discover more about ourselves.

The sense of nationality does not raise very big problems for people from nationally homogeneous areas (who I shall call metropolitans) for the very simple reason that it has few implications in everyday life that they are aware of; most people they come in contact with are citizens of a common nationality sharing a crudely similar national citizen status to themselves. For all its actual deformities a common secular authority over them blurs the question of how far their relations with each other are shaped by this uniform 'national' identity and how far by beliefs in the oneness of humanity. Where this benign accident is missing, as it is when a society is internally fractured by some kind of force relationship, all sorts of dilemmas appear which metropolitans do not experience. A large part of this work is concerned with communicating between the metropolitan and frontier experience.

There is a big difference between seeing the injustice perpetrated through the existence of force relationships and moral judgments about people trapped in their core. Rationalistic understanding often fastens onto concepts such as 'colonialism', 'racism', 'fascism', 'self-determination of nations' (one or two!) and having done so, may read backwards into the situation all manner of motives and interests which are perceived as necessary ingredients of the chosen explanation. In doing so they fail to see that what they are doing is erecting a moral barrier between themselves and whatever people they find guilty of the 'problem'. It is not that the use of these concepts is necessarily out of place. What is out of place is the romantic illusion that divides the world into guilty and innocent parties. One of the implications of René Girard's *Violence and the Sacred* seems to me to be that it is only the sacred qualities of metropolitan institutional order that allow people to believe in their own innocence with a 'good conscience'. This reduces the temptations to engage in militant self-righteousness. But it also tends to suppress the awareness that the oneness of humanity creates obligations we can only begin to shoulder when we first recognise our radical inadequacy to do so.

Common to all of these societies of the frontier was the absence of anything that metropolitans call peace. At best they enjoyed a tranquillity of communal deterrence (ch. 6). The differences between the force relationships operating in the frontier societies looked at here are very real. In the US southern case, to even speak of communal deterrence between whites and blacks only makes any sense at all when we look at the way in which the absence of sacred order allowed vigilante anxieties about black rebellion to generate its own rationalisations. In both the US South and in Algeria, the material inequalities between the ethnic blocs were drastic by contrast with anything evident in the national conflict border lands of Britain and Germany. But the point of the analysis is that once a force field has been generated, it breaks up nearly all the mechanisms that might cancel it. Antagonism—which means being on different ends of a force relationship—is more fundamental than all the various 'things' the antagonism keeps for the dominant and denies to the dominated. The more residual these 'things' are, the more they cause both sides—dominant and dominated—to settle into a circular pattern of violence and response. National conflict strengthens the circle, because the dominated assert themselves as representatives of an alternative metropolis. Thus they are asserting a radical equality with the dominated. In these circumstances, the existing metropolitan power is rendered almost powerless to break the circle.

There are probably some who will see an implied judgment

in making comparisons with German border lands (that eventually produced Nazism) or the situations of racial segregation in the US South and colonialism in Algeria. But there will also be others who for exactly opposite reasons find my treatment of Nazism, white supremacy and Algerian colonisation less heavily laden with moral disapproval than they think proper. No writer can ever be quite sure how what they say is taken up. For example, once upon a time I very nearly changed the opinion of one southern white man about the virtues of Irish unification by explaining the similarities between the position of Irish Catholics and southern blacks—not in the way that I had intended at all. At the end of my remarks, as he sat in thoughtful silence, he eventually said 'Do you mean to tell me that most of the Catholics in Northern Ireland are black?' My purpose in making these comparisons can better be explained by an occasion when a well-known Irish Socialist Republican writer drew out all my own national egoism by arguing (with his tongue in his cheek) that it really was a matter of indifference whether British or German Imperialism triumphed in the Second World War. I detonated, in much the same way that nationalists and unionists in Northern Ireland occasionally detonate each other by arguing the respective merits of their mutually contradictory national causes. It was not long before I heard myself straying from the evils of Nazism to defending (albeit comparatively) all manner of dubious features of the British Empire.

No national power ever has more than a conditional claim to be the guardian of justice. All national self-affirmation is hypocritical. Nowhere is this more true than in nations' relationships with nationalities or ethnic groups that have been shaped in antagonism with themselves on their frontiers. Once no authority has fully legitimate power, any political prescriptions necessarily run the risk of advocating things that inflict injury upon others. I am well aware that my chapter (ch. 9) in which I argue in favour of the 1985 Anglo-Irish Agreement does this. I shall try to show how without some kind of authority that depends upon both the British and Irish governments, there will be no authority in Northern Ireland at all—and therefore a total chaos, more like Cyprus or

Lebanon than the eventually redeemed Algeria. At the same time the very process of moving toward a system of authority that is equidistant between the two communities maximises the *immediate* risk of chaos. This judgment, whether I am right or wrong about it, is political. It is part of the chaos of force relationships and the only thing that can be said in its favour is that I believe it to be the context in which the least illegitimate secular authority can take root that the reconciling forces in this society will flourish. Many others with the same kind of concerns that I have expressed would strongly disagree. Where the legitimacy of authority is undermined by a force-field, political judgments and reconciling faith are radically different things.

Taking risks, discounting what may be quite 'rational' suspicions of others, and in a quiet way softening, qualifying or even repudiating the antagonism at the summit is anti-political. It is a refusal to accept the charge so often made that acts of reconciliation are 'ineffective' or 'insignificant'. There may be a political and a reconciling part in each of us—but the first is opinion with all its imposing implications and the second is the way we live without imposing.

Having been teaching in and about Northern Ireland for thirteen years, I think I came here believing that there was some higher political wisdom that could unravel it if only it could be found. And I owe this confession to many people who spoke to me with unashamed doubts and contradictions about what they felt, that often I did not hear them and listened instead for the decisive statements of political certainty. It was not until Roel Kaptein taught me about the possible implications of the work of René Girard that I understood what I gradually suspected but never altogether recognised, that there are such things as crises which are about everything and nothing at the same time and which can develop into a chaos which makes a nonsense of everything they are ostensibly about.

It is usual when thanking people for the help they have given to acquit them of any responsibility for the final product. In this case, although the faults of this work are obviously entirely my own and the political judgments exclusively so, any positive qualities it may have depend upon its having evolved in relationships with others. Through the Corrymeela Community I have come to understand that the worship of 'decisiveness' and 'effectiveness' is destructive of all hope of reconciliation. It is a part of the chaos itself, differing only in degree and possible consequences from more overtly destructive searches for decisiveness and effectiveness. It is only an accident that in many or most other political situations this particular temptation is any the less dangerous than it is here. I hope that the comparative approach used here will help to illustrate that point.

Finally words of thanks to my MSSc and special subject students at Queen's University and to Adrian Guelke, with whom I have done a lot of team teaching that has put many ideas into my head; to Richard Jay and Mervyn Love who have several times ploughed through various drafts of this book and forced me to sort out things which—when I read them over again now—read like cement or at best thick mud; to Paul Bew and Professors John Whyte, Cornelius O'Leary and Bowyer Bell for encouragement; to Marie Smyth, Margaret Ward, David Goldey, Philip Williams, Alan Laurie, Gillian Rose, Brendan and Sheila McAllister, Alan Falconer, Dr David Hadden, Dr Patrick Bell, Mary Gregory, Maura Kiely, Helen, Harry and Mike Lewis, Angus and Lois McPherson, Shirley and Duncan Morrow, Kathleen Davey, Heather and Alistair Kilgore, Mick Cox, Derek and Dot Wilson, Mathilde and David Stevens, Douglas and Erina McIldoon, my sister, my parents and my neighbours, who have all guided and sustained me in different ways. There are many others I would like to thank, but the list would be endless, so finally thanks also to Margaret McBride for helping me read some French language sources; to Ann Briggs and Debbie Dalzell for typing and editing; to John Morrow and Ray Davey and the Corrymeela Community and to Roel Kaptein for light; and to Fergal Tobin, my editor at Gill and Macmillan, for persistent and always acute demands for clarification of obscurities and for surgery upon what I presented as a final text.

Ballycastle 1987

1

The Ethnic Frontier and the Metropolis

THE BEGINNING OF THE MODERN ERA
IN THE ETHNIC FRONTIER

The places I call ethnic frontiers are places where the populations of citizen and native were fairly evenly balanced numerically. Whether settlement was of recent origin (as in much of West Prussia in 1772) or of much older character (Bohemia and Ulster from the seventeenth century), the citizen (Protestant in Ulster, German in West Prussia and Bohemia) population was not only the overwhelming element in landed, urban propertied or office-holding strata, but also comprised a great part of the lower strata of peasants and artisans. Where the citizen population was so numerous, it was relatively easy for it either to assimilate or exclude natives (Irish Catholics, Poles or Czechs) in urban and commercial society. Even if long established legal restrictions fell into disuse, what mattered was that the citizen society was strong enough in principle to obstruct native efforts at self-organisation.

The Polish and Czech languages, like Roman Catholicism in Ireland, became hallmarks of nineteenth-century nationalisms because at some time or other deliberate efforts had been made to eradicate them. The Irish language receded rapidly in the late eighteenth and early nineteenth centuries as English became the language of commerce and urban intercourse, whereas Catholicism was subject to penalties of law until the 1780s and 1790s. It was Catholicism and not the Irish language which was the bond of Irish nationalism in the nineteenth century. The rise of German as the language of commerce in much of the eastern German lands pushed back the Polish language but the spreading of German by coercive acts of state power generated Polish resistance from the 1760s onwards. Czech remained a language of peasants which was usually shed upon entry into the towns; the rise of Czech nationalism is directly related to efforts to continue this development once it became necessary to enforce it.[1]

The onset of capitalist economic relationships, the extension of centralised state power in opposition to landlords who had previously been the only power in their domains, and eventually democratisation opened up spaces for the native society. The ethnic frontier zones tended to experience the stirring of capitalist development before neighbouring areas of native concentration, partly because citizen status of large sections of their populations freed them of legal risks in economic life. Thus, for example, even when the penal laws fell into general disuse in Ireland, the Ulster bleaching trade—which required heavy investment in fixed immovable assets—was virtually the exclusive preserve of Protestants who could legally acquire long leases. The early economic development in the German northern ring of Bohemia contrasted with the preservation of feudal agricultural relations in central Bohemia. In the areas of Poland absorbed with Prussia, German peasants had been encouraged to immigrate even under the Polish Kingdom in order to provide peasant farmers to tend livestock and bring marshland into cultivation without rupturing the feudal relations between Polish landlord and peasant.[2] But the expansion of commercial relationships between urban and rural society, and the increase in the relative size and importance of towns, ensured that *de facto* dominance of the citizen element could no longer be preserved without more visible and conscious effort. At some point or points in time, this generated a crisis around the question 'Where do the "native" people belong in the new order?'.

I call this crisis one of assimilation. Once it occurred it obliged the native society to build up its own middle-class infrastructure of teachers, clergy, retailers and professionals to replicate the citizen society about them. This strategy the Polish nationalists called 'organic work'[3] and the term can be applied more generally to early native nationalism in ethnic frontiers.

In all three societies in the early nineteenth century, landlords frequently patronised the native culture. In Bohemia they patronised Czech as a way of resisting centralising influences of German bureaucracy; in Ulster, landlords patronised Catholics as peasant voting cohorts; and even in Posen, which was incorporated into Prussia only in 1816, Polish landlords' encouragement of Polish was motivated by a fear that Prussian centralisation would eradicate their limited local autonomy.[4] In none of these cases can we see an exercise of popular self-assertion by the natives themselves. It may indeed be very difficult to pinpoint occasions when collective native self-assertion begins; but by paying attention to the role of education in building up native 'organic work', it is possible to see the shape of the issues involved.

The most notable feature of organic work is the development of an educational system within which the mark of stigma is no longer a stigma but a point of pride. Education is not something children choose for themselves, but something parents choose for their children. In the pre-modern era, when towns and commerce were open only to those who could enter the citizen culture, learning the citizen language might be seen as a mere acquisition of a tool. 'The need or desire for communication produced bilingualism,' said Hagen of the Prussian East.[5] Going to a school run by the citizen religion would create no problem so long as the school did not visibly attack the native religion of the parent.

It became another question when those with power over educational institutions started declaring as their purpose the eradication of the 'inferior', 'reactionary', or 'superstitious' culture of the natives by 'enlightening' the next generation of their children. This was a threat to the relationships between parents and children; a threat that the children would be taught to despise the values and, by extension, the persons of their parents. And such threats were uttered at precisely the historical moment when the parents were in a position to be able to do something about it. It was the evidence of growing native self-assertion, usually in areas beyond those of preponderant citizen population (Southern Ireland, central Bohemia) that first disturbed the assumption that native middle classes would be easily assimilated. The declarations of war against native culture were made at precisely the points when in fact that culture was in a position to defend itself.

Ernest Gellner, upon whose ideas the theme of assimilation crisis is here developed, stresses the growing importance of language facility in a modernising world where old structures (routine relationships) are breaking down, and where it becomes necessary to be able to communicate in unfamiliar and non-routine situations.[6] The difficulty with this present-ation is that it stresses the question of language as such, rather than the circumstances likely to promote the development of an educational system. My argument in relation to ethnic frontiers—zones where there were sound expedient reasons for being 'assimilated'—is that at some point new forces within the citizen society, principally the middle classes, begin to make strident noises about the *need* for assimilation in the very circumstances where they doubt their ability to secure it. Then they can only conceive of sustaining assimilation by methods that are humiliating and coercive, and which tend to revive the stigmatised nature of the native culture.

The three examples below are chosen to emphasise the point that the ostensible issues that generate an assimilation crisis may be entirely different from one situation to another. What all share in common is that sections of the citizen middle classes take stances that represent the native culture as something that ought to be liquidated, and in so doing set in motion a response amongst the native society to minimise their weakness.

In the 1820s, Whig landlords in Britain and Ireland, together with the elites of Irish Catholic society, broadly shared the view that Catholic emancipation (the right of Catholics to sit in the British parliament) should be exchanged for a British veto on Irish Catholic episcopal appointments. Daniel O'Connell's mass campaign for Catho-lic emancipation throughout Southern Ireland took the issue out of the hands of existing elites, and the opponents of Catholic emancipation started what they called the 'Second Reformation', hoping to deny full political rights to those who would not be converted to Protestantism. Until the 1820s the largely Protestant-endowed education system had provided the only funded education in Ireland. In Ulster, Catholics made use of it and there had been little sign of religious discord over educational issues. The 'Second Reformation', however, declared its purpose of using the educational system to 'enlighten' Catholic children, and large-scale Protestant support for it undermined the claims that these schools were not 'proselytising'.[7]

In the 1830s, Whig governments made efforts to conciliate the now powerful O'Connell-clerical bloc of MPs from Southern Ireland, and the National Education system was devised to provide an education free of proselytising possibilities. It was to be a centralised system providing funds for schools at the behest of local ministers and dignitaries, hopefully on a religiously-integrated basis, but not necessarily so if inter-religious co-operation was not forthcoming.[8]

In the North, Protestant opposition to the system crystallised against acceptance of the guardian status of Catholic clergy in relation to Catholic children's education. The effects of this crisis were lasting. Although many Protestants supported the National Educational system and co-operated with Catholics within it, it only secured widespread Protestant support after existing Protestant schools had established their right to join the system without having to recognise the 'visitor' role of Catholic clergy.[9]

When in later years the Catholic hierarchy sought to denominationalise the whole educational system, Northern Protestants began to defend the 'mixed' system for a very wide variety of reasons. Some held that mixed education was an intrinsic good that tempered religious animosities; others spoke of the need to combat 'superstition' and some supported it as a bulwark of Protestant power and the link with Britain. The sincerity of Protestant advocates of religious harmony does not have to be doubted for us to understand why Northern Catholic clergy and school managers were more impressed by the other two arguments as reasons for pursuing denominationalisation. And if these had not been strong enough, the fact that the educational advances achieved thus far had depended on the power of pan-Catholicism in the rest of Ireland was argument in itself for pan-Catholicism in the North of Ireland.[10]

The 1848 revolutions in the German States were a challenge

of rising middle classes to the power of monarchs and landlords. In Prussia, these new forces declared their support for the restoration of Poland; but mainly because Poland would act as a shield against the opposition of the Russian Tsar. When the Frankfurt parliament debated the Polish issue, however, two things emerged. First, they intended to keep all areas of Prussia with German majorities and the environs of the city of Posen (with Polish majorities) for strategic reasons. In this way Poland was to be restored at the expense of Russia primarily. Second, representatives from these areas revealed that German democratic sentiment might not differ much from that of the old oligarchs. Wilhelm Jordan observed how the German liking for Poles seemed to increase the further away it was from actual Poles (a reflection of the foreign policy angle of German support for Polish restoration). He accused Polish clergy and landlords of wanting to restore serfdom—'In the East ours has been the terrible misfortune of having been the conquerors'—and called for a 'healthy national egoism' in treatment of the Polish question.[11]

If there had been some sympathy for Polish claims, none existed for those of the Czechs. When the Czech historian Palacky informed the Frankfurt parliament that the Czechs were not part of the German nation, there was anger. And when Czechs supported the restoration of the Austrian autocracy against revolutionaries in Vienna, they drew the ire of the German radicals. Even Friedrich Engels, who regarded the restoration of Poland as an act of justice to a nationality that had shown itself to have democratic possibilities (the 1846 and 1848 revolts), could say of the Czechs that they were 'the fanatical representatives of the counter revolution . . . [remaining] . . . so until it is completely exterminated or denationalised, as its whole existence is in itself a protest against a great historical revolution'. He asked what kind of Slav state could be erected 'ultimately dominated by the German bourgeoisie of the towns'.[12]

If Engels' sentiments towards Czechs were widely shared by German middle-class and radical sentiment, it helps to understand the meaning of the declaration of the Czech cultural organisation, Sokol:

It is only when we have reached such a degree of

perfection as *to fear no comparison* with the foreigner that
we shall have fulfilled our duty to our own selves,

or, as Ladislav Rieger, the leader of the rising Czech nationalist movement, put it: 'The *less numerous* a nation is, the
greater must be its activity in self-affirmation.'[13]

Writers dealing with 1848 generally agree that it had a
profound effect upon the non-German nationalities of eastern
Europe. Up to that time the leaders of cultural nationalisms
had hoped that it was only German oligarchical power which
opposed them. In 1848 they discovered that the German
populace was scarcely more favourably disposed. The 'Second
Reformation' crisis had something of the same effect in Ulster,
for opposition to Catholic educational claims surfaced in areas
that had supported the 1798 rebellion in favour of equal rights
for all Irish people against the Anglican landlord system.[14]

What consequences flowed from the crystallisation of cultural distinctness? To begin with, it had wholly altered the
meaning of assimilation—which could no longer be regarded
as a 'pragmatic' question. It therefore polarised the embryonic native middle classes. An assimilated Czech said, 'If the
Czechs in Bohemia are made into Germans, that is in my view
no deadly sin, for they rise from a lower step to the sunny
height of a highly civilised nation. But to seek to Czechize the
Germans in Bohemia is quite another thing; that would be a
disgrace unheard of in the pages of world history.'[15]

A converted Irish Catholic, speaking of 'Popery', said 'Its
gentry and wealthy traders are beginning to regard the system
in which they were brought up as rich men regard poor
relations.'[16] The alternative response was the affirmation of
the native culture, which now required a more deliberate
effort to develop interdependence between the native middle
classes and the mass of native society. The interdependence
served the purposes of both. For the mass of native society,
'their' middle class provided services freeing them of dependence upon the citizen society. Whatever else this change
implied, their teachers, clergy, retailers etc. were only able to
exist if they behaved as servants of the community, rather
than its masters. By the same token for the middle classes, the
native masses were their clientele. Seen from a standpoint of

abstract rationalism (the common theme of citizen middle-class liberalism), this arrangement made little sense. But that was scarcely the point. The tranquillity of earlier times had depended upon natives accepting paternalistic liberality gratefully. The new order of 'organic work' confronted the disproportionate power of the citizen society by trying to create a climate in which liberality meant recognising people as people and not as dependents. Polish 'organic work' was thus described: 'If you are a shoemaker make better shoes . . . if you are a housewife make better and cleaner butter . . . than the Germans. In this way you save yourself and Poland. Learning, work, order and thrift, these are our new weapons.'[17]

Organic work in the ethnic frontier can only be regarded as a nationalism in a rather negative sense. Its effort to replicate the citizen society was intrinsically conservative, although it was bound to have some success because the native middle class would grow from its small beginnings relatively faster than the citizen middle class. Yet because the native society coexisted with a numerous citizen population, it had to balance two questionably reconcilable objectives. It needed to secure harmonious and equal co-existence, but it also faced citizen opposition. So, it had to be undogmatic (or opportunistic) about its choices of strategies and allies. In the long run, Ulster Catholics, Prussian Poles and Bohemian Czechs in the German zones were increasingly obliged to depend on their links with Irish Catholics, Austrian and Russian Poles and Czechs of central Bohemia, even when doing so had counter-productive effects on the citizen society about them.

While the rise of a native middle class in the ethnic frontier was the important first step toward equalising the powers of the citizen and native societies, it was also the occasion that gave these communities sharper definition. A related development also tending in an equalising direction was the eradication of institutional devices for protecting citizen labour from economic competition with native labour. Capitalist development tended to reduce all labour to a common status of wage labour and create circumstances that encouraged free movement of labour, placing all labourers in competition with each other. In its early phases it led to antagonistic competition between citizen and native labour. Eventually, once long-distance labour migration became a norm, native labour ceased to be prepared to work for less than citizen labour, and equal pay for equal work became a possible basis for class solidarity between them. We shall see later on that class solidarity was actually difficult to create and even more difficult to sustain as a political force in the face of territorialist antagonism.

In fact this tendency for accepted standards of subsistence of citizen and native to equalise was already an integral part of the character of the society, which the development of capitalism served to bring into sharper focus. Unlike the urban or elite strata of the citizen population, the mass of citizens were never very effectively protected from native competition by extra-economic prohibitions. The Irish penal laws, for example, were a virtual dead letter in this respect. The settlement colonising process had depended in the first place on the wars that created them, in the second on the immediate needs for labour (and particularly labour that only citizen immigrants could provide) in the aftermath of such wars, and in the third place on the preparedness of citizens to face economic competition of defeated and acquiescent natives. The major influx of Protestants into Ulster followed the wars that ended in 1691; but two decades later, when fully-developed farm holding leases expired, there began a massive exodus to the American colonies (which at the time had restrictions against Catholic immigration and settlement).[18] Generally speaking, citizen efforts to prevent displacement by natives only succeeded when the hostilities generalised themselves into total social crises (as in the 1790s in County Armagh). In the areas of Poland incorporated into Prussia between 1772 and 1815, the early economic development—the drainage of the Netze marshes and the growth of artisanship in towns—led to large-scale German immigration until the 1840s. Thereafter the east experienced chronic emigration, disproportionately of Germans.[19]

The lack of dependence of the citizen populations upon special institutional protection has important consequences. Firstly they became and remained the mass base of societies in whole geographical areas and their lack of such protection demonstrated that they had roots in the land virtually as strong as those of the natives. They had to endure in the long run on much the same terms. They were not therefore like nineteenth-century settlers (in Algeria, for example) whose presence could only be sustained if they were backed by institutional proscription of natives. Secondly, when they asserted their nationality as British or German, there was little basis upon which British or German peoples in the metropolis would regard them as different from themselves. They were to some metropolitans (perhaps embarrassingly) like the peoples of the metropolis and were to become more so as the metropolis became more enthusiastically committed to Imperialism—and its conception of antagonism between different races. Thirdly, the history of their societies generated a popular kind of settlement colonial legend. The settlement had survived because of its masses. State power had sometimes conciliated the natives, only to regret the error of its ways. Economically dominant citizens had greedily employed the natives as cheap labour, or encouraged them for their own political ends. But the only kind of leadership that was popular was that which recognised the enduring nature of battle against an unmitigated enemy; an enemy whose calculative accommodation (organic work) was seen as mere tactics disguising a conspiracy. In its most virulent forms this legend grew louder as it corresponded to the kind of territorialist antagonism of the democratic era.

The onset of capitalism tended to create space in which the native societies of the ethnic frontier could undermine established patterns of citizen dominance. But the process involved self-assertion that also sharpened the distinctions between 'citizen' and 'native' and increased possibilites for open antagonism. As political life was gradually democratised, the native middle classes and masses were to become more evenly matched against their citizen counterparts, but the pace of democratisation and institutional reform was set more or less by developments in the metropolis. While the metropolis experienced these changes as advances of popular class forces, in the ethnic frontiers they often appeared as externally imposed changes in the rules for an internal battle that had a momentum of its own. In the rest of this chapter I shall explore the way in which the threat of violence both created national identities and the growing divergence between the metropolis and the ethnic frontier societies.

REPRESENTATIVE VIOLENCE, COMMUNAL DETERRENCE AND NATIONAL IDENTITY IN ULSTER

In this section I shall look at the problem of controlling violence in Ulster, where the central state made a fairly serious effort to subdue it in the 1830s. The importance of this case (to which I return in chapter 6: Comparison with the US South) is that the methods of control proved workable only under pre-democratic conditions. The paradox was that, as the central state functions were generally growing and with it the appearance of increasing state power, in fact state power was becoming weaker.

Very few people in Northern Ireland today would try to claim that the victims of violence are chosen because of their individual characteristics; they are attacked because they are identified as representing groups of people.[20] The point is so obvious that few people dwell on it; it is treated as an 'aspect' of the situation rather than the core of it. But as violence of this kind is in no way restricted to the present troubles, it poses a question. If this kind of thing was always a possible threat, how did people control it? It takes after all very few people to kill enough people to frighten a very large number. How were they prevented from doing so and putting everyone at risk?

This condition of representative violence is very simple. If anyone of a great number of people can be 'punished' for something done by the community they come from, and if the communities are sufficiently clearly defined, there is a risk that anyone attacking a member of the other community can set in motion an endless chain of violence. Even if few aspects of the representative violence enjoy widespread support of the kind that could be established by opinion polls, it is only necessary for people to *understand* what is happening for it to create a generalised danger. Everyone might be a target for reprisal for something done in their name and without their approval. To break up representative violence, an authority had to be able to pursue all people engaged in violence and to criminalise them without any challenge to its authority. But if long-established relationships of violence exist, the law has to be able to obliterate all pleas of mitigating circumstance which the cycle of violence throws up. It cannot for example accept as defence for actions that they are 'deterrence actions', 'pre-emptive strikes', 'anticipatory self-defence', or 'reprisals', even if these correspond to people's actual experiences and perceptions of things. If the law does accept such pleas, it relinquishes its monopoly of the use of force without which it cannot function. And if its capacity to function is impaired, then the only kind of tranquillity that there can ever be is a form of truce or stable pattern of communal deterrence. The law becomes only a balancing wheel in this system. It is not the source of tranquillity.

In Ireland the abolition of the penal laws against Catholicism in the 1760–1780s had different effects in different areas. In the centre of the fine weaving district in North Armagh a displacement crisis between Protestant and Catholic weavers acquired a new dimension when Protestants challenged Catholics' rights to bear arms;[21] Protestant weavers' attacks on Catholic houses became searches for weapons as well as loom-wrecking expeditions. Landlords tried to suppress this activity but their failure to do so led to the creation of armed Catholic defence organisations, the existence of which fundamentally altered the local balance of powers. The landlords then formed companies of volunteers to suppress both kinds of communal organisation, but they drew nearly all their membership from middle-strata Protestants. The backbone of these were the old Volunteer corps formed to extract legislative independence of the Irish parliament from Britain, but some included were judged to be 'controllable' members of the Protestant weaver organisations. The combined effect of this and the inability of (Protestant) juries to convict Protestant wreckers polarised the situation. While the original Catholic defence organisations had tried to apprehend aggressors and hand them over to magistrates, the extension of this kind of conflict into the South Armagh area—still virtually Irish-speaking, overwhelmingly Catholic and unaffected by the development of hand-loom weaving—produced an altogether anti-Protestant counter-force. As the traditional methods of landlord government collapsed, the landlords came to depend upon Protestant weavers to keep 'order', notwithstanding their part in setting the crisis in motion. The threat of a full-scale Catholic revolt was a threat with unknown but certainly dangerous consequences—and all the more so if they had just been enraged by expulsionism of the Protestant weavers.

During the 1790s the Orange Order was formed, having more general popular Protestant membership now that a need for defence was clearly evident. First the landlords adopted it; and then as the crisis spread into neighbouring counties and there appeared to be some common purpose between the Catholics and the Presbyterian United Irishmen in Counties Antrim and Down, the British state absorbed the Orange Order into the Yeomanry, to suppress the rebellion of 1798. After the Act of Union united Ireland and Britain in 1801, there were areas of southern Ulster where law and order depended on magistrates tolerating Orange processions (sometimes as Yeomanry) through Catholic areas to ensure that Catholics were quiet.[22] Protestant plebeian deterrence practices had carved a space for themselves within the law.

When Daniel O'Connell's mobilisation of a mass Catholic movement for Catholic emancipation broke up the authority of southern Protestant landlord-magistrates, the British government completed the centralisation of the constabulary under the control of stipendiary magistrates. In much of Ireland these became the primary arm of the state, but in the North they came into collision with a law and order system that was far from broken up. The law and order reforms, together with the National Education system, were opposed by Conservative landlord-magistrates and in 1834 Orangeism was mobilised as part of a larger British Isles-wide Conservative attack upon the Whig government. When the Whigs returned to power in 1835 dependent on the support of O'Connell, they made a serious effort to confront the Northern law and order system. The constabulary and stipendiary magistrates suppressed Orange processions. Some Orange landlords were dismissed from the magistracy. And the Orange Order was investigated by a parliamentary committee which considered that it was subverting the army. To avoid being declared illegal, its landlord leadership dissolved it.[23]

These centralising reforms, however, only worked because other factors were also in their favour.[24] To begin with, nothing could be done to remove the bulk of Conservative landlords from the magistracy nor could anything be done to the jury selection process without attacking the prerogatives of landlords in general. The centralisation of law and order was already a radical departure from anything in Britain, and landlords generally were sensitive to its implications. So if cases arising out of sectarian conflict came before the courts, despite the influence of stipendiary magistrates and liberal landlords, the chances were stacked in favour of the Orangemen. The main achievement of Thomas Drummond's reforms was that they enabled Catholic priests to exert restraint over Catholics, with the knowledge that Orangemen would be dealt with as a separate problem by the resident magistrates and the constabulary. And as sectarian collisions became more infrequent, Conservative landlords could exert a control over Orangeism analogous to that of priests over the Catholics. The result was to stabilise a less unequal form of communal deterrence and insofar as it worked, the state/liberal-landlord power grew stronger. But this did not create equality before the law. It simply meant that conflicts rarely got into the arena where the law worked unevenly: the local courts.

Not only did the system depend upon the restraining power of elites (clerical and land-holding), but it was vulnerable to shifts in British policy. In 1848 the British government's fears of English chartists and the Young Ireland movement led it to permit the reassembly of Orangeism, which it took the first opportunity of disavowing after the emergency had passed when a major sectarian clash occurred in 1849. Most of the landlords who rejoined the order in 1848 left as quickly in 1850. But the episode demonstrated how British power might rely upon Orangeism in the North, if its own power was threatened in the South.

Cycles of representative violence can only be broken when

they are seen to be broken, meaning that the communities accept the state's repression of their 'own' violence and are convinced of the state's ability to repress the 'others'" violence. During the 1850s and early 1860s it looked outwardly as though this had happened, though there were important exceptions that indicated the growing danger. First there were riots in industrialising Belfast, where the police system was akin to the pre-1830 model, indicating that the centralised police system would have to be much strengthened to deal with urban contests. Secondly, in areas around the southern fringe of Ulster (where there were few Protestants), agrarian violence was used successfully to prevent evictions. These areas were mountainy small holdings used as subsistence bases by migrant labourers already used to physical opposition to the exclusivism they encountered in Scotland and England. In this context clerical discipline was far more difficult to sustain than in situations where the problem was to avoid local sectarian confrontation.

In the mid-1860s, clerical leadership of pan-Catholicism was threatened by the rise of Fenianism—Irish republican separatism. The challenge was very limited in the north, where its impracticability was self-evident. But it had two related effects. First, Orangeism began to revive, partly as plebeian action to attack Catholic institutions (churches and schools) which were seen as 'invading' Protestant territory; partly as a result of the use of Orangeism by Monaghan Conservatives to fight off a Catholic-Liberal electoral challenge in 1865 (in the violent aftermath of which the local judicial system was used in a pre-1830s fashion); and partly as a popular display of strength to match pro-Fenian manifestations. But for Catholics, there was a difference between not responding to provocation so that the law could work and considering the law a source of justice. This difference found expression in the view of Fenians as 'misguided' patriots. Marches were organised for amnesty of Fenian prisoners. In other words, both communities were displaying ambivalence about recourse to political violence, which threatened to break up the Drummond system.

The Orange manifestations ranged across a spectrum from outright intimidation of Catholics to a mere assertion of the traditional 'right to march' (as Fenians' amnesty demonstrations were now doing in the south). The latter enjoyed a degree of sympathy usually denied to their more aggressive manifestations, illustrating the irreducible dangers associated with 'traditions' that have their roots in practices of domination (Orangeism pre-1830). Wherever Catholics did tolerate Orange processions, this was supposed to show that local accommodation was possible; where they did not it showed the need for more Orange vigilance. In the 1850s and 1860s, when the landlords largely deserted Orangeism, it became in many areas simply a fraternity and occasionally a source of democratic opposition to landlord politics. In the late 1860s it included fraternity aspects and supremacism in an uncertain amalgam. When the revived Orange movement gathered momentum during the Fenian period, the state apparatus found it could not physically impose parade bans. And the Catholic clergy were less and less able to prevent collisions with Orange processions. In short, the equivocations about violence were visibly breaking up any capacity for elite restraint and weakening state power in an expanding spiral.

When in 1868, after the enfranchisement of a mass urban constituency, William Johnston—an independent Orangeman—beat the official Conservative candidates in Belfast, the limits of elite restraint were revealed. On the one hand, the breaking of Conservative leadership allowed for the development of popular accommodation (usually expressed in 'equal marching rights') and class politics of urban workers and (more often) tenant farmers in some districts. But on the other hand, it led to more uncontrollable confrontations. Until 1872 it was not obvious how these competing possibilities would work out, largely because the Catholic clergy continued to use their influence to prevent Catholic processions until they were finally legalised. When attempts were made to hold such processions in 1872, on the style of Orange marches, they encountered obstruction and attack, leading in Belfast to a scale of rioting that the constabulary and the stipendiary magistrates could neither prevent nor control.

The 1872 Belfast riots differed from previous ones in several crucial respects. First, the law and order apparatus had (since 1865) been brought under central control and had no partiality toward Orangeism. Second, nearly every section of the Conservative and Independent Orange (plebeian) leadership took the stance that the Catholic march should be left alone. Third, there was clear evidence of labour solidarity in a linen-mills strike only months before. Any suggestion that the masses 'wanted to attack each other' would fly in the face of this evidence. Fourth, when the rioting did begin, Catholic response mirrored Protestant response from the start (unlike 1857 and 1864 where initially Catholic restraint was visible) and developed quickly. Residential expulsionism was reciprocal, and led to a clarification of territorial boundaries in West Belfast that remained fairly stable for a century.

It took this dramatic assertion of communal equality in violence to demonstrate the incompatibility of equality with simple coexistence under the rule of law.

If Orangeism was a form of deterrence, then Catholics must have their equivalent. If one side expelled, the other would do likewise. If one could not walk in 'neutral' ground or the other's territory, then neither would the other. And both discovered that the 'neutral' state could not preserve order, reformed or otherwise. But perhaps most sinister of all, no tranquillity could be preserved except by hierarchical restraint over deterring forces. Any question of criminalising deterrence behaviour was dead and buried, however much it might be disapproved of or feared.

If the violent mimesis revealed an equality in violence, the new truce arrangements reflected the important inequalities that remained. To keep control over 'deterrence' behaviour it is necessary both to legitimise it as a Doomsday possibility and to restrain it simultaneously by appeals to morality, strategy and consequences. The elites, orthodox Conservative and clerical, recovered their power as communal representatives accomodating each other. But as the state had withdrawn (by legalising processions) it left an important space to be filled. The Conservative leaders, in their capacity as magistrates, could give legal sanction to popular deterrence activity suitably ritualised; they could also act as the restraining force over it. They became the balancing wheel between Protestant plebeian assertions of the right to deter and the state's concern for the rule of law. This did not create insuperable difficulties when, as in 1872–4, the Conservative and clerical elites in Belfast both discountenanced processions. But it became a different matter when the state's objectives and popular assertions of deterrence collided. The weakness of state power would then be transparent.

The new form of accommodation was uneven in two senses. First, the elites of the dominant society, unlike their Catholic clerical counterparts, had institutional leverage as magistrates and economic power as large employers, both of which were important not only locally but in the wider context of British politics. Secondly, the division of territory (residential and occupational) would entrench an uneven access of communities to economic resources. As the antagonism between the communities became increasingly severe, two consequences flowed from this. Everything a community had which helped it to sustain its position—control of economic residential and occupational space—would become a resource in battle. Privileges of the Protestant communities would be defended not because they were privileges, but because the defence of every privilege was locked into the defence of everything. The elite leadership sustaining its political control did two contradictory things. On the one hand it was a restraining and disciplining power over territorial expulsionism; on the other, it was a coercive force sustaining a climate in which intimidation of principled opponents of territorial antagonism prevailed. It both upheld the malignant division in the society and restrained its more vicious manifestations. At this stage we need to draw attention to some of the consequences of this method of preserving tranquillity. The process of democratisation and urbanisation broke down forms of restraint which could only be put together on a more precarious basis than before. And whereas before, the cycles of violence did not affect more than particular districts, the more they spread, the more people became aware of being trapped in deterrence communities. The awareness of the need for deterrence posture was the opposite side of the growth of collective responsibility for violence. Hence, preserving tranquillity required an extreme caution not to offend and to restrain others of one's own kind for whose actions one could be held responsible. Tranquillity was always at the mercy of whoever disturbed it for whatever reason. They could never be unequivocally repudiated because they might be a line of defence against whatever threat they might continue to provoke.

There were many who saw the malignancy of communal polarisation but who were powerless to do more than add weight to restraining forces. Even with the best of intentions, often the most effective ways of restraining communal deterrence depend upon tacitly admitting its fundamental assumptions. For example, during the 1857 urban rioting in Belfast, waves of expulsions occurred in which efforts were made to render Protestant districts residentially exclusive. They were often carried out by limited groups and the most effective methods of obstructing their objectives were the ones which came closest to accepting the principle on which they operated. Protestants who told expusionists that there were no Catholics in their streets were better able to protect Catholic neighbours than were Protestants who vouched that their Catholic neighbours were good law-abiding people (i.e. implicitly unlike the ones expulsionists were claiming to be after). The least successful defence was the most heroic—standing in the door and telling expulsionists that if they wanted to expel a Catholic, they would have to expel the defender first. The defended Catholic was not likely to risk staying under these circumstances.

During the 1880s, the Nationalists began the 'Invasion of Ulster', a series of demonstrations of dominance mimicking the long-established practice of Orange (Unionist) demonstrations; plebeian Orange leadership rapidly materialised to obstruct them with counter-demonstrations. Some Conservative elite leaders joined this bandwagon with the intention of controlling and restraining it. But for their doing so, it is likely that in the 1885 elections restraining leadership would have been brushed aside altogether. Publicly endorsing the necessity of such actions and therefore contributing to the intimidatory climate that gave rise to them, it must be conjectured that they were motivated by fear of the dangerous consequences of not doing so and allowing the movement to fall into the hands of those they judged to be bent on confrontation.

When people's experiences of violence tell them that some

forms of it are 'self-defensive' or 'responses' to other forms, it requires a degree of 'hypocrisy' to implement the law against them. If in fact there is not the power to criminalise them, the hypocrisy is diffused into everyday life rather than becoming the special property of the law. In the next section we shall deal with this question of 'hypocrisy' of the law which highlights the difference between the metropolis and its ethnic frontiers. But in both the examples given (and they could be repeated endlessly) it is impossible to know what people's motives are simply from their words or even necessarily from their actions. Restraint of this kind may be immediately effective because it does *not* contradict the logic of communal deterrence. But the long-run consequence of this is to entrench the operation of communal deterrence deeper and deeper into the social order. Conciliatory or pacifying intentions get buried. Turning this around, people are capable of giving justifications (with criticisms perhaps) of some things that metropolitans would see as pure acts of barbarism.

THE ETHNIC FRONTIER AND THE METROPOLIS

In his *Violence and the Sacred*, René Girard shows us that the meaning of sacrifice cannot be understood unless we first see that vengeance and cyclical violence are real problems for primitive societies:

> For us the circle has been broken . . . (by) the judicial system, which serves to deflect the menace of vengeance. The system does not suppress vengeance; rather it effectively limits it to a single act of reprisal, enacted by a sovereign authority specialising in this function. . . . Because revenge is rarely encountered in our society, we seldom have occasion to consider how societies lacking a judicial system of punishment keep it in check. . . . The efficiency of our judicial system conceals the problem and the elimination of the problem conceals from us the role played by religion.[25]

As the judicial system in the ethnic frontier clearly does not conceal the problem of revenge, Girard's exploration of the meaning of sacrifice ought to throw light on the differences between the metropolis and frontier.

For Girard, man's propensity for Violence is rooted in Desire. Man does not have definable limits to his desires. Desire is mimetic. We desire what other people have and our striving for what other people have alerts them to the desirability of what they possess. Cultures are systems of restraint upon mimetic rivalry. Without culture, mimesis can expand without limits. When rivalry is strong enough and violence is used to protect or grasp desired things, it does two things. First it proves the enormous desirability of the thing being striven for; secondly it teaches the lesson that the things you want most can only be secured by violence.[26] If this is true, then it raises a seemingly unanswerable question: where does Culture come from in the first place and what holds it together?

Girard's argument is that Culture was created by the sacrifice of a scapegoat which ended epidemics of violence arising from the breakdown of the culture that was there before. In all sacrificial rituals he observes that the victim is always like the people of the community while at the same time being critically different in some respect (it does not matter what). In the period of epidemic violence there must have come a point when, in fear and exhaustion, people found a scapegoat who could be blamed for the disorder. But to be a scapegoat he or she had to be universally pronounced guilty, so that his or her death would bring no risk of vengeance. Once the scapegoat is murdered, the violence stops. But this pragmatically effective way of ending violence only has lasting effect if the source of its success is hidden from view.[27] Culture is a product of the sacrificial crisis transfigured as Myth. The victim becomes in Myth either the source of all evil (an expelled Devil) or the source of all good (a God whom we are all equally guilty of murdering). The rituals of religion prohibit or restrict the kinds of rivalry that lead to epidemics of disorder (murder, theft, adultery etc.). The new Culture abolishes the 'justifications' for all past violences and views all infringements of its codes as isolated criminality. The unanimity with which law-breakers are punished conceals the violence implicit in the notion of punishment because in the relationship between sacred justice and the individual criminal the inequality of powers is such that there can be no rivalry. Culture conceals from view the violence in all of us.

Girard's theory of religion and sacred authority fills the gaps in Hobbes's theory of political authority. Hobbes's Leviathan was an all-powerful ruler in fear of which all men lived in order that they should not fear each other.[28] For Girard, it must be surmised first that this is a description that is more or less valid for any regime that enjoys undisputed legitimacy and second that no such authority can ever be created by the rational designs of men. If Leviathans exist, it is through sacrificial crisis transfigured as myth. It is the illusion about the origin of sacrificial ritual that gives it the power to curb mimetic violence. And all distinctions between power, authority and force rest at some point on the sacred qualities of culture. The more culture and institutions of power are revealed to be hypocritical, the more the distinctions between power, authority and force collapse into the chaos of sacrificial crisis.

To return then to the question of criminalisation and hypocrisy which I raised in discussing representative violence and deterrence community: law is not absolute because it is just. It is just, insofar as it is, because it is absolute, meaning that it shatters challenges to its supremacy, and breaks cycles of violence before they generate their endless justifications. It may be hypocritical—indeed it must be because when it counterposes its absolute power to that of the individual criminal it conceals the relationship of violence between them—but without its supremacy there is a mimetic chaos. However hypocritical the law may actually be, the success of its 'hypocrisy' has important consequences. Suppressing certain kinds of behaviour, it puts a damper on the escalation of rivalries. Firstly, people are less likely to break its law for fear of consequences. Secondly, because of the confidence it creates that people will not meet violence in everyday life, it enables them to assume that non-violence in their dealings with anonymous others, so human trust becomes relatively risk-free and self-reinforcing. Thirdly, the lesson of mimesis—that what is most valuable is that which is contested for with violence—is suppressed. In other words, the non-violence of culture which the metropolitan world could, broadly speaking, take for granted is not so much a product of the conscious effort of its peoples, but rather a direct reflection of how little effort had to be put into the avoidance of violence.

As a picture of metropolitan society this raises several difficulties. Since the establishment of the rule of law and the democratic abolition of statuses in favour of the citizenship of everyone, actual history has been full of denunciations of the hypocrisy of captialist law. The law that treats all citizens as equal before it included all manner of prohibitions that affected the poor and which it suited the rich to enforce. Why, then, did the rise of socialism not spell the death of the absolute qualities of the judicial system in the way that communal deterrence did in the ethnic frontiers? This is not a question of why did not Marxist revolution succeed; it is a question of why class conflict did not initially polarise western societies into 'proletarian' and 'bourgeois' deterrence communities. The best short answer that I can offer is provided by Georges Sorel. With little of the intellectual sophistication of Marx—whose writings were sufficiently universal in their scope to enable different people to find in them either pro-Sorel or anti-Sorel implications—Sorel advocated proletarian violence against the hypocritical and degenerating bourgeois order. The Girardian implication of this would have been that *either* as the working class became stronger and stronger it would eventually be able to scapegoat the bourgeoisie and erect upon the ashes of the capitalist system its own socialist religion, *or* the exposure of 'hypocrisy' of the bourgeois order would have precipitated chaos. In a society where the cult of proletarian violence enjoyed some popularity, Sorel criticised Jean Jaures, the leader of French socialism, for threatening the bourgeoisie with proletarian rebellion not because he meant it in earnest, but merely as a lever for securing the rights of trade union organisations and extending the power of parliamentary socialism. Sorel was also put out that the ruling groups gave in to this 'blackmail' and admitted the existence of a 'social problem'. From his standpoint, the redeeming hope was that 'proletarian violence confined employers to their role of producers and tends to restore the separation of classes, just when they seemed to be on the point of intermingling in the democratic marsh'. This was to be the remedy for the 'new and unforseen fact—a middle class which seeks to weaken its own strength' (i.e. were accepting as legitimate new working-class definitions of 'rights').[29] If

Jaures's strategy was as Sorel described and was the dominant strategy of French socialism, it becomes clear why in practice the class struggle did not destroy the supremacy of law and generate mimetic chaos. Jaures's strategy depended not on uprooting the system of law or the institutions that wrote the law, but upon building up a force that would oblige the bourgeoisie to recognise the distinction between 'good' and 'bad' law. This descent into the 'democratic marsh' meant elevating the instruments of power above conflict, so that they could be used for other purposes than upholding narrow interests and cease to be a mere appendage of dominant class interests. In short, it *created power* by tolerating necessary forms of hypocrisy.

It may be argued that this was not much of an achievement from the standpoint of revolutionary socialism—into that question I cannot go here—but it does mean democratic socialism secured the basis for such twentieth-century civilisation as there has actually been. Implicitly or explicitly, democratic socialists and bourgeois liberals who conciliate them recognised that only the existence of transcendent Culture and its associated authority shields us from chaos. An inescapable element of hypocrisy is involved in enabling this to happen. Girard says:

> As soon as the essential quality of transcendence—religious, humanistic or whatever—is lost, there are no longer any terms by which to define the legitimate form of violence and to recognise it among the multitude of illicit forms. The definition of legitimate and illegitimate forms becomes a matter of mere opinion, with each man free to reach his own decision. In other words, the question is thrown to the winds. Henceforth there are as many legitimate forms of violence as there are men to implement them; legitimacy as a principle no longer exists. Only the introduction of some transcendental quality that will persuade men of the fundamental difference between sacrifice and revenge, between a judicial system and vengeance, can succeed in by-passing violence.

All this explains why our penetration and demystification of the system necessarily coincides with the disintegration of that system. The art of demystification

retains a sacrificial quality and remains essentially religious in character for at least as long as it fails to come to a
conclusion—as long, that is, as the process purports to be
non-violent or less violent than the system itself. In fact
demystification leads to constantly increasing violence, a
violence perhaps less 'hypocritical' than the violence it
seeks to expose, but more energetic, more virulent and
the harbinger of something far worse—a violence that
knows no bounds.[30]

If, by and large, metropolitan societies did secure the rule of
law and the ascendancy of the judicial system, the areas which
threatened these achievements most were the expanding
colonial empires. The new colonies developed after the 1870s
depended on limited strata of colonial officials, military
personnel and capitalist entrepreneurs establishing
ascendancy over vast areas and populations. No such under-
taking could ever have been carried out without the (at least
implied) possibility of backing these very limited presences
with a massive display of punitive or retaliatory violence. The
development of Imperialism would have been impossible if
governments hesitated to send out such expeditions to back up
carriers of the flag. Enthusiastic Imperialism in the
metropolis—the denunciation of the 'treachery' of liberal or
internationalist opponents of Imperialism—was a way of
creating representative violence as a system for sustaining
colonialism. So long as the denunciations were largely verbal
(like the abuse hurled at Gladstone for his lack of punitive
zeal) they did not import representative violence back into the
metropolis. Put another way, it was still a crime to intimidate
liberals and internationalists with anything more than verbal
obscenity. So long as the metropolis could be insulated from
the realities of imperialising violence, the rule of law could
remain supreme.

The danger, however, was that there was only a thin line
between creating conditions in the metropolis that sustained
representative violence abroad, and importing them back
home (as the Dreyfus affair showed in France).[31] But so long
as that line was not crossed, the people of the metropolis were
not obliged to live, as did people of the ethnic frontiers, in the
shade of such dangers.

Seen in this context the ethnic frontiers acquire a clear significance. For the citizen society of the ethnic frontier, the principle that defenders of the flag should be upheld by metropolitan force is an absolute guarantee of their power not to be subordinated to the native society in their midst. The ethnic frontier offered the same challenge as the far-flung imperial outpost. In both cases, it was imperative to defend those who showed the flag. Not to do so on the domestic frontier would have subverted the logic of the imperial frontier.

The incorporation of 'defence of the ethnic frontier' into the mainstream of imperialising political alliances was therefore involuntary. But it was fraught with great dangers. The representative violence of the ethnic frontier might spill over into the metropolis, a development which many metropolitan politicians grasped in one way or another. The easiest way to prevent it from doing so, to keep it localised in the frontier, was to ensure that the citizen society at least considered itself an upholder of the law. And that meant fashioning the application of the law so that in practice it left spaces for the citizen to take precautions against the native. Instead, in other words, of allowing the law to be a *visibly* feeble pivot in an antagonistic conflict, the law should disguise its own weakness by upholding legitimate forms of citizen communal deterrence practices. The weakness of the law and of state power could only be concealed by allowing it to become a partisan instrument which, however, guaranteed that eventually it would produce an antagonistic opponent. The right of Orangeism to public procession is an example of a citizen society's right to deter. The battery of anti-Polish legislation in the German east made the law a tool of Germanisation. Yet in both cases the law also remained an instrument of restraint upon 'excesses'.

Hannah Arendt, in her *Origins of Totalitarianism*, suggested that the differences between the various twentieth-century democracies and dictatorships depended upon how far the conduct of normal law in the metropolis could be insulated from their practices of Imperialism abroad.[32] The real battle to preserve democracy and the rule of law, especially after the rise of Imperialism in the 1880s, was never a battle for absolute (liberal) values. It was a holding operation to prevent the Imperial cancer from spreading into the metropolitan core. Only when the essentially hypocritical basis of this operation is understood does it become possible to see that, even if representative violence was consciously developed as an instrument for sustaining particular forms of economic exploitation arrangements in the new Empire, Imperialisation of human relationships is something much larger.

It is the undermining of sacred values of democracy and rule of law by thinly veiled relationships of force. It is as instrumental as it is controllable. But where the force relationship is between two peoples who have similar capacities to respond to each other's aggression and similar causes for anxiety about such aggression, Imperialisation is a thinly disguised chaos.

National Conflict in the Ethnic Frontier

By the time of the First World War, national conflicts in the ethnic frontiers had been integrated into the wider framework of Imperial rivalries. Internally political life had degenerated into a perpetual territorial conflict with each nationality attempting to maximise its power in relation to the other. Power depended upon numbers, whether in electoral battles or more menacing confrontations with implied or actual violence. In the German situation, the German-Polish ethnic frontier alone was within German territory. The much larger ethnically Polish areas were in the Russian Empire and Austrian Galacia. In both the British and Austrian cases, the larger ethnically Irish and Czech areas were, together with the British-Irish, German and Czech ethnic frontiers, inside British and Austrian territory. But in all three cases the dominant political strategy of the citizen bloc was to force the metropolitan state to uphold their position and to prevent efforts to conciliate the natives. Through all the variations on this theme one conclusion stands out. The metropolitan state was forced to recognise the limits of its power in the frontier, where it could not govern without the support of the citizen peoples. The development was self-reinforcing insofar as it was also the source of increasingly clearcut native nationalist alienation. Whether the state itself initiated a policy of opposition to native nationalism (as in Germany), or whether its attempts to conciliate native nationalism were thwarted by defiance actions of the citizen population, the result was in the last analysis the same.

Throughout this chapter several themes will be brought

out. First, the way in which the ambivalences of early native nationalists are swept aside in favour of a more cohesive nationalism that demands a nation state, embracing not only areas of native ethnic predominance but also ethnic frontiers. Second, the way in which the citizen society's territorialism mirrors some of the aspects of native organic work. Where the interdependence of organic work was initially a way of asserting equality with the citizen society, the onset of territorialism gave the interdependence of classes a new meaning for citizen and native society alike. By the 1880s the practice of exclusive dealing[1] (buying only from one's own kind) was widespread in all three societies and more significantly the dominant classes of the citizen society were able to sustain their political leadership only at the price of partially subordinating their rights as property owners to the imperatives of territorialist strategy. Thus lignite mining capitalists who employed cheap Czech labour in the 1860s were evicting or sacking employees who registered in the census as Czech in the 1890s. Catholics expelled from the Belfast shipyards in the 1864 riots were reinstated by peace committees composed of middle-class liberals and capitalists, but the expulsions of 1886 could not be reversed. German landlords (Junkers) who brought Poles across the Russian border as seasonal labourers in the 1860s found themselves deprived of this labour supply between 1885 and 1892.[2] Enforced interdependence of classes was the essence of territorialist defence of position.

Thirdly, we shall explore the way in which state power became locked into the ethnic conflict. There are two tendencies operating that cannot be easily separated. On the one hand the citizens of the ethnic frontier had to be upheld if the Imperial projects of the 1880s were to get off the ground, as we argued in the last chapter. On the other hand, when metropolitan governments attempted to conciliate the natives, a defiance action could threaten to expose the limits of their power. These two tendencies were bridged where the citizen elites in the ethnic frontier could articulate strategy that clearly bound both tendencies together in a pro-Imperial alliance. Under these circumstances the popular base of citizen territorialism could be led in 'martial' fashion. But when citizen territorialism and the priorities of Imperial politics clashed, the former could appear as an unvarnished plebeian movement, and still retain serious powers of defiance even without elite leadership and integral membership of Imperialist alliances. The reason why this possibility is fairly thoroughly disguised is that, by and large, it suited Imperial purposes to pre-empt it. The Austrian exception proves the rule.

BOHEMIA AND MORAVIA[3]

Until 1866 the Austrian monarchy rested on a centralised bureaucracy, its army, the Roman Catholic church and heavily property-weighted representative bodies, in all of which the German speakers were dominant. When Prussia defeated Austria in 1866 and successfully united all the other Germanic states into the German Reich in 1870, the Austrian Empire was forced to recognise that it could not rest its legitimacy on its German minority. In 1867 the eastern half was ceded to Hungarian control and between 1867 and 1871, Polish Galacia was granted effective autonomy within the German-dominated western half.

But the German Liberals—dominant in the German Austrian heartland and in the provinces inhabited by Czechs— were determined to resist any such autonomy for Bohemia and Moravia. In these the large German minorities could sustain control by property-weighted franchises. The weakness of the Czechs' position was severalfold. To secure any leverage within the electoral system, they had to ally with landowners of Bohemia whose interest in Bohemian 'states right' was based on opposition to the centralising and anti-clerical tendencies of German Liberalism and support for Imperial designs. The Old Czech leaders—aware that Bohemia was surrounded to north, west and south by Germans—had always seen the Austrian state as the best framework for the advance of Czech nationality. Their hope lay in the eventual recognition by the state of the need to treat all its national components equally. But to prove this necessity to the Imperial centre, they had to draw attention to the consequences of continuing to uphold German dominance. Hence, in the 1860s, the Czech leaders made clear their cultural affinity to Russia, a veiled threat to the Germans. However Russia had suppressed the 1863 revolt in Russian Poland, so the Polish landlords who dominated the Lantag of Galacia and who were able to secure their own autonomy had neither will nor interest in promoting the collateral cause of the Czechs. When a government backed by the big landholders and Catholic clericals attempted to grant Bohemian and Moravian autonomy in 1871, in accordance with the then perceived weakness of the state structure, the popular German opposition was so great that the proposals had to be withdrawn. The German Liberals, restored to office, devised a direct electoral system for the Reichsrat calculated to entrench German urban and bourgeois interests, and attacked the power of the church in education and civil law. This last measure threatened the *de facto* language accommodation within church schools and was intended as a Germanising measure. The Czechs resorted to political abstentionism.

When Palacky had advocated a federal system as the basis for Czech membership of the Austrian Empire, he had accepted that German areas of Bohemia and Moravia might be linked to the German Austrian units rather than the Czech. The thwarted scheme of 1871 had provided for all officials and judges to speak both languages, for administrative divisions to follow language frontiers and for a separate voting system for Czechs and Germans in which a two-thirds majority of either nationality could block any measure. Both Palacky's vision and the 1871 scheme contained protection for the German minority: the first by excluding them and the second by giving them veto powers. But the first would have required an acceptable way of defining a 'German area' while the second could only have worked by communal consent.

Bohemian German defiance appeared to have locked the Austrian state into an antagonistic relationship with the Czechs. But the nature of the Imperial state prevented it from carrying this development to its logical conclusion. It could not rest its base on its German citizens alone without placing itself in a relationship with the rest of its peoples that would degenerate into pure coercion. Had it for example linked the defence of Germanism at home with any prospect of Imperial expansion, the very process of extending Empire would have exacerbated national conflict at home and imperilled the Imperial expansion itself. In fact, for this very reason the Austrian Empire was unable to develop an Imperial expansionism along the lines of the British or German models. Even if the development of capitalism within its territories had reached the point of stimulating the quest for economic expansionism, this fact would not have altered. The Austrian imperative to Imperial expansion was far more limited and based on the need to balance Russian expansionism in the areas of the Balkans where Turkish power was collapsing.

The major move of the Austrian state forward toward conciliation of the Czechs was a direct consequence of the opposition of the German Liberals to the occupation of Bosnia in 1878.[4] They opposed it both on classical liberal grounds of opposition to the military and to expenditure—and also because its likely implication was to strengthen Slav influence in Austria, whether through the integration of the occupied provinces or because rule over them would be based on the Catholic church and Croats from within the Empire. Either way, it would clearly not strengthen Germanism within Austria. Thus the Taaffe government which replaced them in 1879 depended on the traditional landed and clerical bases of the regime plus the conservative leaders of the Polish and Czech nationalities. Its policy toward the Czechs was part of its wider aim of keeping all nationalities in a state of 'equal and well-modulated discontent'. Instead of insisting on bilingualism, it required officials to use the language of those they were dealing with (implying the necessity of bilingualism in mixed and Czech areas). Otherwise the franchise reforms made it easier for Czechs to compete in the various electoral curias (in the first, the great landowners, by easing the purchase of big property). And the division of the University of Prague into Czech and German units, together with a commitment to extend the provision of secondary schools for Czechs (a central state responsibility) enabled the upper tiers of a Czech education system to develop.

But these reforms, which did not extend the autonomy of the Bohemian and Moravian Lantags, left open the question of primary education, which was a local government responsibility. The letter of the 1867 constitution, providing public education for each nationality in its own language without compulsion to learn another, had been interpreted to mean that a national group of 40 children had a right to a public elementary school. But local governments were also responsible for taking the census and might be tempted to describe a bilingual Czech as German. The important subject of primary education for Czech minorities in German districts now hinged upon ensuring that the minority was built up and able to assert itself.[5] The Taaffe reforms, unlike the 1871 proposals, did not attempt to provide comprehensive solutions. The scale of German opposition to these indicated that their use of the blocking provision would have paralysed them if they had been enforced. The Taaffe reforms simply provided a framework for territorialist confrontations over whether an area was mixed or German.

With the main bulwark of German dominance breached, the German Liberals still entrenched by the undemocratic franchise system began to decline. The German Radicals who attracted popular support in Bohemia adopted a programme of separating off much of the non-German area of Austria (but continuing to include the Czech areas), democratising the franchise and making German the state language. Democratic majority rule could thus be reconciled with undiluted German dominance. They otherwise supported trade unions and social reform measures in opposition to the elitist Liberals. But they quickly became militantly anti-Slav and anti-Semitic. Anti-Semitism meant many things in Austria. Among the clericals in the core area of Austria it was aimed at Eastern Jewish refugees from Russia as well as against the assimilated Jewish financier element which identified with the German Liberals. But in the Czech provinces, it acquired another meaning. It could be used against all Germans (and most Jews were assimilated Germans) who showed themselves to be less than fully committed to Germanism in the territorialist battle with the Czechs;[6] Jewish and German employers who employed cheap Czech labour in lignite mines and German and Jewish Socialists who preached union between workers of different races in opposition to employers. As Jews had been assimilated in the way that a powerful bloc can absorb any numerically harmless group of people, they supported Liberals and Socialists who had welcomed their assimilation. Anti-Semitism necessarily threw them on the defensive alongside all other German exponents of racial tolerance of any kind.

The ground rules for fighting the language struggle were simply to keep Czechs out of 'German' areas. The spirit behind this is revealed in the opening chapter of Hitler's *Mein Kampf*: 'Only a handful of Germans in the Reich had the slightest conception of the eternal and merciless struggle for the German language, German schools, and a German way of life.' Hitler described the post-Taaffe regime in Austria as a 'policy of Czechisation from above': 'Purely German towns, indirectly through government officialdom were slowly but steadily pushed into the mixed language danger zones . . . Czech pastors were appointed to German communities . . . becoming the germ cells of the de-Germanisation process.'[7]

The Taaffe reforms enabled the Czechs to increase their representative power and to build up a Czech educational system. Rieger, the leader of the Old Czechs, became increasingly reconciled to the regime despite the earlier disappointments. The temper of the schools and electoral contests, however, gave greater strength to the more radical Young Czechs whose greatest strength was in areas of contested nationality. In 1889, after the Czechs won a majority in the Bohemian Lantag, Rieger tried to bargain with German Liberal leaders for a new settlement, which could only in practice involve either administrative partitions that left each in control of areas where the other had minorities or entrenching provisions to protect minority rights. The territorial conflict had, however, destroyed the legitimacy of headcounting as a way of settling disputes. Rieger's plan was denounced by the Young Czechs as a betrayal and a partition abandoning Czech minorities to German harassment. Where German Radicals used direct action to reduce Czech numbers to assert control over as much of Bohemia and Moravia as possible, Czech Radicals began to preach that all of Bohemia and Moravia was once Czech and that it was a national duty to recover 'lost lands' from usurping Germans. When the Young Czechs displaced the Old Czechs as the major Czech party, the possibilities of compromise shrank. The Taaffe regime's efforts to conciliate were now self-evidently incapable of fulfilment.[8]

But the impasse did not produce symmetrical results. When the Young Czechs displaced the Old Czechs electorally, they could not be included in any governing coalition—their anti-militarism, anti-clericalism and pro-Russian stance made them a permanent opposition notwithstanding the fact that, despite their popular following, their leadership represented propertied elements, entrenched in the diets and local governments. The regime's stance toward the Czechs hardened as it governed against them and made increasing use of emergency law in Czech areas. In an effort to deal with this crisis that was undermining normal law in Bohemia, the Badeni government in 1897 published decrees requiring all public servants in Bohemia and Moravia to be bilingual. The reaction to this was civil disorder on a massive scale, in which German territorialist organisations made the running. The army warned of the effects of these disturbances on its own unity; the German government made disapproving noises and the Badeni government buckled. Defiance had worked conclusively, transforming its leader Schönerer 'from a despised former convict . . . into the leader of a large fanatical party'.[9]

The Young Czech leader Kramar, who had ridiculed the notions of 'reconquest of Bohemia', now spoke of Czechs as a living wedge between Germans, whose first duty was 'to be strong and healthy that not the slightest anxiety exist lest it gave way to German pressure'.[10]

Whereas in the Polish and Irish cases, frontier territorialism became locked into the question of Imperialism, the absence of a clear alignment between Bohemian German and Imperial power precipitated a far more chaotic and popular form of territorial conflict. But the absence of Imperial commitment to the Bohemian German supremacy did not mean that the Imperial centre could be neutral. In Moravia, where the German presence was thinner, more strictly urban and of elevated social class, the compromise of 1905 between conservative leaders of both blocs rested on the condition that 'what is German today remains German'. It permitted German elitist local governments to restrict Czech upper primary schools and gave Germans a blocking power in the Lantag not unlike that provided for in the 1871 aborted scheme. In Bohemia no such compromise was evolved.[11] The Lantag remained without a fifth (universal franchise) curia such as was introduced in Moravia in 1905, so that popular forces were expressed electorally only in Reichsrat elections. The conflict on the ground was fought out in a more openly territorial manner. The absence of Imperial commitment led to two tendencies, both outside elite control. First, the social democrats attempted to build a transnational class party on a basis of compromise of the kind that the Imperial centre would have liked to have imposed (of which more in chapter four). But secondly, the German Workers Party and pan-class plebeian parties such as the German Radicals both competed with the Social Democrats for working-class following. Two examples illustrate their appeal. The town of Gablonz was unusual in that its surrounding worker villages were more nationalist than the town itself. Here, German workers in small-scale unorganised craft work (glass production) were facing Czech competition and the weakness of labour organisation made it difficult to create an 'equal pay for equal work' compromise. The DAP's programme mirrored the Social Democrats in most respects except in its internationalism— 'Work in German districts for German workers only!'—and as the state fell back on its bureaucratic and military base before 1914, they stopped talking of 'maintaining' German territory and began speaking of increasing it. In overwhelmingly German Eger, plebeian nationalism had (by direct action) prevented a Czech school from ever being set up and obliged a Czech association to pack up its bags.[12]

The national conflict undermined the working of representative institutions. When the Czech radicals disrupted the Reichsrat the Imperial regime fell back on its executive arms which were largely German at the highest levels. And when Bohemian Germans disrupted the Bohemian Lantag (the Reichenberg district threatened to secede and set up the core of 'German Bohemia') eventually it was suspended and rule based on executive arms. In this way, despite the state's efforts to be neutral, it was in fact forced by abstentionism and boycotts to rest its power on its German apparatus.

In 1908 Austria secured the support of the German Reich for the annexation of Bosnia-Herzegovina, while lining itself up ever more clearly against Russia and its client Serbia. The implication of growing Imperial rivalry was that the regime had to rest more and more on its German base and become more and more antagonistic to the Russophilic Czechs. The suspension of the Bohemian Lantag in 1913 fitted the Reichenberg German demands admirably. Even if Kramar ridiculed 'reconquest' notions, Czech-German antagonism had pinioned the Imperial centre to the Germans and reduced the Czechs to placing their hopes on an external *deus ex machina* in the probable shape of Russia.

PRUSSIAN POLAND[13]

Poland's nationalism, unlike that of the Czechs, was perpetually bound up with international politics in a very immediate manner. The 1815 partitions of Poland between Prussia, Austria-Hungary and Russia meant that changing relationships between each were reflected in the Polish areas. Up until the 1830 revolt in Russian Poland, the three empires competed for the support of the Poles. And in the Prussian zone this was reflected in the relative autonomy of Posen and its Polish landlord leadership (notwithstanding the active Germanisation of West Prussia). After 1830, Posen was subjected to increasingly close absorption into the rest of Prussia and an active policy of buying up Polish landlords' properties set in motion. Unlike the other partitions of Poland, the Prussian area was roughly half populated by Germans, so although any question of restoring Poland depended on international developments, none the less the logic of seeking accommodation with the Prussian regime was strong, if for no other reasons than that it could not be dislodged and could be more repressive than Russia or Austria to Polish interests if it chose so to be.

In 1870, Prussia completed the unification of all the German states (except Austria, forcibly excluded) under its leadership in the German Reich. As far as the Poles were concerned they faced now two distinct legal arenas of power. The Prussian Lantag was elected by a three-class franchise that over-represented Junker (and Polish) landlords. Here their representation decreased through the loss of Polish estates and the influence of Archbishop Ledochowski, who drew Polish Catholics toward pro-Prussian political currents. The all-German Reichstag, however, was elected on a relatively democratic franchise and provided much greater possibilities for Polish representation.

Bismark was concerned by the possible centrifugal effects of Catholicism on the southern and eastern borders—and in particular the possible effect of the autonomy granted to the Poles of Galacia by Austria in 1871.[14] The Kulturkampf of 1872–5 was intended to subordinate the Church to the state, and in a manner of speaking succeeded in creating a compromise in most German areas. But when applied to the Poles in the east, it broke up the fabric of *de facto* accommodation as to the use of Polish and German languages in the Church and in the educational system. Secularisation of education meant Germanisation. The Polish language— hitherto the language of instruction in many elementary schools and some Catholic high schools—was to be replaced by German. In 1876 German became the exclusive language of all administration. Ledochowski and many priests were imprisoned for their opposition to state interference with the Church. The net effect of the Kulturkampf was to arouse Polish resistance and political organisation not only in Posen but also in West Prussia and Upper Silesia. But some of this political opposition was channelled into the Catholic Centre party, as the substantial German Catholic minority in the east (where most Germans were Protestant) had ended up opposing the Kulturkampf if they had not done so from the beginning (e.g. Ledochowski).

The difficulty created by the Kulturkampf now came home to roost. When the central state declared war on 'Polishness', it was difficult to disengage. And more so as the secular trend of population movement was tending to 'polonise' the east. The Junker landlords who monopolised the ownership of land and the local powers of the state were mechanising the threshing of rye and so reducing their labour needs to the harvest season only. The chronic underemployment amongst farm labourers, magnified by the final death throes of handloom weaving of linen,[15] accelerated mass emigration of both German and Polish speakers to the industrial areas of western Germany. But their places as seasonal harvesters were taken up by Poles from Russia, where underemployment was much worse, who tried to establish permanent holdings from accumulated earnings.

The National Liberals, whose Germanising enthusiasm sustained the Kulturkampf, had been denouncing this tendency for some years. They advocated buying up Polish estates to settle German farmers and closing the border. In 1885 Bismark expelled some thousands of non-citizen Jews and Poles. His reasons for doing so were a combination of pressure from officials and small traders in the east and perhaps an effort to send a diplomatic message of solidarity to the Russian government.[16] But the result was the only censure motion ever passed against him in the Reichstag.

The censure of his 1885 Polish policy by Progressives, Centre (Catholic), Socialist and Polish parties provided the occasion for embarrassing both the Progressives and the Centre. Instead of reversing his policy, he initiated—through the Prussian Lantag—a policy of buying up Polish estates in the east to create settlement farms for Germans and continued the exclusion of migrant labour. His opponents saw themselves as defending rule of law and now found themselves accused of lack of zeal for Germanism. The Progressives' alarm at the anti-Semitism and the Centre's alarm at the anti-Catholicism of the expulsions were now thrown back in their faces, because none of the opponent parties (except the Poles) favoured contributing the ethnic frontier to a restored Poland. Unlike Bohemia or Ireland there was no mass zone of overwhelming Polish population within German frontiers. For the same reason there was not much popular German concern with Polish power in the east. But Bismark's adoption of the National Liberal concepts of Germanising the east irreversibly connected that policy with the defence of Empire. If Empire could only be created by a definite commitment to upholding the national flag in far-off continents, and stigmatising metropolitan opponents of that policy as traitors, here was a domestic variant on the same theme.

The split between the National Liberals who supported

Bismark's system and the Progressives who supported classical democratising reforms (such as the abolition of the three-class system in Prussia) was in some respects a model of the general problem of liberalism at the outset of Imperialism. The Progressives opposed Imperialism out of opposition to militarism, support for a loosely internationalist conception of the relations between states, and concern to uphold rule of law. In this they were not unlike Gladstonian Liberals in Britain or Clemenceau's Radicals in France. The National Liberals, like Liberal Unionists in Britain, were attracted to Imperialism by the need to extend markets and secure raw materials, to open up new areas for trade for a highly developed industrial capitalism. The anti-Polish policies and ventures into overseas Imperialism in the 1880s cemented that division within Liberalism

The state inaugurated a form of territorialist confrontation with the Poles from which it would have been difficult to disengage and which gradually made the opposition support for rule of law a more and more abstract solution to national conflict in the east: in much the same way as Empire was actually extended, linking business interests to those of militarism and colonial adventure, it became increasingly difficult to disengage from Imperialism. The juggernaut of Imperialism created an argument in favour of itself—all rival Imperialisms were engaged in it also. So opposition to Imperialism increasingly gave way to demands for restraints upon it. Thus, for example, more or less the same forces that opposed the 1885 expulsions were later responsible for the dismissal in 1897 of Carl Peters, the governor of German East Africa, whose excesses embarrassed many Imperialists. Imperialisation, whether of ethnic frontiers or overseas, generated situations which one-time opponents of Imperialism could not unmake.

Just how difficult it might be to disengage from the anti-Polish actions in the east became clear during the Chancellorship of Count Caprivi between 1890–94.

The Caprivi-Koscielski compromise by which the Polish deputies agreed to support the government secured some gains to the Poles, although they were vulnerable to the charge of not being enough. Thus the use of the General

Commissions to finance land purchases for small and medium holdings (Poles as well as Germans), the reopening of the frontier (which benefited Junkers primarily and immigrant Poles secondarily), and the relaxation of anti-Polish language laws were gains. But Caprivi, whatever his intentions, was hamstrung by the Prussian Lantag and the Colonisation Commission continued to operate; the temper of the bureaucracy was now conditioned to conflictual relations with Poles; and Junkers had coercive powers to frustrate Poles applying for General Commission loans.[17] In short, the accommodation could not break the momentum of conflict between its own state arms and the Poles in the east.

The Caprivi administration and its Polish supporters faced massive opposition from a variety of quarters. Its trade treaties and reform of manorial self-government in the east were an attack on Junker interests, though the first was a source of wider agrarian protest. The Polish votes for naval estimates were denounced by more popular currents of Polish nationalism, while the dependence of the government on Polish votes made it a butt of increasingly vocal German nationalism.

With the fall of Caprivi in 1894, the HKT or Society for the Protection of Germanism in the eastern Marches set the pace of Polish policy until 1914. The Society was founded by three untypical Junkers—untypical in that the Junkers' class interests were opposed to closing the border to migrants and to any form of colonisation except that which created an extra supply of farm labour (i.e. small holdings). It acted as a watchdog on the administration, complaining when its personnel patronised Polish businesses or failed to impose anti-Polish laws. Initially, it fashioned the compromise that bridged the interests of Junkers and territorial German nationalism—the requirement that seasonal labourers be held under tight supervision and displaced across the border after the harvesting season was over. But gradually it began to adopt such proposals as support for medium-scale settlement farms (i.e. of no use to Junkers as sources of labour) and it strongly supported the expropriation law of 1908 allowing the state to purchase Polish estates compulsorily, a measure described by some Junkers as 'pure Marxist dogma'. The Junkers were not enamoured of the new settlers. Some in the Gnesen area protested for a greater voice in local government, went hunting and did not address Junkers as 'My Lord'. The numbers of Germans of the Polish provinces in HKT probably never exceeded 6 per cent of adult males eligible, but it made its presence felt by parades with banners on German Day. In the last years before the war its leadership began to acquire a more popular character and the followers of Wolfgang Kapp were drawing the logical conclusions of HKT territorialism: the Junker states should be refashioned as peasant farm holdings, obviating the need for Polish seasonal labour and facilitating the settlement of permanent Germans.[18] In the Prussian east, the pace of territorialist political development was clearly set by the state and HKT pressure; a fact which disguises the inflexibility of the state to a reversal of policy. If the mass of Germans initially had little to do with it, they could not escape the consequences.

Just as in every other territorialist degeneration of political life, there is an opposite side. For every mesure the HKT and Prussian government took, there was a rebound effect. Once it became clear that the intent was to thin down the Polish population, it became un-national for Poles to leave their holdings. Polish migrants to the Ruhr invested their earnings in peasant plots in Posen. The German government attempted to prevent Poles building homes, thereby creating a Polish demand for German holdings at tempting prices. When efforts were made to prevent the use of Polish in schools, there was a schools' strike. And a rule that Polish papers had to carry a parallel German text was only reconsidered when someone asked whether it might not encourage Germans to read Polish. The political results were the displacement of accommodative Poles by the National Democrats, strongest in the Prussian partition but rising in all three. Roman Dmowski spoke of 'struggle' as the basis of life and regarded the Prussians as the most firmly opposed to Polish aspirations of the partitioning powers. His radicalism was neither liberal (he was anti-Semitic) nor socialist (which he saw as atheistic). It was a mimesis of the HKT, a reflection of the stance of Prussia toward Poles.[19] Any German government attempting to restore normal rule of law in the east would have found itself attempting to use a wholly Germanised state apparatus to conciliate an irreconcilable enemy. The 1885 opponents of the expulsions would, as a hypothetical governing coalition, have discovered a limited power to achieve any conciliatory effect, even if not confronted with local defiance actions.

ULSTER

Ireland's distance from Continental Europe deprived her of the international significance of Poland or the possibilities sought by the Czechs, until the emergence of the United States as a factor in European politics in the twentieth century.[20] From the 1830s, the centralisation of the education system and law and order materially strengthened Catholics in the North, and from 1843 onwards all British governments regarded an accommodative stance towards the Catholic hierarchy's educational claims as a precondition of retaining consent to its rule in Ireland outside Ulster. This arrangement suited Northern Catholics' interests as the forces potentially destructive of organic work were far stronger in the North than elsewhere.

Fenianism directly opposed this accommodationist strategy by armed separatist revolt. The massive (and now heavily Catholic) emigration from Ireland during the Famine of 1845–50 had the twofold effect of creating the American-Irish and exposing the perpetual debilitation of Irish rural society. Though the Fenian rising was firmly opposed by the Catholic hierarchy, it was also the occasion that persuaded Gladstone of the need to abolish the explicit claims of Anglican Protestant ascendancy and to reform land laws. This enabled clerical accommodation with Liberalism to evolve a new working relationship between 1868 and 1873. Until 1874 no Catholic ever represented an Ulster constituency in the Westminster parliament. The franchise extension to farmers with middle-sized properties in the 1850s was a dead letter under the system of open voting; or else, as in Monaghan in 1865, a condition permitting electoral contests to turn into open warfare and exposing the use to which Conservative landlord control over local government institutions could be put. But the borough franchise reforms of 1868 and the Secret Ballot

Act of 1872 created a mass urban constituency and facilitated challenges to landlord conservatism. Catholic political participation became more important and was generally supportive of Liberals who followed Gladstone's policy.[21]

But Fenianism and the subsequent rise of the home rule movement created real difficulties for Northern Catholics. On the one hand the pan-Catholic link southwards had been the source of all effective leverage on British power and a tacit source of strength in relating to Protestants within the North. But on the other hand, the reactivation of Orangeism bore down on them as a potential support for any kind of Irish nationalist challenge to British power. These effects were compounded by the break-up of the *de facto* accommodation of Presbyterian and Catholic educational interests in the national education system, leading Northern Protestant liberalism into increasingly direct conflict with Catholic efforts to establish a wholly separate and explicitly denominational system.

The first movement toward home rule, initiated by Isaac Butt, was supported by some dominant Anglican landlords. Its principles were intrinsically accommodationist. Only after the Galway election trial of Catholic clergy (1872), the challenge to clerical authority raised by the Callan School case (1873) and the defeat of Gladstone's Irish Universities Bill in 1873 did the Catholic hierarchy lend home rule much support. But home rule also drew in Fenian strands as well, which gradually strengthened and became more important as Butt's conciliatory approach encountered total resistance.[22]

Within the North, home rule acquired a distinctly regional meaning. It was the ideological riposte to Orange supremacism; it exploited the hostility of Liberals to denominationalised education; and it stressed the importance of arresting the tide of emigration that began to accelerate in the North in the late 1860s, when the weakening market for domestically-produced flax undermined small tenantry. When Parnell displaced Butt from the leadership of the Irish Parliamentary Party, the temper of home rule organisation changed. Instead of being a somewhat ritual expression of linkage with the South, manipulable for clerical ends in the field of educational policy, it produced a more agrarian, radical and anti-Orange confrontationist leadership in the North.[23]

In the North, the Land League campaign of 1880–81 effectively became two campaigns operating in tacit alliance, each aware of the benefit to common ends. The Ulster Liberals' agitation was designed to strengthen Gladstone's hand in formulating the eventual Land Act of 1881; while the Land League's concept of itself as a national movement articulating agrarian demands was conceived as coercing reforms out of an alien power. Both were concerned however to avoid an Orange v Land League territorial contest in the North, which would have occurred if the Liberals had chosen to regard the Land League as essentially a nationalist challenge, even if the Land League had in those circumstances picked up support from even more Protestant farmers than it did in the event. But at all events, the Rev. R.R. Kane's efforts to mobilise Protestant tenants (ostensibly supporting land reform) to oppose the 'rebel invasion' failed.

When, after the 1881 Land Act, Parnell's challenge to Gladstone was renewed in more clearly nationalist terms, the 'Invasion of Ulster' provided Kane with his opportunity. The only strategy Liberals could advocate in this context of threatened sectarian collision was to keep their distance, leave the separation of contesting forces to state power and hope that the government would take care of the crisis. But Conservative landlords, being the local representatives of the state (as magistrates), used their position both to secure control over Orange demonstrations and to cast a mantle of legitimacy over them. The Liberal government might fire a warning shot (such as the dismissal of Lord Rossmore, one of the more reckless landlords, from the magistracy), but it would not challenge the Conservative magistracy as a bloc. When the government banned both demonstrations and counter-demonstrations, it played into the hands of the Conservative leaders and angered the Nationalists; when it decided to ban counter-demonstrations only, the Conservative landlord leader, Lord Arthur Hill, who had orchestrated the counter-demonstration movement, had difficulty sustaining the Conservative leadership against plebeian Orange rivals. The martial leadership role of the landlords, now largely deprived of economic power by the 1881 Land Act, began to rest upon their important residual constitutional powers.

They were the pivot between government authority which they represented locally and Orange territorialists over whom they sustained an uneasy leadership.

The 1884/5 franchise and seat redistribution acts extended the democratic basis of the electoral system including most of the adult male population. In the 1885 elections, the non-Nationalist seats in Ulster were represented either by Conservatives or prominent figures in the Orange counter-demonstration movement, the Liberals being entirely eliminated. The social radicalism of the independent Orange candidates was sharply tempered by their deference to Lord Arthur Hill, whose arbitration they sought in disputes with orthodox Conservative leaders in Belfast.

When Gladstone's conversion to Irish home rule became clear after the election, the pivotal role of 'martial' Conservative leaders was undermined and Orange confrontationist leaders now competed with each other in mobilising defiance. Protestant rioting against Catholics turned to full-scale warfare against the Constabulary who, it was believed, were present in force to impose home rule. The momentum of the conflict was such that even the defeat of the Home Rule Bill did not immediately arrest it.[24]

It was only when the Belfast Conservative magistracy were fully convinced themselves that there was no secret coercive plan—indeed when a commanding general reassured them that if there were, he would not be a party to it—that it became possible to restore order and to face down the Reverend Kane. The defeat of the 1886 Home Rule Bill buried the problem so acutely manifested at that time.

If the ethnic frontiers were not in any sense products of the new Imperialism of the 1880s, they were none the less affected by its development. Gladstone's commitment to Irish home rule contained at least three dimensions with direct bearing on Empire.[25] First, he feared Irish terrorist actions in Britain if home rule was not conceded—a concern to uphold the fabric of normal law in Britain. Secondly, his denunciations of the injustices of British rule in Ireland (perpetual recourse to coercion acts in particular) had moralistic implications for British rule everywhere. Thirdly, the modelling of home rule on the Nova Scotia Act suggested that his solution to Ireland was to put it on the same level of democratic free association with Britain to which the colonies of mass white settlement were moving. Gladstone's problem, unlike that of German Liberals who opposed Imperialism that had not yet gotten underway, was to develop principles and policies that would restrain the new Imperialising impulse and enable the existing Empire to approach norms of free association rather than coercive unity.

When the Conservative opponents of home rule spoke of Gladstone 'plunging the knife into the heart of the British Empire' or of the 'highest interests of the Empire precluding . . . any licence to the majority in Ireland to govern the rest as they please', they may indeed have cared little about Ulster. But that does not lead to the conclusion that they could have done other than they did and sponsored Imperialism at the same time.

The Unionists were supported by some Liberals (such as John Bright) who were in other respects anti-Imperialist. To have failed to uphold Ulster's Unionism would have rendered talk about upholding the flag anywhere else a self-evident hypocrisy. All that was required was for Ulster Unionists themselves to define the issue in terms of their rights not to be cast adrift from the mother country (as Randolph Churchill put it, for the Ulster Unionists to become an 'ace' rather than a 'two') for the effect to be coercive.

The only thing that is unusual about the Ulster frontier is that the national communities were denominated by religion and not by language. This is a result both of the pre-1830 decline of the Irish language and the erection of Irish nationality round Catholicism (the stigmatised character of the penal era); and of efforts made by Gladstone to represent the Protestants as Irish for the purposes of granting home rule. The fact that Irish nationalism proclaimed its non-sectarian character and secured some Protestant members is no more or less important than the fact that Czech and Polish nationalisms welcomed and secured bilingual supporters whose family origins were German. Representative violence creates deterrence communities and the symbols which denote them are ultimately of little consequence: all that matters is their mutually threatening character and the dissolution of all politically transcendent values or institutions which might bind them together.

The difference between the 1885–6 home rule crisis and the subsequent one in 1892–3 was that after the defeat of the 1886 Bill, the new Unionist alliance in Britain—composed of Conservatives and Liberal Unionist opponents of Gladstone—explicitly upheld Unionism and could be relied upon to use its overwhelming majority in the House of Lords to obstruct future home rule measures. That gave Ulster Unionist leaders a firm basis for a strategy of ritualised (rather than actualised) defiance that enabled them to sustain martial leadership over potential confrontationists. In this way, plebeian territorialist currents could be subsumed within an Imperialist alliance. It is no accident that they had to compete for leadership with confrontationist demagogues of the kind who actually made the running in German Bohemia. The hidden dimension of Ulster Unionist leadership was its role in disguising the essential weakness of British state power in the ethnic frontier between 1887 and 1912.

The UVF mobilisation of 1912–14—orchestrated by Ulster Unionists to oppose the introduction of home rule after the blocking power of the House of Lords had been broken—demonstrated that territorial conflict had broken the basis of any possible standards of justification. Irredentist native nationalist claims to Protestant Ulster, German Bohemia and German West Prussia were often expressed in terms of the sacred integrity of historic territories. But the minorities in the ethnic frontiers had strong reasons from their own experiences to sustain these notions. The British claim to Ireland was similar to the Austro-German claims to Bohemia. They could not rest on democratic headcounts in respect of the entire territory in question. Democratic principles could only be invoked for the ethnic frontiers where there were citizen majorities. Territorialism was a way of turning democratic values upside down (if we have to have a majority, then we will make one wherever we can) but in turning them upside down they were deprived of any sacred quality.

While the Gladstonian Liberals had hoped to rest the Empire as nearly as possible on free association and prevent the extension of metropolitan support to new situations where its coercive basis would have a much thinner disguise, their Liberal successors were faced with what amounted to a *fait accompli*. The flag flew over more precarious peripheries and its maintenance in Ireland was part of the new sacred principle of Imperialism. Preventing the Empire from feeding its coercive possibilities back into the metropolis was a question of preventing a domestic outcry against 'traitors' to the Imperial cause. A distinction had now to be drawn between aggressive imperialisation and the maintenance of the Empire as such. This tendency is reflected in the changing nature of post-Gladstonian Liberal criticism of Empire. During the Boer War the Radical Liberal opposition (as distinct from the Irish, which was pro-Boer) concentrated on the way reckless business interests had suborned Imperialism; it attacked the concentration camps and after the war the scheme for importing Chinese labour to work the gold mines. The line of attack was to draw out potentially popular interests in Imperialism in opposition to its economic monopolist initiators. Otherwise the criticisms of recklessness fused a general humanitarianism with warnings about the risks of destabilising the paternalistic possibilities for colonial rule.[26] If this was a policy it was essentially one of freezing the growth of Empire, to create some kind of leash over its administration to ensure that metropolitan power was not sucked into commitments of colonial adventurers. Paternalistic rule-governed authoritarianism might be a far cry from the rule of law and democracy in the metropolis—it might be more hypocritical than naked colonial oppression—but it was a way of reducing the risks of Imperialist tails wagging metropolitan dogs.

What brought people of the metropolis to see the dangers of Imperialism was the evidence that supporting flag-carriers everywhere led nations into adventures for narrowly defined interests and that Imperial rivalry threatened to create wars that would involve them. Their distance from the actual theatre of Imperialism enabled them to change their minds about its implications without threatening them with reprisal for the imperialising violence they might earlier have supported. So although Imperialism trapped metropolitans in a larger deterrence relationship with other Imperial nations, the relationships still had the appearance of being adjustable by state initiative. Opposition to Imperialism was not so much a root-and-branch criticism—which pointed in no intelligible policy direction—as a fear of its possible consequences. It might more appropriately be labelled Liberal Imperialism. But whatever else it was, it clung tightly to the achievements of liberal reform in the metropolis—the classical liberal concepts of rule of law and democracy—which both Empire and ethnic frontier threatened.

This Liberal Imperial position is illustrated by the apparently contradictory implications of Liberal support for Irish home rule after Gladstone. Post-Gladstone Liberals showed visibly declining enthusiasm for Irish home rule; yet it could never be abandoned. It was not just the point of honour involved but the fact that the Irish Nationalists had 85 seats in the Imperial parliament and that without that commitment, Irish votes might have been given to Conservatives (on the basis of Conservative conciliation of Irish Catholic educational interests), or become altogether less accommodationist. Preservation of an approximation to rule of law did indeed require conciliation of the Nationalists. But in practice, Conservative policy and Liberal policy (between 1906–10 when the Liberal majority was large enough not to depend on Irish votes) was very similar. The differences between the tentative devolution scheme of 1904–5 and the Irish Council Bill of 1908 are not spectacular. Both involved the reservation of important power to the British government (not least control of the police).[27]

Liberal moves in the direction of Irish home rule were not made in earnest until after the conflicts between the Liberal government and the House of Lords over the budget in 1910. Having broken the Lords' veto power on legislation and become from 1910 strictly dependent on Irish votes, the Liberals moved towards home rule.

As the bill passed through its various stages, Edward Carson organised the movement of defiance in Ulster.[28] The signing of the Covenant, the formation of a provisional government to take over should home rule be passed, and the mobilisation of the UVF secured first the enthusiastic support of the Conservative leader Bonar Law and then in 1913 the support of officers in the army (The Curragh Mutiny). The Liberals discovered first the scale of opposition in Ulster itself, then the Conservative threat to support defiance action and finally the impossibility of using the army to put down the defiance action. This does not make the Ulster Unionist opposition to home rule 'right' or 'wrong'. It does mean that British power could only have attempted to coerce it at the cost of possible failure (and total loss of control of what was actually happening in Ireland) and at the cost of exposing itself to charges of Empire treachery multiplied by the inevitable consequence of revealing Empire governmental weakness. Arguably the credibility of the Liberal Imperial position depended upon sustaining liberal order in Britain and preserving the outward appearance of order in the Empire. The threatened revolt would have undermined both. It has often been suggested that a revolutionary current in Britain would have swept aside the Imperialist/Defiance opposition if the Liberals had only had the 'courage' to take it on. This belief depends critically upon the assumption that large sections of the population would have rejected the Ulster Protestants as people 'unlike themselves'. This is an unlikely hypothesis. Of all sections of the Empire where the flag was threatened, Ulster had been made the touchstone of Conservative and Liberal Unionist unity. The Liberal retreat in the face of this defiance and the acceptance of the principle of partition (but obviously not an agreement on where the partition line might be drawn) was probably the only way of preventing the Irish question from doing to the metropolis that which Liberals most feared.

It might be argued that the Conservatives could have imposed home rule and deprived the Ulster defiance action of the necessary back–up. The essence of this argument is that as the Conservative Party embraced all the likely agents of defiance, logically any home rule measure of its making would have been without opponents of note. The difficulty with this argument is that as it did indeed embrace all the likely agents of defiance, it would have needed a very compelling reason to do this if it was not to impale itself on its own weapons. I shall argue later that the collapse of Imperial power might indeed have made this necessary, but that leads on to the far more important question: if Imperial power collapses, how is the possible antagonism between citizen and native nationalism prevented from moving into a cycle of representative violence that makes a mockery of peace?

CONCLUSION

The replacement of the moderate Nationalist leadership was probably inevitable once it was clear that the Imperial centres were locked into an interdependent relationship with defiance actions. The moderate Nationalists always knew they would have to coexist with the citizen society, and feared the consequences of conflicts which would spawn reasons for antagonism. As Rieger put it, 'For small nations it is particularly dangerous to tread on the quagmire of "might makes right".'[29] A peaceful and equal coexistence could scarcely be a product of warfare between them. But once a defiance action had worked, or the state became locked into upholding its citizens, it became more and more difficult to argue that observing the law in the face of provocation was not a form of weakness or acceptance of domination. The new 'radical' leaderships attacked old leaders for their conservatism (intrinsic to organic work), their timidity (their sense of responsibility for sustaining tranquillity), and their legalist hopes (which increasingly concealed the absence of any possible strategy that would subdue the claims of dominance). But the new strategy could only work by gambling for higher stakes—in effect the defeat not only of the citizen society but of their metropolitan state by a wider crisis. The ultimate polarisation of the ethnic frontiers—in which the citizens' links to the metropolis were matched by hopes for counteracting assistance from elsewhere—crystallised during the First World War. There were mass defections of Czech regiments to the Russians and military rule became an increasingly blunt German influence in Bohemia; the 1916 Easter Rising in Ireland, the executions in its aftermath and the effort to introduce conscription, all put nails in the coffin of the Irish constitutional Nationalists, already shaken by the Carson Defiance of 1912 and acceptance of partition; while Dmowski set himself up as Poland's representative in London.[30] In the

Czech and Polish cases, after the overthrow of Tsarism in Russia and the withdrawal of the Bolsheviks from the war in 1917, the future hung upon the defeat of Austria and Germany. For the Irish, it depended upon the influence of the Irish in America. When President Wilson announced his support for the self-determination of nationalities as the basis for peace, these hopes all seemed nearer to fulfilment.

But the doctrine of self-determination could only be applied when sanctioned by power. The history of the three frontiers has shown us how the legitimacy of the principle of head counting had been largely discredited. The major difference between what happened to Ulster on the one hand and Bohemia/Moravia and West Prussia/Posen on the other was that Britain was on the winning side and both Germany and Austria lost. The new settlement in Europe was the work of the victors, and everywhere issues that could not be settled according to simple ethnic criteria were settled in accordance with strategic considerations. The strategic considerations, however, were those of the distant United States and the more immediately concerned France and Britain.

Thus, France in particular was keen to ensure German weakness and the new states of Poland and Czechoslovakia were seen as helpful allies, so large German minorities (including the whole of Bohemia/Moravia and Posen/West Prussia except for Danzig) were incorporated into the new states. The Irish weakness was not lack of US support: in fact, American pressures that Britain solve the Irish question were made at the time of US entry into the war—Congress voted by a large majority that it hoped the Peace Conference would favourably consider the claim of Ireland to self-determination.[31] The difficulty lay in the fact that Britain was not a vanquished power and that left her in a position to apply the doctrine of self-determination in Ireland in accordance with her own priorities judged only in relation to the strength of forces internal to Ireland. Had Britain as a losing power been faced with a peace equivalent to the Treaties of Versailles (Germany) and St Germain (Austria), it would unquestionably have had to grant independence to a united Ireland.

One of the difficulties involved in getting this rather simple proposition into perspective is the fact that Poland and Czechoslovakia were formed as they were. Both appear to be a vindication of national separatisms which claimed 'historic lands' even where these included localised majorities of Germans. This makes it appear that there is somehow not only a necessary empirical progression between the accommodationist leaderships of the old nationalisms and their less accommodating successors (which we have argued that there is), but that this progression was necessarily a 'good' or 'righteous' thing. Such judgment is only vindicated at all by the results. In 1918–20 the metropolitan powers that sustained the dominant Germans were indeed cancelled by an external power, allowing this 'progression' to appear natural. In the Irish case this displacement of the old nationalists by the Republicans is also seen to have been progressive in both senses and leads to the view that Irish national self-determination was thwarted by the 'unjust', 'artificial', 'Imperialist' designs of the ever-malignant Britain. I am not suggesting that this view of the sacred unity of the island of Ireland was not provoked; it clearly was, in the same way that similar claims of the Czechs and Poles were provoked. But what Ireland suffered from in 1918–1920, when compared with Czechoslovakia or Poland, was not so much an injustice in an absolute sense as a different and opposing application of the doctrine of might makes right.

Colonialism and Mass Settlement: French Algeria and the US South

The US South and French Algeria resembled the ethnic frontiers of chapter two, in having large citizen populations (white and French) and being institutionally parts of the national territory of the USA and France respectively. They were, however, products of far more recent settlement colonisations and in both cases contained explicit institutional devices for super-exploitation of native (in contrast to citizen) labour. There is a contradiction between populating a land with citizens and at the same time depending on a cheaper and/or more easily coercible form of labour. In the US southern case, where blacks had been imported as slaves, the boundary between citizen and slave space was preserved by a combination of exclusionist barriers and the relative shortage of slave numbers. In the Algerian case, the process of colonisation generated a massive rural Moslem underemployment which became the absolute barrier to mass citizen settlement. This chapter starts with the contradiction between orthodox colonialism and mass settlement extension and then explores the cases of Algeria and the US South. These societies which were neither ethnic frontiers nor orthodox colonies help to illustrate the relationship between imperialisation of human relationships and colonialism as an instrument of economic plunder.

Orthodox colonial structures of nineteenth-century empires required the expropriation of large areas of land and cheap native labour to work them. Frequently the imposition of liberal concepts of property rights—individual ownership as distinct from tribal trusteeship—was a mechanism for securing colonial landownership and the resulting shortage of native land resources generated the native labour supply. But where the colonising presence was slender, it was essential to generate some indigenous support for the system. Liberal property rights might be a weapon of plunder in the beginning, but they tended to become the source of legitimacy of the system once it had established itself. Lesser native property ownership became an outer rampart for the institution of property itself.

In the early phases of colonial economic develoment, cheap labour and the scarceness of tropical productions generated profit levels for colonial capital much above average levels in the metropolis. But as the colonial production extended, and relatively freer competition developed between colonial capitalists, profit levels tended to equalise between the metropolis and empire. The low costs of production using native labour then meant not so much high profits as low metropolitan prices for colonial products. The cheap labour of the colonial world produced advantages which, instead of being monopolised by colonial companies were partly 'socialised' to the advantage of metropolitan citizens. This relationship described by Arghiri Emmanuel as 'Unequal Exchange' depended upon the absence of any significant movement of labour from the colony to the metropolis.[1] In theory free movement of colonial labour to the metropolis would have tended to eradicate the differential wage levels between the two zones. In its absence the system was self-reinforcing. Low colonial labour costs obviated incentives to invest in technology that would raise labour productivity; the low levels of colonial incomes discouraged investment in production for the limited domestic markets; which in turn might have increased demand for labour and lifted wage levels. Against this, however, the limited economic development that did occur, notably in transport and communications, together with the growth of administrative professional and teaching occupations, created opportunities for some natives. Furthermore, the system of economic exploitation could be preserved with reduced resort to coercion, once underemployment was a self-reproducing reality.

Independence movements tended to emerge eventually

amongst the section of the population in the 'developed' sector. They faced obstacles that retreated when they protested against them. Political sovereignty was much easier to achieve than any transformation of the impersonal structure of economic exploitation. Metropolitan governments could calculate the costs and benefits of resisting such political oppositions free from any consideration for colonists who numerically speaking were insignificant. The overall development tended to reduce rather than to intensify the long-term temptations to colonial repression.

The presence of settlers complicated this process not so much during the formative and overly repressive stages of colonial development but rather when its structure had matured. Once general wage levels began to reflect the low costs of native labour, made available by the dislocation of pre-colonial society, settler labour had either to exclude natives from its sphere, combine restricted native entry with an 'equal pay for equal work' formula, or accept the downward revision of its own wage levels. Otherwise settlers abandoned sectors of economic, life retreating to occupations protected from native competition. Furthermore, settlers often pre-empted spaces in the administrative sectors; and small capitalist settlers, vulnerable to competition from natives with comparable property rights, tended to seek restrictions upon them. Settlers in these positions were interested not so much in upholding the system of colonial exploitation of native labour as in avoiding being themselves drawn down into that world. Hence while metropolitan administration and larger colonial property holders might look upon admitting natives to spaces occupied by settlers as a way of stabilising the system in general, any such development jeopardised the ability of ordinary settlers to live at metropolitan levels in the colonial world. Unlike the citizens of the metropolis who benefited from unequal exchange and were only very indirectly affected by the competition of cheap native labour, citizen-settlers confronted this competition in their immediate lives. The main reason why there are in fact so few zones of the world that are 'intermediate' between ethnic frontiers (where a large body of citizens coexists with natives at similar levels of labour subsistence) and colonies proper (where the small body of citizens is restricted to a limited range of high-income occupations) is that a large gap between settler and native subsistence levels tends to displace the settlers from every occupation the native could undertake at lower rates of labour pay (either directly or through imputed income to himself as a small capitalist). Thus any tendency on the part of metropolitan governments or larger colonial capital to open either economic or political spaces to the native is likely to encounter a plebeian settler reaction, not unlike an ethnic frontier defiance action.

As far as the native society is concerned the presence of mass settlers altogether changes the implication of colonialism. Instead of a largely impersonal system whose ultimate malignancy is beyond his reach, the small settler in whose interest restrictions on native access to the 'developing' sector are upheld is very immediate. He becomes both a model of what the native himself might be and the obstacle in his path.

ALGERIA[2]

Although never more than 15 per cent of the Algerian population, the colons of Algeria were at one time looked upon as the means of making Algeria part of France. The French citizens included the French settlers, non-French Europeans born in Algeria (from 1889) and the indigenous Algerian Jews (granted citizenship in 1870). The great mass of indigenous Moslems could only become citizens by renouncing their civic status under Koranic law (tantamount to repudiating Islam) which virtually none of them ever did. By 1914 however, even the nuclei of French colonisation—the *communes de plein exercice*—contained only 600,000 citizens compared to a million Moslems. Rural mass settlement had reached its peak and was already decaying.

From the first conquest in 1830 to the downfall of the Second Empire of Napoleon III in 1870, Algerian settlement had been limited in order not to antagonise native rulers who were prepared to make their peace with the French military presence. The settlers' opposition to the military regime was spurred by a desire to secure access to more tribal lands. Their demand for democratic citizen rights (for settlers) created a link with French Republicans, who viewed ordinary settlers as pioneers extending French national territory. The natives whose lands were shielded by their accommodation with the Bonapartist military were seen as lesser clients of despotism. Thus when France was defeated in the 1870–71 war with Prussia, the settlers revolted against the military in support of the Republicans, securing for themselves full citizenship of the new Republic. And when this demonstration of French weakness was followed by a Moslem rising, the despised military was sent out to crush it. Between the forfeiture of tribal lands on the principle of collective responsibility for the rebellion and the extension of liberal concepts of individual property ownership imposed thereafter, vast areas of coastal Algeria were taken into European ownership. Seizure and purchase on terms amounting to seizure made available lands for a mass settlement.

Between 1871 and 1898 the French rural community rose from 120,000 to 200,000. Two forms of settlement proceeded side by side. The popular settlement consisted of roughly 10,000 grants of 40 hectare holdings which were free on condition that settlers remained on the land for five years. Simultaneously the pre-1870 system of selling large holdings to big concessionaires continued now that land could be more easily purchased.[3] Although some of these lands were worked by European labour, the tendency was to employ Moslem labour made available by the disruption and dispossession of traditional society and its need to pay French taxes. The system of local government through *communes de plein exercice* provided settlers with entrenched three-quarters majorities on councils empowered to raise taxes primarily on Moslems. After 1884 more and more Moslems were incorporated into these zones to expand their tax base. Moslems were subjected to a special legal code imposed by European justices of the peace. The system allowed the French settlement more or less unrestricted means of fleecing Moslem society in order to build up its own. The extension of vine culture between 1880 and 1900, made possible by free trade into France stricken by vine disease, increased the demand for labour; while the indigenously held land fell by 30 per cent in the 20 years to 1893.[4] But the depression in agricultural prices in the 1890s put more marginal producers under serious economic pressures.

Once the appropriation of Moslem lands and imposition of taxes on Moslems had generated a large supply of super-exploitable labour, a depression in agri-prices exposed European agriculture labour to its competitive effects; and more marginal European farmers felt the squeeze, leading many to sell up their holdings. The danger of the system which permitted participation of settlers with no initial capital was that it contained no limiting mechanism to prevent them resolving their own difficulties by further increasing exactions from Moslems. Sufficient pressure might, whether by starvation, disease or other causes, not only provoke rebellion but jeopardise the labour supply of larger, better capitalised plantations. Jules Ferry, the leading Republican supporter of Empire and a supporter of Algerian settlement in the 1870s, was very critical of the developments he witnessed in the 1890s. What Algeria needed, he thought, was more capital and fewer poor settlers. When Jules Cambon (Governor General 1891–97) tightened restrictions on settlement, so that lands had to be purchased, he was represented by colon politicians as engaged in a struggle against European colonisations. But the drift of French governing policy clearly reflected the remark of Ferry. 'The fundamental error in all that concerns Algeria is to have wished to see there anything other than a colony.'[5]

It is obvious that any extension of popular small-scale colon farming that depended not only on extending European land ownership but also on European labour would have involved genocide on a scale greater than anything that actually occurred, prejudicial to the existing structure of large-scale agriculture and to metropolitan government concern to limit its coercive commitments. In fact, even by the 1890s, many of the small colons had sold up their farms and moved to the cities and towns, which expanded rapidly during this period. The French character of Algeria, such as it was, depended essentially upon these areas. Until 1913 Moslems' movements outside their home districts remained legally restricted and the development of French education for Moslems—a precondition for securing any job requiring the French language—

was slow. In 1904 there were only 20,000 Moslems in such schools. Thus the port cities' European populations remained dominant even up to the 1930s (Algiers 1906, 75%; 1930, 67%; Oran 1930, 80%; Bone 1930, 59%).[6]

The small rural colon had been the original symbol on whose account the French of Algeria had been given full metropolitan citizen rights, including representation in the French parliament. The official retrenchment in the 1890s, however, generated a political revolt, which bore some resemblance to an ethnic frontier defiance action but had significantly different results.

France in the 1890s was convulsed by the controversy over the guilt or innocence of a Jewish Captain Dreyfus accused of spying for Germany.[7] The issues of fact became submerged as the Radical leader Clemenceau, the one-time standard-bearer of liberal democratic anti-Imperialism, and the Socialist leader Jaures, rallied to the cause of Dreyfus. The greater part of the supporters of the Republic were also Dreyfusards, on the argument that an injustice to one threatened all. Against them stood the opponents of the Republic, ex-Monarchists, Bonapartists, the religious orders and the greater part of the army. Anti-Semitism (of which more in chapter five) became the rallying cry of reactionary, ultra-Imperialist anti-Republicans.

In Algeria, where the administration was attempting to protect Moslems from unbridled exactions at a time of economic stagnation, a colon anti-Semitic movement appeared with secessionist overtones. It demanded the withdrawal of citizenship from the indigenous Algerian Jews, the only section of the indigenous population who were at that stage absorbed into French urban society. Hitherto, the small colons had been regarded as a popular Republican cause, but their alignment with the anti-Dreyfusards cast them as a threat to the Republic. The Algerian Jews were a tightly organised community who cast bloc votes for the conservative Republican leaders of the colonial lobby, Etienne and Thomson.[8] Jews were accused of illegally immigrating from Morocco and Tunisia and swelling the numbers of Algerian Jewish French citizens. A few aggressive incidents between Jewish men and non-Jewish women were made the focus of great attention, demands for collective revenge and excuses for municipal anti-Semitic regulations. In 1898, a violent anti-Semite, Max Regis, was elected mayor of Algiers and four out of the six Algerian deputies elected to Paris were anti-Semites. For a while, Algiers was in tumult, which subsided partly with the collapse of the anti-Dreyfus campaign in France and partly when the government announced the creation of the Delegation Financieres (a body which was to entrench European interests, but in particular those of established rural property holders) having its own budget. At the same time, the governor firmly clamped down on the anti-Semites and refused their municipal ordinances. The final blow to this defiance action came when in 1901 a small Moslem rising occurred which drew the colons' attention to their ultimate dependence on the French military. In the debate on the rising, Etienne and Thomson proposed a resolution backed by the Dreyfusard supporters which expressed confidence in the government and attacked 'fanaticism and bigotry' of the anti-Semites.[9] In 1902 the anti-Semites were electorally defeated.

After the Dreyfus affair, the shape of French Liberal Imperialism crystallised. Clemenceau, who had fought the anti-Republican influence of the Church and army at home and opposed Imperialism, became a supporter of Imperialism in which the Church and army played a conspicuous part abroad—a good example of what Barrington Moore describes as the tendency of liberal democracy to channel its repression outwards rather than against its own citizens.[10] But the implications of this democratic victory in Algeria were altogether more ambiguous.

Until the 1930s, the French parliament periodically debated various measures of reform from Algeria, such as the removal of specifically Moslem taxes or subordination under repressive law (the major impact of the 1898–1902 crisis for Moslems was the imposition of a new form of administrative internment in the wake of the 1901 rising) or various schemes of limited enfranchisement either of small numbers in the citizen electorate or larger numbers in separate electoral institutions. But the pressures upon them were limited. In 1912 a small group of French-educated Moslems, the Young

Algerians, made demands of this kind, all having the tendency to facilitate gradual Moslem assimilation to French citizenship. In fact, the Algerian socialists supported moves of this kind together with 'equal pay for equal work' as a way of dealing with Moslem migration to urban areas (very limited before 1914 and only on a massive scale during the 1930s depression). French discussions of assimilation tended to operate on the assumption that issues in Algeria would be defined by Frenchmen for Moslems rather than by Moslems for themselves. The whole framework of debate could be maintained within paternalistic parameters.

Defiance actions of plebeian citizens, just as in ethnic frontiers, tend to be targeted against 'alien' groups, who are in the process of replicating their own institutional structures (providing their own schools, cultural institutions, professional and retail services) and against powers who are conceived as assisting or tolerating this development. The 1898 anti-Semitic action focused on a secondary target of ethnic antagonism: the Jews, their conservative colonial and metropolitan Republican allies. This indicated that the real contradiction of settlement colonisation between Europeans and Moslems had still to crystallise. But anti-Semitic expulsionism had no attractions for any forces that wanted to preserve the rule of law and democracy in the metropolis nor for anyone concerned to stabilise the colonial status quo in Algeria. The colon defiance action's choice of target indicated their fundamental weakness—the mass of the rural sector depended on Moslem labour which inescapably branded Algeria as colonial. While Liberal Imperialism continued to talk of assimilation, however gradual in relation to Moslems, it could not countenance the reverse of assimilation in relation to those already assimilated.

THE AMERICAN SOUTH[11]

If the claim that Algeria was French was in the long term to be totally undermined by the limited extent of French citizen presence, this was not the case in the southern states of the USA. Rather than colonising an existing population, southern society was built on the labour of imported slaves and their descendants. Before 1860 slave cultivation of short staple cotton moved across the interior of the South in harness with free farming. So long as the westward expansion proceeded and slavery was concentrated on cotton productions, slavery permitted slave owners to profit from cheap labour without threatening free non-slave–holding whites with its competitive pressures. No southern state ever had much less than a 40 per cent white population and after the Civil War, all but three had white majorities. Even if the slave states were oligarchical by US standards, the non-slave–owning whites had more formal institutional leverage in the tentatively democratised systems than did commoners anywhere in Europe before 1848. In Alabama before the esclation of the North/South sectional conflict, the abusive term 'aristocrat' was used to denigrate political leaders accused of having pretensions to be superior to ordinary whites and who might contrive to reduce free farmers to 'serfdom'[12] by such means as foreclosing bank loans and then using slave labour to cultivate lands they engrossed from failed farmers. This rather loose and imprecise way of alluding to the potential contradiction between settlement and exploitation of subordinated (slave) labour might have become politically sharper had the issue of slavery not become the axis of regional conflict between North and South.

Slave plantations became increasingly self-sufficient (in provision of food and artisan services). Gradually slavery was adopted to industrial production and the practice of permitting slave artisans to hire out their own labour placed non-slave–owning whites in more direct competition with slave labour. White artisan protests and petitions against these practices were generally unavailing.[13] Secondly, some of the potentially best lands in the South were speculatively priced to reflect what they would be worth after the river levees had been built and the cypress forests cleared by slave labour. With slave and land prices rising, the greater part of the white populations became more clearly excluded from the booty of slavery.[14] Thirdly, the tide of European immigrants that accelerated during the famines of the 1840s avoided the South, anxious to steer clear of the depressing influence of competition with slave labour. The population base of the northern states grew relatively to the South.[15] Northern politicians, aware of both the increasing weight of their section and much of the hostility to slavery that lay behind it, began to articulate 'free soil' programmes to exclude slavery from the newly developing western territories. If the northern desire to avoid competition with slave labour took the form of wanting to keep slavery as far away as possible, the southern version of the same desire pointed to ensuring the expansion of slavery into the very territories from which the 'free soilers' wanted to exclude it. Hence the focus of the major conflict in the Kansas-Nebraska territories in the 1850s. When the Republican party linked support for free soil policies in the new territories with a programme of tariff protection which would permit industrial growth despite high US wage levels, its victory in 1860 brought to power an administration that had neither political obligations to, nor any significant support, in the South. Within the South itself the thirty years before the Civil War had seen slavery justified with an increasing vigour, proportional to the fear of free soil and abolitionist influence in the North. Whereas federal government forces had helped to suppress the Nat Turner slave rebellion in 1831, John Brown's rising in 1859 evoked echoes of northern sympathy.[16] The arrival of the Republican administration made it increasingly uncertain how the federal government might react to slave rebellions and was swiftly followed by the start of the US Civil War.

The convergence between northern opposition and southern support for slavery—fear of competition with slave labour—is strongly indicated by the Republican notion that abolition of slavery should be followed up by the emigration of freed slaves from the United States. Indeed, southern opposition to planters' power frequently adopted the same proposal. A working men's organisation in the only large southern city, New Orleans, proclaimed this objective after the federal occupation of southern Louisiana. And in the border states the extent of liberality toward blacks displayed by supporters of the federal side often went little beyond the mere abolition of slavery.[17] It is not clear that, taken *en masse*, the supporters of the federal government and of the southern Confederacy were sharply differentiated on this question. It is possibly not far from the truth to suggest that the primary animus against slavery was directed at the power and influence of slave owners rather than in favour of the slaves as people. Blacks were feared for the same reasons that slavery as a system had been feared, but now within the South for another reason also.

Although there was no slave rising against the Confederacy, about 85,000 blacks who had joined the federal army were stationed in the South until they were withdrawn by the end of 1866. Every sympton of black self-confidence or aggression was noted with anxiety and the removal of these troops was a major preoccupation of southern white leaders. In Mississippi, risings to secure lands of the plantations were anticipated at each Christmas in 1865, '66 and '67. General Sherman's experiment of land reform in the coastal areas and sea islands of South Carolina and Georgia was terminated by Congress for fear of the precedent that would be set for other projects of expropriation; but the hope remained for a while that this policy might be revived, despite the use of federal forces to put down the risings in parts of Georgia in 1869 and 1870.[18] Some of the earliest manifestations of white violence against blacks were directed against those who managed to buy or rent land as independent farmers; it was occasionally directed against planters who made such transactions. Thus it appears that the sale of land to blacks in the Natchez area was limited, but that nearly all such sales occurred before 1875.[19] The same preoccupation appeared when the white conventions in the Deep South, having abolished slavery as a precondition for re-entry into the Union in 1865, created a series of legislative devices known as Black Codes. With much of the South devastated, farmers and planters denuded of capital, and the hitherto coerced labour supply now free, the Black Codes were intended to thwart black powers of self-organisation, effectively to exclude blacks from urban and rural property ownership and to confine them to agricultural labour. Until 1867 the states maintained militias which were often composed of ex-confederate forces.[20]

When the congressional Republicans took the lead in Reconstruction in 1867 they struck down the Black Codes, abolished the militias and made admission to the Union conditional upon the enfranchisement of blacks. They intended to break the political power of the planters and create a southern Republicanism that would enable them to sustain the Republican high tariff deflationary monetary policy against a revived agrarian coalition of the South and west. They hoped that the Union army in the South would provide adequate support to sustain alliances between southern whites and blacks which would realise black citizenship and introduce orthodox capitalist development of railroads and industry. Subsequently the Reconstruction administrations were allowed to form militias of their own.[21]

The relationship between whites and blacks had rested in the last analysis on the use or threat of violence. The new order of Reconstruction would tend to attract those whites who had least to fear from a quantum shift in the force relationship and most to gain by seizing the opportunity. As far as native southern whites were concerned, Stampp observes they could be divided into two categories. First, whites from predominantly white free farming areas who sought railroad extension, public education, a more equitable taxation system and wanted to break the back of planters' power. For them, perhaps like northern 'free soil' Republicans, small black minorities posed little threat regardless of the overall shift in the balance of force relationships. Alliances made with blacks elsewhere in the state could be judged on their pragmatic merits. But once the possibility of land reform had passed by, the other group of whites who could capitalise on non-coercive relationships with blacks were plantation owners on richer soils (notably the Mississippi Delta) who were able to offer share-cropping tenants high returns for the labour planters eagerly sought. This second group's purposes were directly opposed to those of the first.[22] Those most threatened by black freedom were farmers and planters on poor soils unable to keep black labour voluntarily and sections of urban populations (notably artisans) threatened with competition. The first wanted coercive devices to subordinate black labour and the second wanted to exclude blacks. The blacks themselves sought education and to organise their own lives, to which end black churches were erected and institutions of self-help and solidarity (such as Loyal Leagues). Full legal and political rights increased their capacity to secure schools and some kind of protection of the law. Political offices also—in the absence of accumulated capital—provided important sources of income.[23]

But the very fact of being organised was bound to be a threat to a social order that once rested on ensuring their total disorganisation and which had recently tried to curb their power of organisation by Black Codes. The question was whether this new power could be made an argument in favour of conciliating their interests rather than seeking new forms of control. Between 1867 and 1900 the effective support of the northern Republicans for southern black citizenship sank from a very strong commitment before 1872 to practically nothing by 1900. Reconstruction was ended in 1876–77, when the conservative leaders of the southern Democrats assented to the election of a Republican president despite a disputed electoral count. Although the real reasons for the arrangement included southern hopes for railroad subsidies and a share of presidential patronage, the publically proclaimed reason was the agreement of President-elect Hayes to withdraw federal troops from the South and thereby to let the three remaining Reconstruction governments fall. Even though a Democratic president would have done as much, it was highly significant as it marked a clear public break between the Republican Party and Reconstruction. From the late 1870s to the mid-1890s, black influence was curbed but not eradicted.[24] White politics divided between the economically con-servative–led Democrats and various Greenback, Indepen-dent Readjuster and Populist popular reactions to the distress associated with the agricultural depression and problems of agrarian indebtedness. Both sought black electoral support, the Democrats on paternalistic principles and their opponents on a basis that approximated to class solidarity. Finally in the 1890s, federal obstacles to full-scale disenfranchisement and legalised segregation were removed and by the early twentieth century blacks were under a regime not unlike that originally conceived for them in the 1865 Black Codes. The outward thrust of American Imperialism in the 1890s reconciled the northern Republicans and southern Democrats at the expense of the southern blacks.

The changing phases of the Reconstruction regime in Mississippi, one of the three states with a black majority, suggest a method of understanding the concept of paternalism.[25] In the overwhelmingly black counties of western Mississippi, the planters were interested in attracting as much labour as possible to their highly productive lands. There were relatively high economic returns for share-cropping in this area. During Reconstruction, black office-holding (including black sheriffs whose surety bonds were often subscribed by white planter Republicans) and the development of schools replaced a coercive race/class relationship by a voluntary class/race compromise.[26] At least three factors shaped the meaning of 'paternalism'. First it contrasted sharply with what blacks experienced in other parts of the state, notably the counties in the east of the state with poorer soils where violence was used not only to control blacks but to drive out labour agents and to murder or intimidate Republican office-holders and school teachers.[27] Faced with a choice of 'paternalists' seeking black labour and others either trying to exclude black competiton or to coerce them, the former was obviously preferable, particularly if one of the incentives was the recognition of legitimate black influence and if it was tacitly guaranteed by the sheer relative weight of black numbers. Even after Reconstruction was overthrown, blacks still held minor offices in these areas in a one-sided fusion arrangement with (now) Democratic whites. And when whitecapping expulsionism developed in south-east Mississippi in the early twentieth century, the Delta counties were still *relatively* speaking a refuge, even if their forms of labour control were by then highly coercive. In other words, a paternalistic arrangement, however coercive it had actually become, still could be described as such, so long as it was to be compared with a worse alternative.[28]

The second factor influencing the balance of the paternalist system was the disposition of the external guarantor, the federal government. The early racist violence in 1869–70 in the eastern counties was relatively easily put down. The knowledge that Reconstruction had substantial white support and federal force in the background were mutually strengthening. The federal force reduced the risks faced by white southern Republicans from racist violence; and white support lent credibility to the federal policy. But in 1873 the Mississippi Republicans divided between the Alcorn faction which wanted to preserve the balance of office-holding that had sustained white leadership and the Ames faction which supported black claims for increased leadership roles in the alliance for which they provided the votes. In this election Ames won but the overwhelming part of the white vote (Republican and Democrat) went to Alcorn.[29] The implied class/race compromise in the Delta counties broke down. The level of taxation and public debt became closely linked in the eyes of the property holders with the ascendant political forces which levied and expended them. Initially the taxpayers' revolt which took shape in Vicksburg and Warren County was 'a major attempt by the old leadership to keep the conservative movement focused on concrete issues, avert the social disruption that accompanied racial violence, and prevent the federal intervention that many believed would follow the employment of all-white tactics'(Harris).[30] The taxpayers' revolt in Vicksburg and Warren County focused all-white opposition first against an effort of blacks to secure a majority on the city council and then to remove a black sheriff who, lacking white bond sureties or any creditworthy alternative, was held to be unfit to exercise his function as a tax collector. The defection of the propertied white strata from Reconstruction, and federal reluctance to use force to sustain the increasingly unpopular regimes that depended ever more heavily on black votes, were mutually reinforcing tendencies. They now came round in full circle. Although federal military assistance was sent to restore Ames' supporters in Vicksburg after a confrontation that left 36 blacks and 2 whites dead, in all subsequent encounters Ames was told to exhaust all his own resources before federal support would be forthcoming. His own resources (by his own account) depended on black militias and black ministers' exhortations to their congregations to support the evicted sheriff.[31] In other words, when the paternalistic Republican alliance disintegrated, white challengers could confront the regime sure in the knowledge that it could protect itself only by falling back on its black supporters. In such circumstances confrontationist logic was self-fulfilling. Direct action against 'black rule' might be a misrepresentation of the current reality; but if the attack had failed it would have been defeated principally by blacks and the aftermath might be something much more like 'black rule' than anything that had appeared so far.

A third element strengthening the paternalistic voice was the absence of any reliable alternative alliance for blacks, a tendency which the paternalistic 'alliance' or arrangement magnified. The more effectively blacks were excluded from other areas than plantation agriculture and the more plantation owners preferred black labour to white (being more pliable when less able to exert its rights) the more were the 'cultural' differences between blacks and whites perpetuated, not least their preparedness to accept low wage rates and oppressive labour conditions in work elsewhere. Thus the Grange or farmers' movement, whose membership may have had ambivalent feelings about black political rights, was drawn into the 1874–5 revolt against Ames by charges of oppressive taxation and profligacy.[32] Once the barriers against anti-black violence crumbled, any group whose interests might be served by the overthrow of Reconstruction was magnetised. And all except the heroic opponents of such violence were silenced.

Overt political class conflict amongst whites did not break out until after the overthrow of Reconstruction and the consolidation of conservative Democrats in power in the southern states. The strength of populism in the 1890s has been directly correlated with the growth of tenancy among farmers in mostly white counties.[33] Populist attitudes toward alliances with blacks covered the whole range between outright opposition to positive support. Their public pronouncements were consequently ambiguous. By means of an uncertain mixture of coercion, fraud, inducements in the shape of schools and office-holding, and doubts about populist intentions towards blacks, Democratic candidates secured the black vote in many plantation areas. In other areas, notably North Carolina where the populists allied with the Republicans, the black vote went to the popular side (as earlier to the Readjusters in Virginia). The eventual disintegration products of populism ranged between whitecapping expulsionism in southern Mississippi (driving away black tenants placed on farms by merchants who had taken them from bankrupt white farmers), increased white Republican voting in northern Alabama (often an expression of electoral opposition to 'White Supremacism'), socialism (among white and black lumber workers in northern Louisiana, subsequently broken by company violence) and sheer non-participation (magnified by post-1900 poll tax requirements for voting).[34]

Where popular regimes did succeed in taking power at state level, Virginia (1879–83) and North Carolina (1896–98), they were subsequently overthrown by campaigns that focused on particular towns where it was held that they had led to black rule. In neither case was this true in any literal sense. But in both Danville and Wilmington, there were some black office-holders, notably policemen, alongside relatively self-confident black communities which contained professional and commercial elements. If there was a common denominator (including say Vicksburg) it was evidence that blacks were organising themselves free of controlling (i.e. white) leadership. In much the same way, even after virtual disenfranchisement, a campaign for a more comprehensive disenfranchisement in Georgia could be orchestrated in 1906 because in McIntosh County there were a substantial number of black farmers who still elected black county officials.[35] Rabinowitz shows that formal disenfranchisement was actively supported in order to rid white factions of the need to promise black offices in exchange for black votes (in controversies over prohibition which preceded the similar contest between Democrats and Populists) and to assist the process of imposing the rule of white police over young urban blacks who displayed collective resistance to arrests.[36] Thus even if substantial numbers of whites may have wanted to live and let live, have voted with blacks for common ends, it seems as though lines were drawn whenever blacks secured any kind of leverage over the exercise of the law independently of white authority. I will return to this subject in chapter six.

The US South is not usually referred to as a settlement colonial society. I have done so to draw attention to its experience of the contradiction between super-exploitation and citizen settlement (illustrated in a manner of speaking by the way its white population failed to grow while that of the north far outstripped it). The greater weight of the white population meant that metropolitan power, far from having to reckon with black protest at exclusionist restrictions, had to reckon with white protest at its own interventions on the blacks' behalf after 1867. Thus the line of least resistance was to restore virtual white autonomy.

Similarly, the blacks could not be held in a super-exploitable condition by mere underemployment (as in a usual colonial context) but only by being actively excluded from other spheres, whether by law or permitted extra-legal possibilities of violence. Paternalism remained as real for blacks as the expulsionist/exclusionist threat from which it was a protection; paternalism also perpetually regenerated that threat.

Contrasting the black post-1867 experience with that of natives in ethnic frontiers, several themes emerge. First the federal government's reason for sustaining black political influence was essentially instrumental and therefore revers-ible. There was no compelling external force to which atten-tion needed to be paid (Irish Catholics outside Ulster; Czechs in central Bohemia; or even the Russian and Austrian Poles). Secondly, and expressing the same point in another way, as federal support receded, even the most limited evidences of black self-organisation and local power were regarded as 'dangers'. There was nothing left that resembled black space: the areas that in a European context might have become such, the overwhelmingly black plantation counties, were firmly controlled by white oligarchies. If the gist of this presentation seems 'segregationist', the point is made by Rabinowitz's study of southern cities that the notion of separate facilities (and therefore territorial separation) was common to the Reconstruction era as well as to the periods that followed. What changed after Reconstruction was that black facilities became progressively less equal or less of an asset (as with the replacement of black school teachers by white, and the eventual reversion to black teachers only when they could be paid lower wages) and *de jure* segregation was effectively extended to what were once common but then became white–only facilities. After 1900 blacks were squeezed out of urban commerce and craft occupations. They had, in other words, no means of building up anything that resembled an interdependent sub-society of their own (organic work).

Booker T. Washington's outward acceptance of disenfranchisement and the notion that blacks should concentrate their energies on industrial education and build up their society through economic self-improvement may have been open to all manner of criticisms (not least that it was exactly what southern employers and plantation paternalists wanted to hear). But although W.E.B. DuBois observed that without the ballot, blacks would be powerless and antagonism with working-class whites would be regenerated to the advantage of ruling-class whites, Washington's approach had the practical advantage that it intended to exploit the only significant cleavage in white society that could actually be exploited.[37] Faced with pressures that might have driven blacks out of every urban occupation that whites might have sought (and might also have destroyed black educational institutions), it was a calculated gamble that paternalist whites interested in efficient black labour would provide the cover under which some kind of self-organisation could develop. The temptations to black nationalism were obviously very real. The idea of concentrating blacks in coastal Georgia (where McIntosh County lay) so that black territory on the US mainland would be linked to predominantly black zones of the Caribbean which could not be 'surrounded' may have been a dream.[38] But seen alongside European ethnic frontier zones and their experiences of territorial antagonism, the dream looks quite 'normal'.

4

Class Solidarity and Practical Internationalism

Having dealt with the question of how the values of the liberal era were deprived of sacred quality by territorial conflict in the ethnic frontier, it now remains to speak of the power of workplace solidarity and socialism to undermine the integrity of national antagonisms. Socialism in this context appears as the highest form of restraint upon violent malignancy. In Bohemia, in the context of the collapse of Austrian and German Imperial power at the end of the First World War, it was largely responsible for ensuring the peaceful transition to the new Czechoslovak state, which for about ten years was one of the most harmonious examples of multinational democratic government in Europe. Study of this example throws further light on the question of what obstacles lay in the path of the unification of an independent Ireland in the same period.

The creation of workplace solidarity was only a relatively late possibility in the ethnic frontier. Until a fairly high level of labour mobility had been established (mostly since the famines of the 1840s), native migrants could be used by employers as cheap or strike-breaking labour to break up craft unionism. This transposition of the displacement effect to urban settings gave a new thrust to communal conflict, being as it was a source of real division of interest within the working class. Only the establishment of 'equal pay for equal work' could break up this divisive possibility; then, for example, a mining capitalist would no longer be able to exploit German-Czech antagonism for his own purposes.[1]

'Equal pay for equal work'—absolutely essential to class solidarity—could still be a two-edged sword. If German workers imposed this policy on employers and a token number of Czech workers, it could then be used as an instrument for facilitating the virtual exclusion of Czechs, once the employer's economic interest in securing them had been broken. So, however necessary 'equal pay for equal work' was as a compact between workers, it could only be the source of solidarity so long as it was not seen as a way of strengthening exclusionism. The trouble was that it *could* be used in this way, and so the question of visible intent necessarily became very important.[2] If ethnic antagonisms continued, then from the native worker's perspective 'equal pay for equal work' would be viewed as a disguise for discrimination, never intended as a measure of justice. Put simply, once a society has experienced the virulence of representative violence, even the significances of workplace solidarities were open to doubts and suspicions. Just as we have seen the way in which democratic principle, rule of law etc. were destroyed by territorial antagonism— eradicating the sacred basis of liberal values—now the same danger threatened the principles and values of socialist solidarity.

This relatively formidable obstacle was overcome in many places and times in Bohemia and Ulster. But the next layer of obstacles—the translation of such solidarities into political forces that could operate on the same plane as and in opposition to national antagonisms—was an altogether more awesome task. To demonstrate why this should be so, it is necessary to explore the ways in which working-class and plebeian members of the citizen society related to the ruling classes. With the onset of territorialist national antagonism, the plebeian nationalist ideologies attacked dominant economic classes for their lack of vigour and solidarity in the struggle against native nationalism. These currents also tended to articulate orthodox support for dominated classes—trades union rights, social reforms—against capital and landownership. The German Workers Party in Bohemia combined the plebeian nationalist and working-class critiques explicitly. But even if the nationalist stance of the German Workers Party was unreservedly opposed by Social Democrats, there were still other dangers. Much nineteenth- and early twentieth-century socialist theorising was concerned with the question of which nationalisms were 'progressive'; meaning which nationalisms would tend to further the cause of democratisation most effectively. This type of reasoning may have made sense to abstract theorists and people far away from ethnic frontiers. But within the ethnic frontiers themselves, describing a nationalism as 'progressive' was simply a licence to align the weak and embryonic currents of socialism with a strong and already well-established pole of a national conflict.[3] Even nominally internationalist socialist parties that declared the 'progressive' quality of an existing nationalism were in danger of being absorbed into either plebeian citizen nationalism or native nationalism.[4] The only release from this dilemma was to find a national formula which was, in the circumstances then prevailing, a compromise.

We have already seen how in Ulster in 1880–81 a major tenant-farmer agitation was orchestrated simultaneously by the (Nationalist) Land League and the Ulster Liberals. The intervention of the Liberals prevented Orange territorialists from repulsing the Land League as Nationalist invaders and allowing them to uphold practices of plebeian dominance; it also obliged the Land League to concentrate (in the North) on its agrarian objectives rather than to make a display of explicitly nationalist force. The Liberal intervention was possible because it aimed to mobilise a class to secure land reforms in alliance with a metropolitan ally that gave this strategy credibility. Class unity on this occasion subdued national antagonism. It could be seen as a class action because even though it was Unionist in its national implications, it explicitly attacked the concept of Unionism as a form of domination over the Catholic community. But it was able to do this because its metropolitan alliance gave it a means of securing a reformist action within the existing national context. The conversion of Gladstone to home rule in 1886 deprived Northern Liberalism of this strategy thereafter.[5]

The rise of mass trade unionism in Belfast during the first decades of the twentieth century, though it demonstrated the strength of class organisation, had very limited political implications. In the period before 1905, the climate for

Labour Party organisation was facilitated by the simultaneous appearance of the Independent Orange Order which, like the German Workers Party in Bohemia, combined orthodox class attacks on capital and landownership with attacks on ruling class conciliation of the opposing nationalism.[6]

The Belfast Nationalist leader Joe Devlin in this period of stand-off in national conflict—frozen by the Liberals' commitment to home rule and the Nationalists' consequent strategy of legalism—supported the appearance of Labour both for its own sake and as a means of weakening official Conservative Unionism.[7] The Labour programme, however, was drastically weakened by a two-fold difficulty. First, it advocated the continued union of Britain and Ireland as the context in which working-class power might be realised in both, in spite of the fact that the British Labour Party itself supported home rule. Second, in advocating the continued union from the context of industrial Belfast, it showed no appreciation of the sources of nationalism in the south which it attributed to essentially 'moral' faults. Had it analysed the implications of uneven economic development of capitalism in Ireland, Henry Patterson argues that it might have recognised in the protectionist ideologies of Southern nationalism the basis of another legitimate nationality, and separated itself from mainline Unionism which opposed home rule for any part of Ireland.[8] The practical implication of this criticism is that it did not advocate the partition of Ireland in the period when this might have been an intelligible basis for national compromise. Whatever its intentions, its national programme could scarcely be differentiated from that of Conservative Unionism. When the home rule crisis loomed large in 1911–14, Labour lacked an independent standpoint supported by an intelligible strategy. Any ambivalence it displayed over supporting Unionism left it vulnerable to the prevailing intimidatory climate.

Whereas Belfast Labour had no metropolitan ally with which to develop this alternative national solution, the Social Democrats in Bohemia had considerably more freedom of movement. In 1897, at the time of the conflict over the Badeni decrees, both the Czech and German Social Democrats—whose only access to institutional representation was the newly introduced fifth curia in the Reichsrat—had opposed the decrees because they would perpetuate the oligarchical system of the provincial diets and local governments. While they supported a democratised federation arrangement as an alternative, the Czech Social Democrats were vulnerable to the charge of helping pan-German opposition. Although the greatest part of the disorder at this time occurred in German majority areas against Czech minorities and their cultural institutions, some fighting occurred between Czech and German workers in overwhelmingly Czech areas, in two of which (Pilsen and Kladno) Social Democrats subsequently lost their seats to Czech National Socialists. The fighting took both wings of Social Democracy by surprise but their capacity to limit the damage in the longer run depended on the continued credibility of the democratised federal concept.[9] After 1900, the notion that Bohemia would have to be either partitioned or else governed by a strictly bicommunal system was becoming clear. The imperial centre wanted to achieve such a result and it held out a concept of 'triple' partition as a possible compromise (German, mixed and Czech districts), although as we have seen, neither Czech nor German main-line blocs were prepared—or able—to reach any kind of consensus on how this should be done. The Czechs were ambivalently perched between wanting to uphold Austria because of German encirclement and looking toward Russia (and pan-Slavism) as the Austrian monarchy and the German Reich became increasingly locked into Imperial alliance; the pan-Germans oscillated between wanting German (and Czech) areas of the Empire incorporated into the Reich and tacitly supporting the increasing resort to direct German bureaucratic rule as an alternative to increased Czech power in Bohemia. In a sense then, the central state looked more 'neutral', not just because a lot of its lower officials and gendarmes were Czech (many of the Irish equivalents were Catholic), but because its central state apparatus was obliged to preserve a higher profile in Bohemia and because it still appeared more 'equally objectionable' to both camps. The Social Democrats' opportunity arose because its policy of national equality corresponded to the state's desired formula: 'Nothing can show more clearly the abnormal state condition of the Danube monarchy than the fact that the strong parliamentary progress of Socialism could be regarded as a gain for the State.' Paradoxically, the state's confession of its weakness—its inability to uphold either bloc—was the Social Democrats' opportunity.[10] Even though Social Democracy split up into national sections, by 1911 it had about 25 per cent of the German and Czech seats in the Reichsrat. The failure of Austria to develop an Imperialist system of the kind developed by Britain and (to a lesser extent) Germany, gave an internal transnationalism a coherent meaning, even if it was beginning to lose it as the war approached.

However, putting things in this way only explains why the pre-war possibilities for establishing a transnational socialism were better in Bohemia than in Ulster. In Ulster during the war, and especially in the local elections of 1920, Labour became stronger.[11] It might have been that once partition was seen as a policy with metropolitan allies, it could have become the basis of an explicit Labour policy of national compromise. But that is conjecture. The important point is that whereas in Bohemia, Social Democracy had a vital part to play in the transition to a relatively peaceful and stable Czechoslovakia, its relative weakness in Prussian Poland and in the North of Ireland was part and parcel of the story of a thoroughly antagonistic take-over by Poles in 1918–20 and of the violent beginnings of Northern Ireland.

The upsurge of socialist revolt in the German and Austrian armies in 1918 led to the Armistice, the fall of the old regimes and the establishment of socialist governments in Germany and the German zones of Austria. The Austrian socialists had been the first to respond to President Wilson's peace proposals by announcing their support for the principle of national self-determination. The fact that this stance appeared not only just but realistic, together with the generalised opposition to war, provided Austrian and German-Bohemian Social Democrats with massive popular support. The Socialist government in Austria (unlike the one in Germany) replaced the old army by popular militias over which they were able to keep tight control and prevent 'interventions' against Czechs.[12] Even though the mass of Germans in Bohemia wanted to be incorporated into a German state (whether Austria, Germany or a unified state of both), the Socialists actively discouraged opposition to the entry of the Czech Legions, insisting upon discipline and appeal to the peace conferences, thereby preventing any 'defiance' actions.

Thus the Bohemian Social Democrats themselves—when prevented by the Czechs from participating in the February 1919 elections—organised peaceful marches in favour of the principle of self-determination 'to prevent individual protest'. And when fighting broke out at Kadan between demonstrators and Czech troops, leading to twenty-five deaths, an agreed version of the incident was arrived at which neither justified nor condemned either side (one demonstrator threw a brick, one soldier shot without orders to do so), an outcome which anyone familiar with these kinds of situation knows very well could never have been reached if the German and Czech leaders had not wanted to reach it. Secondly, the Austrian government was in a position to keep under control any possible 'interventions' and to deprive the Czechs of the reason or excuse for heavy precautionary measures against German irredentism. And thirdly, the German government, preoccupied with Polish claims over Posen where they were allowing interventionists to fight Poles (or Bolsheviks in the Baltic), were keen to avoid appearing annexationist by interfering with Czechoslovakia. Fourthly, most German capitalists despite outward displays of national feeling preferred to operate behind Czechoslovak tariff barriers (rather than face German industrial competition), and were not sorry to see Czech militias take over from German workers' councils.[13]

Although it may be considered that the inclusion of the German minority into Czechoslovakia was a disaster (in the light of what happened in 1935–39), what stands out most sharply here is the role of Socialists with half the German Bohemian vote in preventing the kind of national conflict that would have poisoned Czechoslovakia from the beginning. The Bohemian Germans clearly did not want to be incorporated, but the restraint exerted by the Social Democrats was a key element enabling the Czechs to demonstrate an authentic liberality towards their national minority.

Defeat of the Imperial centre in war was not enough on its own to permit Czechoslovak-style transitions. It was necessary that *no* significant actions be taken that set the circle of violence into operation. That meant not only practical internationalist leadership of the people of the contested zones, but also the paralysis of those forces of defiance that could create situations to which everyone might have to respond. The Polish case, for example, demonstrates these dangers. In 1918, the Independent Socialists in control of the soldiers' councils attempted to organise a handover to the Poles in Posen. But between the allied concern about Bolshevism and the German government's continued licence to the German high command, periodic battles occurred between German and Polish forces which had implications for civilians. When Poland became engaged in war with Russia, Germans fled Poland to avoid conscription and German dockworkers in Danzig obstructed the transport of munitions to the Poles (whether out of a conception of internationalist duty to the Bolsheviks or sheer animosity to the Poles it would be hard to sort out). Polish-German relations in the old Prussian zones—without any significant earlier leavening effect of transnational political co-operation—were often characterised by overt efforts to thin down the German presence. Apart from German civil servants and those who fled to avoid conscription, the Polish governments not only displaced all who had opted to retain German citizenship but they attempted to evict all 'settlers' (whose introduction was part of the post-1885 colonisation schemes) and only relinquished their rights under the Versailles treaty to liquidate German property in 1929–30. The SPD's charge that the Polish policy of eviction was a consequence of the policy of the German Right before the war did not prevent the issue being a stick with which the Right could beat democratic governments in general and the SPD in particular (see chapter five).[14]

Bruegel's account of the formation of Czechoslovakia (the analogue of a united Ireland) should draw our attention away from the non-problem of working-class militancy failing to turn Ulster Unionist workers into socialist Irish nationalists. The 44-hour strike which spread through Belfast in 1919 indicates the scale of trades union activism which expressed itself in some class conscious form or other. But even if the strength of Belfast labour in early 1920 had approached that of the Bohemian socialists, no comparable mechanism would have existed in Ireland for peacefully creating an independent united Ireland.

It is only necessary to consider the hypothetical condition of Britain, defeated in the First World War and its Imperial apparatus paralysed by the appearance of socialist councils in the army, to see that a Carson-style intervention might then have been arrestable. Under these circumstances the leaders of the Belfast labour movement might very well have been able to secure a policy of active retraint, being able to point to the potentially disastrous consequences that might flow from work-place expulsionism. It is, I think, futile to attribute what actually happened to a 'lack of class consciousness', because class consciousness developed within national communities. Its internationalism could never be a denial of the reality of national communities; it could only be a source of restraint upon their antagonistic exacerbation.

Once the British government, neither defeated nor encumbered by internationally sanctioned armistice agreements, collided with Republicanism in the South, the pre-war matrix of ethnic frontier-metropolis relations were easily reasserted. The British state's limited powers in the North were again exposed by a supremely violent defiance action.

Unionist strategy was to demonstrate to the British government the strength of Unionist force and feeling, the dangers of not absorbing it into a legitimate force and the disadvantages arising from not using it. On the assumption that the British might concede control to the Republicans in the South, then the more the indigenous Unionist forces in the North were involved in the opposition, the more difficult it would be to make any arrangement eventually opposed by them. In other words, the British government would find itself pinioned to support of the North because it lacked the instruments with which to put down Ulster defiance of its power. This was remodelled defiance strategy. In the accounts of both Buckland and Farrell, it becomes clear that the Unionist leaders sought always to maximise their freedom of action from Britain: threatened revolts of their own followers (whether intentionally or not) became the lever for prising this freedom. British government preparedness to bestow this freedom depended on whether it facilitated negotiation with the Southern leaders (enabling it to claim that it could not coerce the North) or embarrassed them.[15]

Patterson shows how before the expulsions from the ship-yards and engineering works in mid-1920, a group of Labour Unionists had been created by Unionist leaders worried about the challenge of the labour movement and the possible interpretation that would be placed upon Labour votes by British politicians then engaged in the conflict with Sinn Féin in the South. This initially not very influential group started organising a campaign to have Catholics displaced from the shipyard to make way for returning ex-servicemen. Once Republican violence spread to the North in early 1920, this issue was turned into a question of territorial infiltration and advance legitimacy was given by Unionist leaders to the anti-infiltration movement. When the expulsions began, Catholics, socialists and other 'rotten' Protestants were driven out (including some socialists recently elected city councill-ors).[16]

Socialism in ethnic frontiers was confronted with a national conflict which no amount of clever theorising or wishful thinking could ever dissipate. Stripped down to its essentials, it was an assertion and a warning that national antagonism—in these contexts between workers of opposed nationalities—was lethal. Working-class solidarity was both a constructive instrument of class power and a way of bringing out the grisly fact that national conflict was both an unpleasant evil (rather than a righteous cause) and something that could suck everything worthwhile down into the gutter. The importance of the Bohemian case is that its (perhaps short-lived) success draws our attention to a particularly powerful case of effective restraint and makes the meaning of the less successful efforts of socialists in Ulster and Posen more comprehensible.

The history of these societies is apt to bury efforts of this kind and in so doing to bury their most redemptive moments; the greatest achievement of socialism in ethnic frontiers was to erect barriers of restraint against real possibilities of madness. It is immaterial that in the course of doing so, they often spoke as though the dangers of madness arose from malignant class interests and selfish individuals, rather than being embedded deep in the social fabric. These barriers erected by socialist internationalism were nowhere near absolute, but they were a lot stronger than anything else available; and their failure is a tragic statement about these societies, not a condemnation of themselves.

Fascism and the Metropolis

In this chapter I shall look at the impact of ethnic frontier antagonisms upon the metropolitan core areas and the rise of fascism. Democracies can only be said to be stable when the results of elections are treated as binding and the operation of law and order and justice do not generate collective protests from large sections of the population. Yet in ethnic frontiers which were institutionally part of metropolitan societies, territorial antagonism undermined the sacred qualities of democracy and rule of law; and in both Algeria and the US South large sections of the population were explicitly denied even approximations to democratic rights, let alone equality before the law. Studies of the stability of British, French and US democracy do not spend much time on Northern Ireland, Algeria or (say) Mississippi. They concentrate understandably on what went on in the metropolitan core areas, on the assumption that frontiers are 'different'. On the other hand, ethnic frontier areas of Germany, Austria or Italy occupy a more central place in the study of fascisms.

How is the potential chaos and violence of frontiers kept at a distance from the metropolitan core? The cue for these comments is taken from two sources. Barrington Moore develops the thesis that democracy was consolidated whenever liberal middle classes generated by industrialisation took the leadership of peasants and working classes, breaking the grip of pre-modern landed classes and uprooting institutions that contradicted the spirit of democracy (notably repressive labour institutions such as the Junker's three-class franchises and manorial self-government, but also southern slavery). This process required some decisive break with the past. Where this did not happen, the landlords found ways of adopting anti-democratic institutions to the period of industrialisation. Under these conditions, sections of the middle classes were drawn into an anti-democratic alliance with landlords, while the democratic sections of middle class, without the means of reshaping this order, were squeezed between it and the rising socialist working class. [1] Eventually when socialism became formidable, the landlords and others attempted to popularise reaction in fascism.

This thesis seems to separate neatly the Liberal Imperialist democracies from Nazism. Hannah Arendt, by contrast, stresses the later period of middle-class development from 1875 onwards and points to the role of the middle classes in sponsoring the development of Imperialism, to extend markets and opportunities for investment abroad. For her, empire is intrinsically lawless and the future of democracy depended in large part on insulating the metropolis from empire. The very last page of Barrington Moore's epic suggests that he has thoughts along these lines which he had not developed, when he speaks of the repression of liberal democracies during the Imperial era being directed outwards rather than against its own citizens.[2] Indeed, when we look at empire in the countries that did not succumb to fascism, it is hard to escape the view that this is indeed the basis of the distinction. Fascisms identified their enemies as 'traitors' and it cannot be an accident that they attacked socialists and communists for their 'internationalism'; or that the radical aspects of fascism focused on the internationalism of finance capital and free trade liberalism; or that the identification of 'internationalist' enemies tended to suit particular circumstances, such as the anti-Catholicism of Nazism in the German east where it attacked the Catholic church sympathy for Poles; and most strikingly of all the 'internationalism' of the Jews, who, without a nation state of their own, were citizens of many states. Nor can it be an accident that fascisms often secured their first major success in zones of disputed nationality. Even if the fascisms of these areas were not typical—they usually contained more radical social strata and a higher proportion of workers than elsewhere[3]—they may have been important in setting precedents.

Otto Bauer implied that 'threatened' or 'besieged' ethnic frontier zones played an important part in getting fascisms past their first obstacle: securing a degree of legitimacy for anti-socialist violence outside the law.[4] I stress this theme because it seems to be this particular layer of ice that remained intact in the Liberal Imperialist countries. Remaining uncracked it allowed their non-socialists to believe—or believe that they believed in—the supremacy of the rule of law and democratic principle. When it was cracked and ambivalent legitimation accorded to non-state violence against the left, the same process we saw chronically in ethnic frontiers developed acutely as violence generated reasons for itself (fear of the socialist response) and magnetised reasons to itself (all the ancillary ends that will be served by a fascist victory). This ice-breaking development corroded the distinction which is crucial to liberal empire between the metropolis and the frontier. The problem then is: under what circumstances could socialists, or others accused of 'internationalism', be isolated as 'traitors' and the violence used against them be accorded widespread (even if 'critical') legitimacy?

The socialist parties throughout Europe supported their countries' entry into the First World War (except Italy and Serbia). As Max Adler, the Austrian Marxist leader, said in 1915: 'this option of the proletariat for its own country and its own nation is something quite different from an identification with the power politics of individual classes in the same. It occurs in spite of, not on behalf of, imperialism, which has plunged it into this situation; and it requires, *given the identical goal*—defeat of the enemy—a clear distinction in the realm of ideas and feelings.'[5] Realistically the identity of the goal also confused the distinction in the realm of ideas until the Russian revolutions and mutinies in other armies began to encourage resistance to the war and internationalist conceptions of peace—'peace without annexations'. In the final stages of the war, the rulers of the defeated powers were replaced by liberal and socialist administrations that sued for peace on the basis of President Wilson's Fourteen Points. They were in their turn displaced briefly by socialist regimes resting on workers' councils (Germany, Austria, Hungary). Meanwhile the hitherto subordinated nationalities began to set up their own governments in anticipation of peace on the principle of national self-determination.

In no instance (that I know of) did socialists or liberals approve of leaving their self-proclaimed nationals to the rule of others in the abstract. What they often did do was to argue that the primary objective of securing peace ruled out renewing hostilities on any pretext or pressing demands to incorporate disputed nationality areas, especially when the peace conferences ruled against them. This stance, which in its actual context was clearly 'internationalist', put some countries' socialists into sharper opposition to their national egoisms than others. When in opposition to such internationalism, sections of the state apparatus either jointed or assisted freelance actions to 'protect' nationals who were likely to be cast adrift, they achieved three things. First, they created the impression that the governments had failed to 'protect their nationals', not because such action was impossible, but because the governments and their supporters were 'treacherous'. Second, they successfully dislocated the subordination of the state apparatus to its ostensible master, generating a disorder in which they were able to extend their actions against 'traitors' and 'enemies' within the metropolis. Third, they provided a focal point not only for those who felt strongly about the besieged frontier citizens but also for any other elements which might gain from the escalation of their activities. These focal points provided the starting point of fascisms, enabling non-state elements to usurp state functions and destroy the rule of law.

In the German case, the seeds of the subsequent developments toward fascism were unwittingly sown by the leaders of the majority Social Democrats. Whereas in Austria the Socialists effectively replaced the Imperial military by their own Volkswehr, avoided sponsoring rearguard actions in Bohemia or relying upon anyone but themselves to contain their extreme left, the German Social Democrats fell back on the Imperial army both to conduct rearguard actions against the Poles and to curb the socialist extreme left. Even so, in January 1919 it looked as though they had successfully orchestrated a transition to liberal democracy. Neither the extreme left nor the parties of the old imperial order were

more than marginally represented and the bulk of the constit-
uent assembly was composed of Social Democrats, the Centre
party and Democratic party.

The full implications of permitting the Reichswehr to
recruit volunteer Free Corps to put down limited revolts from
the extreme left, to engage in rearguard efforts to keep Poznan
or even (with Franco-British approval) to fight Bolsheviks in
the Baltic states had not yet materialised.[6] However, when the
terms of the Versailles treaty became known in mid-1919, the
shock notwithstanding, there was little that the existing
leadership could do but accept, unless to engage in a hopeless
reactivation of hostilities. The treaty included unexpectedly
large loss of territory, limitation of the Reichswehr and
economic reparations. The old right could afford themselves
the luxury of opposing it verbally without responsibility for
the consequences of doing so. The Free Corps organisations
turned their attacks inwards upon 'Versailles Traitors', creating an epidemic of political murders that lasted until 1924, with
ambivalent legitimation from the unreconstructed forces of the
state apparatus. When the government attempted to suppress
the Free Corps in early 1920 they staged a coup which the
Reichswehr refused to put down and which the old right
cautiously welcomed. The short-lived regime of Wolfgang
Kapp (mentioned earlier in connection with pre-war efforts to
Germanise the east) was paralysed by the general strike. But
the summer 1920 election brought a revival of the Peoples and
Nationalist parties (DVP and DNVP) at the expense of the
Democrats. Barrington Moore's argument that the incom-
plete development of pre-1914 German democracy led to the
inter-war rise of fascism depends not only on the appearance
of Nazism but also on the intervening continuity of middle-
class support for the somewhat anti-democratic DVP and
Junker-led DNVP. Clearly the defeat in the war and the
Treaty of Versailles are a crucial element in that continuity
which was puntuated in January 1919 by middle-class
German support for the Democratic party.

In 1921 Free Corps were recruited by the Reichswehr to
fight an undeclared war against Poles in Upper Silesia in
order to 'influence' the results of the border plebiscite. Their
role in this and other anti-Polish conflicts, in the areas of the

east where about 750,000 refugees from Poland settled, 'convinced many Germans that these bands . . . were the true defenders of the nation'.[7] Although they were virtually disowned by the Reichswehr after 1923 when Stresemann secured Reichswehr support for the Republic—in exchange for social democratic acceptance of a subordinated place within it—they never altogether lost their 'legitimate' claim to pre-empt the official role of the state. The opposition to the Versailles settlement was rechannelled into the Junker-led and largely agrarian DNVP which secured over 20 per cent of the vote and was strongest in Protestant rural areas of the east. Together with the Reichswehr and the Protestant churches it was exceedingly critical of any move that appeared to confer legitimacy on the existing Polish frontier. Its paramilitary formation, the Stahlhelm, provided much of the manpower for the semi-official Grenzschutz, a civilian part-time border defence force in East Prussia, which was extended through the whole Polish frontier region after 1928.[8] Although the DNVP entered governments and secured agricultural tariff protection after 1925, the onset of the agricultural depression broke up its following amongst smaller farmers and farm labourers. The tariff protection, weakened by trade treaties, was counter-productive for the dairy and livestock farmers (whose prices fell while that of rye feedstock produced by Junkers did not) and the re-introduction of Polish seasonal labour exposed Junkers to the charge of 'polonising' German agriculture.[9] Already losing ground in 1928 to various rural protest movements, the extreme nationalist Alfred Hugenburg who took over the leadership in 1929 orchestrated a referendum campaign against the Young Plan (for reorganising reparations payments and incidentally making Poland a reparations creditor) and mass meetings in protest against the Liquidations treaty with Poland in 1930. Although the referendum only received 15 per cent of the popular vote (heavily concentrated in the east) the campaign's noisy denunciations of 'Versailles Traitors' provided the occasion for co-operation between the DNVP and the hitherto marginal Nazi party. A year later when the depression had begun to generalise itself and the Nazis secured 18 per cent of the popular vote, old Free Corps leaders were elected to the Reichstag as Nazi deputies.[10]

Italy, unlike Germany, was on the winning side in the First World War, which it entered in 1915 having been promised various zones of the Austrian empire by France and Britain in the Treaty of London. These included South Tyrol (mostly German); Istria; Venezia-Giulia including the port of Trieste (mostly Italian but with very substantial Slovene and Croat minorities); and Dalmatia (largely Croat with Italian urban populations notably in Zara and landlords in rural areas). The entry of the US into the war put the Dalmatian claim in doubt. But the Italian-populated port of Fiume (between Dalmatia and Istria) had not even been scheduled to Italy in the London Treaty. The major allied powers saw Fiume as part of the future Yugoslavia (the proposed expansion of Serbia to form the state of Serbs, Croats and Slovenes). In November 1918 the Italian city authorities of Fiume secured Italian naval intervention to prevent the establishment of Croatian authority. After a period of tense coexistence French military occupation was withdrawn and the Italian force remained in possession. The city authorities called for the annexation of Fiume to Italy and, as Michael Ledeen puts it, by mid-1919 'many Italians who had never heard of Fiume a year before had become convinced that the honour of their country was involved in the resolution of the Fiume question'.[11]

The Italian socialists had opposed the entry into the war and, in its aftermath, revolutionary agitation spread throughout much of the industrial north. The government of Francesco Nitti hoped to bring the socialists and the mass Catholic popolari parties into a reforming coalition, to dispose of the frontier questions and secure badly needed US loans to revive industry and fend off inflation. But in September 1919 the poet Gabriele D'Annunzio led a march at the head of a body of Arditti—wartime stormtroopers—to take over Fiume, ostensibly in opposition to but in fact with connivance of much of the army. Just before the November election he took an expedition to Zara where he secured the commitment of the commander, Admiral Millo, not to evacuate Dalmatia. Nitti responded by calling on the workers to defend Italy against sedition and the election created an absolute majority for the socialists and popolari; their inability to cooperate magnified the debilitating effects of the defiance action in Fiume on the Italian state.

D'Annunzio's action acted as a magnet for various strands of nationalism. Strongly supported by propertied and institutional interests, it revealed the powerlessness of the government over its own state apparatus, prevented Nitti from settling the frontier questions while exposing him to the charge of 'betraying' Fiume and Dalmatia. But though it raised the temper of popular nationalist protest and cries of betrayal, it failed to generate a new mass electoral base. The recently formed Fascists had secured a derisory vote. D'Annunzio's contribution to the destablisation of Italian democracy was to preserve this focus for a year more and to delay the settlement of the frontier with Yugoslavia. Yet neither he nor Mussolini were keen on exacerbating direct national conflicts. Before 1914 Italian-Croat conflict in Fiume had been secondary to the opposition to the ruling Hungarians. D'Annunzio's next moves were clearly not intended to make Fiume itself a zone of frontier warfare.

After the election, D'Annunzio shifted the base of his regime away from the established Imperialist elites toward leftists who had supported the intervention in the war. Instead of making Fiume a confrontation zone between Croats and Italians, in which condition it might conceivably have polarised Italians more sharply over the 'besieged' Fiume, he and his lieutenant—the anarcho-syndicalist Alceste De Ambris—attempted to build an alliance with Croats. They aimed to secure Croatian acceptance of Italian Fiume and Dalmatia in exchange for support for Croat separation from Yugoslavian 'Serb domination'. Although the Croat peasant party was indeed opposed to Serb domination, it seems highly improbable that it would have traded Italian support for the loss of Croatian Dalmatia and Fiume.[12] Only the Croatian party of Rights which got 2 per cent of the Croatian vote in 1920 was interested in such antics (it was this party incidentally that was eventually installed as a puppet in 1941 during the German/Italian occupation). This strategy cut across rather than exploited the crystallisation of ethnic antagonism in Fiume. Italians opposed the proposed creation of Croatian educational institutions; and De Ambris had difficulties when unemployment generated anti-Croat expulsionism. Finally the effort to create a leftist-national rising depended on linking the Fiume regime with the Italian socialists whose position in Trieste, where they were a multi-national alliance with Slovenes, made this improbable, to put it mildly.

In mid-1920, with the frontier questions still unsettled, Arditti appeared (now as Fascists) in the Venezia-Giulia, Istria and Trieste area where their role was far less complicated. Here Fascists acted in league with the police in a wave of repression of Slovenes. The first big Fascist breakthrough came in Trieste, where the socialists were an Italian Slovene alliance; the Fascists 'secured' a nationally disputed territory. But the crudely national egoist mechanism for its development accorded with neither D'Annunzio's nor even Mussolini's plans.

By the time the pre-war liberal prime minister Giolitti returned to office and the major Versailles powers agreed that Italy and Yugoslavia resolve their differences directly, the virus of fascist violence was well entrenched. Under Giolitti the state apparatus again responded with greater compliance to political direction and D'Annunzio could be displaced from Fiume by a minor Italian naval bombardment. Fiume became a free city, the environs of Trieste were annexed to Italy and nearly all of Dalmatia except Zara was incorporated into Yugoslavia. Had these frontier issues been settled in mid-1919, it is less likely that the various species of nationalist-fascist violence would have been able to carve out the space for themselves that made them a tempting weapon to use against the socialist factory occupations which peaked in the later part of 1920. As it was, the Fascists were able both to make themselves indispensable to Giolitti's electoral coalition in 1921 and to destabilise it from within, although they had secured only 35 seats in the 1921 elections. Their effective power depended upon their having inserted themselves into the relationship between the state and the socialist left as an 'auxilliary' of order. Their most direct challenges to the authority of the governing parties (as distinct from attacks upon socialist local authorities) were the fascist takeovers in Fiume in February 1922 and in Bolzano and Trento (the principal cities of the recently acquired South Tyrol).[13] If Mussolini's ideological positions were a rag-bag of changing elements, the forces of national egoism on the ethnic frontiers sharpened them in practice.

Class conflict heightened by the Bolshevik revolution was something of a European norm but it did not everywhere generate fascisms. In both Britain and France, anti-German sentiment consolidated rather than weakened the force of the existing order. When Millerand in 1919 formed the Bloc National composed of parties 'free from the taint of inter-nationalism',[14] the victorious Bloc synthesised anti-Bolshevism and anti-Germanism but the whole transaction was contained within the parameters of the electoral process and the containment of socialist strike waves was left to the state apparatus. Such an 'anti-internationalist' coalition differed from Giolitti's 1921 coalition (whch included Fascists) not so much in its 'tolerance' toward socialists and foreigners as in its capacity to contain the whole within the established framework of state authority.

If this argument about the role of severed frontiers is credible it would, however, have to cope with the objection that French democracy had survived between 1870 and 1914 despite the loss of Alsace-Lorraine to Germany (recovered in 1918). In doing this, the parameters of the argument can be drawn more sharply. First the various later nineteenth-century challenges to French democracy—such as that of Boulanger or the anti-Dreyfusards—did call for revenge against Germany. Second, however, the French left was not, in the aftermath of the Paris Commune, vulnerable to the charge of having helped to lose these provinces. The circumstance of their loss placed that onus on the Bonapartists and secondarily on those conservative monarchists who had repressed the Commune. Indeed Gustave Hervé, the extreme left leader, once suggested that some French colonies should be exchanged for Lorraine—a backhandedly patriotic way of being anti-Imperialist.[15] But third and probably most important, non-state initiatives to recover or protect ethnic frontiers have to generate the charge that the government itself is somehow avoiding doing something it could do to protect its own citizens. Bearing in mind that German power in Alsace-

Lorraine was not to be lightly meddled with, it was probably crucial that the soft method of doing this by orchestrating a 'back to France' movement in Alsace-Lorraine was largely impossible. The great mass of the peasantry spoke a language akin to German.[16] Before 1870 there had been conflict about language between the French education ministry and the Catholic clergy who controlled elementary education. French was the language of the bourgeoisie and the administration; but the clerical insistence upon the use of German in primary education was a potentially popular cause. So it might be more to the point to ask how the language issue would have developed if these provinces had remained part of France after 1870. Once incorporated into Germany, they experienced the Kulturkampf not as an attack upon language (as the Poles had done) but as one on Catholicism. Hence in its aftermath they became aligned politically with the German centre party. Alsace-Lorraine after 1870 therefore lacked an essential ingredient as a zone from which to start a successful frontier defiance action to weaken French democracy.

If Alsace-Lorraine was an unsatisfactory base for such actions before 1914, the case of Northern Ireland was unsatisfactory afterwards. British power, unconstrained by Versailles-type treaties such as it imposed on others, confronted Irish republican separatism from late 1919 with a relatively free hand. Although the December 1918 election had given Sinn Féin a total victory in nearly all areas outside Ulster (and some areas within), in June 1919 the Irish deputation heard President Wilson's rebuff to the effect that no small nation should appear before the peace conference without the unanimous consent of the whole committee. Thereafter the Anglo-Irish war escalated. The British attempted to enforce acceptance of the 1920 Government of Ireland Act providing for two home rule parliaments in the North and South linked by a Council of Ireland.

Nicholas Mansergh points out how the Foreign Office was preoccupied with the problem of preventing Irish appeals to the peace conference. An argument clearly designed for US consumption in favour of leaving as much discretion as possible in the hands of Allied Powers was that 'it would be inadvisable to go even the smallest distance in the direction of admitting the claim of American Negroes or the southern Irish . . . to appeal to an Interstate Conference over the head of their own government.'[17]

The local elections in Ireland of January 1920 unhinged unionist control of district councils in large areas of the North where the new nationalist authorities declared their allegiance to the Dáil, the parliament set up by the Sinn Féin representatives in Dublin in defiance of the British. But although at this stage Unionist paramilitary activity began to escalate, the Ulster unionist leadership accepted the principle of a separate northern parliament for the six-county area over which they would have a two-thirds majority. In this they were guided by a fear of what might happen if the British Labour Party or the Asquith Liberals returned to power and the knowledge that possession of a secure local majority was crucial for their future. The shipyard expulsions of mid-1920, mentioned earlier, rather than dislocating the link between the metropolitan state and Ulster Unionists, lent force to the argument that Unionists should be incorporated into and restrained within legitimate forces. Hence the creation of the Special Constabulary in November 1920.[18] When the government of Northern Ireland was formed in 1921, they became its physical backbone.

So long as they were contained within the ethnic border land context, the activity of the irregular Imperial Guards that surfaced during the period of the Anglo-Irish truce, those of the Austrian Heimwehr in the Slovene-German borderlands of Carinthia and Styria, the Free Corps in Pozen or Upper Silesia, the Fascists in Venezia-Giulia and Istria or the Arditti of D'Annunzio in Fiume (until the effort made to adopt an alliance with Croats that effectively deprived the Arditti of any local action possibilities) differed only in degrees.[19] What was clearly different was the implications of these kinds of activities for the metropolis to which they were attached.

The post-war British government that won the 1918 election was a continuation of the wartime coalition between Conservatives and Lloyd George Liberals. As in France the fact of victory enabled the existing political leadership to use anti-Germanism (making the Germans pay) as a way of consolidating their hold. Not only were the unionist threats of defiance channelled in such a way as to ensure a new *modus vivendi* between British Conservatism and unionism—based on the devolution of powers to the NI government—but the dominant political powers in Britain had no incentive to encourage the overspill of the Irish conflict into Britain. They were far from falling back upon any appeal to the rights of self-determination of Ulster Protestants but rather attempting to erect a mechanism for sustaining an Imperial hold over all Ireland. The only point where Ulster self-determination might have surfaced was if it came into contradiction with efforts to impose the Treaty settlement over the whole of Ireland in which case it would have been an unpopular cause even with metropolitan Imperialists. When Chamberlain stated that Northern Ireland was an 'illogical and indefensible' compromise and 'you could not raise an army in England to fight for that *as we could for crown and Empire*', he alluded to the danger that Sinn Féin forces in the South might accept the Treaty on the condition that it terminated partition of the North, which had already exercised its option for partition under the Government of Ireland Act.[20] Under those circumstances any further military repression required to impose the Treaty would have been demonstrably necessitated by the Northern Unionists' demands for partition. But the fact that British power had not been obliged to retreat to a much more defensive posture by international constraint prevented Irish issues from assuming a 'European' form.

In conclusion, frontier citizens were often elevated to the status of a symbol, most important when they were 'lost' and least important when securely retained. They became as important to metropolitan political 'culture' as they were visible symptoms of the weakness of national state power shackled by external constraint and undermined internally by internationalist 'treachery'. Their situation personalised and focused issues of national kudos that otherwise lacked sharp definition. Victory in the First World War not only shielded the French and British left from fascist attacks upon 'internationalisms' but in so far as it also preserved the over-extended French and British empires, it consolidated the consensus base of Liberal Imperialism. An over-extended empire with a large component of orthodox colonial structures could only be kept by a process of conciliating (however grudgingly and ungraciously) such protest movements as they generated. Colonial capital and metropolitan cost/benefit analysis of the costs of coercion tended to point in the same direction as humanitarian concern for colonial 'reform'. The more over-extended empires were, the stronger the *de facto* convergence between metropolitan forces into a liberal imperial consensus, which blurred the distinction between national egoism and political internationalism.

Liberal Imperialisms earn that title not through any pecu-liarly national virtue but because liberal imperial consensus preserves the metropolitan democracy and the distinctions between all the parts of empire. In relation to ethnic frontiers and settlement colonial frontiers it is a source of restraint upon antagonisms, however feeble. Thus even in the case of the US South, during the early twentieth century, however repressive paternalism became it was a shield against or refuge from something worse.[21] Likewise, the defeat of the anti-Semitic outburst in Algeria in 1898 was a victory of Liberal Imperial-ism. Once a native population has acquiesced as labour, its employees and metropolitan state power have no interest in permitting its extermination or expulsion. The interests of property, the state calculus of the costs and benefits of the use of state violence, and humanitarian acceptance, however hypocritical, of natives as people all point in the same direction. The only conceivable purpose of expulsionism and extermination would then be to create spaces for plebeian labour or small farmers in order to extend the citizen national population of a territory. But pressures for this kind of action are very unlikely to be generated within the frontiers by plebeian citizens alone. They require external 'supports' (which should more accurately be called temptations or coercions) to get any such project off the ground. The most decisive of these is a metropolitan fascism, which elevates frontier nationals to the status of a national symbol.

At a minimum, fascist radicalisation of nationality amounts to removing legal protection from organised forces of the left and therefore strengthening the hand of capital and (in the Italian case) landed property. But in principle radicalised nationality strips away all restraints upon the expressions of national egoism including those which limit and define liberal imperialism. Nazism did do this, successfully channelling the mass reaction to the great deflationary crisis of 1929–32 into an assault upon external restraints (the Versailles Treaty and reparations), internal 'traitors' (the socialists, centre and liberals) and discredited conservative imperial leaders (the DNVP.) Nazism was able to exploit the ambiguity between recovering German ethnic areas beyond its frontier on the principle of 'self-determination' and a form of settlement colonising warfare that it unleased in eastern Europe in 1939.

Despite the high proportion of early Nazis who were refugees or ethnic frontier residents, the Abel-Merkl survey found that among Nazis they were the least disposed to violence. They also tended to refer to their aspirations for Nazism as 'national renaissance' rather than expansionism.[22] And it is probably no accident that the early working-class supporters of the German Workers Party in Bohemia were impediments to Hitler's assertion of total control over the Nazis and subsequently his opponents.[23] They presumably had some idea of what Hitler's hyperbolical visions of *Lebensraum* might mean in practice, being themselves used to a much lower level of ethnic contestation. Hitler's vision of the world took the most antagonistic ethnic frontier vision of territorial conflict to its logical conclusions, which required the break–up of the restraints of Liberal Imperialism.

Hitler's *Mein Kampf* is dominated by a dream of *Lebensraum* or living space to be carved out in eastern Europe. This had nothing to do with mere conquest or conventional colonisation. He explicitly repudiated even the Prussian colonisation scheme of the pre-1914 period: 'Half–hearted was the Polish policy. It consisted in irritating without seriously going through with anything. The result was neither a victory for the Germans nor conciliation of the Poles, but hostility with Russia instead' (which was able to pose as a protector of Poles and to use the weight of its own Polish population to deter Prussia) and 'We must break off the colonial and commercial policy of the pre-war period and shift to the soil policy of the future.' Speaking of the German achievements of the last 600 years he identified the Germanisation of the Ostmark (Austria, Bohemia) and the territory east of the Elbe (i.e. extending out to the Polish border lands): 'Without them our nation today would no longer have any importance at all.' And on the DNVP's demands to restore the pre-1914 frontiers: 'In particular it is morally dangerous to regard the last pre-war developments as binding even in the slightest degree for our own course.' Even if fascists everywhere became a tool for the destruction of socialism, Hitler was well aware that it was not only socialists or the Catholic Centre party but also the conservative and Junker-dominated old Imperial leadership that stood in the way of settlement colonising *Lebensraum*.

In view of Hitler's description of a genius as one with a talent for 'making adversaries far removed from one another seem to belong to the same category',[24] it is striking how few Nazi party members were simple 'dupes' of his use of anti-Semitism for this end. (According to the Abel-Merkl survey only about one-seventh of pre-1930 members gave anti-Semitism top ideological priority.)[25] As with most really vicious ideas, even ones which end up by translating into gruesomely real practice, their mass voters have other reasons for supporting them. The enemy chosen did in part have to represent all possible sources of restraint. No particular enemy of national egoism would have sufficed for their purpose: Marxism, the Poles, the Russians, international capital, the Versailles powers, were all real powers to which opposition was already articulated by existing forces. To have focused upon any particular manifestation of 'internationalism' would have contained Nazism within an alliance (of the kind Italian Fascism was contained within).[26] The perfect symbol of all internationalisms had to be a group that could be identified in all of them (and was therefore in reality ·dominant in none of them). The Jews as people who were in fact citizens of many nations were usually assimilated by whatever nations would assimilate them; they tended to support the most positively tolerant currents (socialist and liberal) within them—and were, more or less, universally accepted when they were seen as a powerless religious minority. Even Imperialist nationalisms which were highly antagonistic to foreigners often proved their tolerance by acceptance of Jews, as the French had done in Algeria. To a non-paranoid mind, the liberal Jews' rejection of Zionism might be taken at face value in a country with less than 2 per cent of its population Jewish. To one who came to see all internationalisms as a form of treachery, 'the so-called liberal Jews did not reject the Zionists as non-Jews but only as Jews with an impractical, perhaps even dangerous, way of publicly avowing their Jewishness. Intrinsically they remained unalterably of one piece.'[27] Liberal Jews were 'really' the secret arm of Zionism behind all forms of internationalism and had ensnared *all* existing political forces. Anti-Semitism was the absolute in anti-internationalism.

Hitler's advance description of his subsequent mass electoral support as 'bourgeois voting cattle' neatly sums up the relationship between the initiators and the followers. After the stabilisation of 1924 and the channelling of militant anti-Versailles sentiment into the DNVP, the vulnerability of the Weimar Republic to a radicalised anti-internationalism depended on convergence of a wide range of issues that could be grouped under the heading of external constraints. The post-1924 economic strategy that held the socialists and middle-class parties together depended on financing the payment of reparations, industrial development and public investment by an influx of US loans, a system often denounced by agricultural spokesmen as an alliance of export capital and Marxism. The economic revival of the 1925–9 period depended heavily upon the growth of exports and the series of post-1925 trade treaties tended to promote export industries at the expense of agriculture and domestic heavy industry (coal and steel). The 1929 collapse of Wall Street rapidly led to the withdrawal of US short-term loans and shortage of new credit, precipitating a spiral of bankruptcy, unemployment and collapsing prices against a background of high interest rates.

But so total was this system's dependence on the activity of the export industries and so limited was the government's freedom to reorganise the trade environment while other countries put up tariff barriers (or, in the case of the larger imperial powers, reorganised the actual and *de facto* empires into protected trading zones), that it had little choice but to adjust to the crisis by deflationary measures designed to cut back public expenditure below the falling tax yields and avoid generating a balance of payments deficit and a further outflow of foreign capital. When protectionism extended in the rest of the world, even the export industry began to collapse. The 1931 bank collapses and the French veto on the projected German-Austrian customs union magnified the appearance of total bankruptcy of government policy. Trying to uphold the free trading, export-oriented system and continuing to pay reparations created a sense of governments attempting to appease external powers, supported or tolerated by 'self-interested' exponents of various internationalist doctrines, liberal, clerical and socialist, and in doing so plunging Germany into an even deeper 'interest slavery' or high real interest rates on outstanding debts.

Demagogic attacks upon 'parasitical' capital (as distinct from 'productive' capital) were not a monopoly of Nazis. The French Popular Front and the New Deal Democrats attacks upon 'walls of money' or 'speculators' were also attempts to exploit hostility to credit institutions while blurring the edge of any more trenchant attacks upon 'productive' capital. What was quite specific to Nazism was that the deflationary crisis was represented as an 'internationalist' (Jewish) conspiracy orchestrated by the Versailles powers and the international bankers together with domestic internationalist 'traitors'. In 1929, during the Young Plan referendum, the Nazis challenged the SPD in Silesia, calling their popular defence organisation, the Reichsbanner, 'a protection squad for capital'.[28] They managed to generate a physical force confrontation in which they demonstrated their power in spite of the SPD's electoral strength and its control of the Prussian government (and the police). Nazis took a major part in resisting forced sales of indebted farms, which placed the SPD-Centre Prussian government further on the defensive.

In a work which concentrates the most detailed attention on the ebbs and flows of class alliances, David Abraham states that 'Germans of nearly all classes believed that agriculture's interests and well being were more "national" than those of industry', because of agriculture's supposed role as 'a border "bulwark" against the Slavic and Semitic tide'. He continues: 'Only if one appreciates this does the success of agrarian propaganda become comprehensible, particularly in portraying most of industry as "internationalist" compared to patriotic and "national" agriculture.'[29] The economic collapse, its specific effects upon agriculture, reparations, the loss of eastern territories and the limitations of the size of the Reichswehr were all effectively locked together as interdependent issues subsumed under the head of throwing off the shackles of Versailles, of Jewish domination.

If Nazism in power resolved most of the domestic pressures that accelerated its growth to 1932 by a programme of reflation within an autarchic trading context and tight discipline over labour costs, Hitler's method of rule preserved and institutionalised the imperialising thrust that was eventually unleashed in 1938–9. Martin Broszat shows how after the seizure of power, the competition between the authority of the normal adminstrative arms of the state (even after being Nazified) and the various specifically Nazi institutions generated a system of polyarchy in which jurisdictional boundaries remained fluid and depended on the ultimate arbitration by Hitler himself.[30] Within the old Reich area, the tendency was for authoritarian rule governed procedures to be gradually undermined by the overlapping jurisdictions of Nazi agencies (most notably the SS). But once the Reich expanded from 1938, the balances shifted especially in the case of the annexed areas of Poland where the existing administration was destroyed and the eastern Nazi gauleiters took over. Here, after Hitler terminated the military occupation regime, the competing jurisdictions were those of the Nazi party and its eastern leaders and the rapidly expanding SS, both laying claim to special Germanising tasks devolved to them by Hitler. The potentially chaotic and lawless tendencies of these areas then percolated back into the old Reich, undermining what remained of authoritarian order in favour of unrestrained racist chaos.

The existence of the Nazi state with its imperial ambitions which could initially be expressed in the language of rights to self-determination had a magnetic effect on Germans beyond the borders, binding them 'together in a new species of imperial unity'.[31] Where Nazism secured some temporary accommodation with the eastern European regimes (as in

Poland) the greater freedom accorded to Nazi organisation and concessions granted to German minorities drew the Germans towards Nazism. Where by contrast the eastern European regimes responded by taking precautions against the Nazi menace (as in Czechoslovakia) the attraction of Nazism rose as a means of securing 'liberation' from these precautions, which could be represented as oppressions. And in Austria with its overwhelmingly German population where the Catholic clericals attempted to suppress the socialists and the Nazis simultaneously, the pro-Anschluss forces were strongest in Styria and Carinthia—the German-Slovene ethnic border areas where political Catholicism tended to be a restraint upon opposition to the Catholic Slovenes.[32] The magnetic effect of Nazism on ethnic frontier Germans operated, whatever stance other governments took towards it.

In Czechoslovakia, the rise of the Nazis introduced a sharp twist into the process of internal accommodation between the Czech and German populations. The early success of the Nazis forced the Czech state to ban both it and the German Nationalist party, to replace German municipal police by Czech gendarmes and to reconsider plans which had been developing for greater autonomy for German districts. In all of these measures they were firmly supported by the German Social Democrats who were in the coalition government. But the effects of Nazi autarchic policies on the export-orientated industrial border areas of Czechoslovakia were disastrous and led to unusually high levels of localised German unemployment.[33] This could lead to one of two lessons: either that incorporation of Bohemia into Germany would bring the rapidly rising levels of employment in the Reich or that the monster which was a threat to democracy and to working class self-organisation needed to be resisted more firmly. Had it not been for the presence of the German Social Democrats in government and their control over the welfare ministry—a very solid evidence of transnational co-operation—the appeal of the first argument would no doubt have been even stronger than it actually was. As it was, the nebulous Sudeten German front which campaigned for greater 'autonomy' for German areas collected about 63 per cent of the German votes in 1935 and in the process halved that of the Social Democrats. In the circumstances, what is rather more remarkable is the continued existence of the 'democratic German third'. Having been placed in Czechoslovakia against their will and denied the right to self-determination by the Versailles Powers in 1919, they and their Czech counterparts developed a transnational co-operation that made Czechoslovakia the only state of its kind in Europe. When those same Versailles powers were confronted with Nazism and discovered so-called moderate tendencies in its Sudeten front organisation, they began to recognise rights of self-determination claimed by dictators which they had previously denied to democrats.[34]

The Polish frontier zones had a much more direct effect upon the rise of Nazism, which absorbed the DNVP's support more or less bodily, lifting radicalised anti-internationalism away from its original border reservoir to a new level of comprehensiveness.

In the November 1930 Polish elections, German representation was drastically reduced, in an election marked by fraud and violence. Polish authorities showed increasing suspicion of German organisations. In 1929 an attack on the Polish national opera in Oppeln in Upper Silesia led to an anti-German cultural boycott and German minority leaders were tried (but acquitted) of treason for organising military draft evasion. After the success of the Nazis in the September 1930 election, the German government could not get a majority to ratify the Polish trade treaty. With the French evacuation of the Rhineland, the Poles feared increased German freedom of action against themselves in the east. The extension of the Nazi SA in the east created new difficulties for the Reichswehr, Stahlhelm, DNVP alliance, because as the Nazis ate away the electoral base of the DNVP their relationship with the Grenzschutz became increasingly important. In East Prussia the SA and Reichswehr co-operated fully in the Grenzschutz; in other areas, notably Silesia, Hitler's opposition to letting the SA support the 'system' reinforced plebeian notions of confronting and reorganising the 'reactionary' army.[35] Scares about possible Polish invasion contributed to the military reasons for opposing Brüning's ban on the SA and SS in 1932, paving the way for his ejection from office.[36] This was one of the elements of intrigue in which the ruling elites around President Hindenburg, deprived by the Nazis of any electoral base of their own worth mentioning, allowed Hitler to take power.

Had the Poles actually launched a pre-emptive strike against Germany after the Nazi seizure of power, the relationship between the SA and the Reichswehr might have developed in a very different manner from the way it did. But Hitler's Non-Aggression Pact with Poland in January 1934 lifted the pressure so that it became both possible and more necessary to curb SA ambitions to 'revolutionise' the Reichswehr. The 1934 June SA purge did not so much destroy the Nazi 'left' as the elements in the SA who were the greatest obstacles to cooperations with the Reichswehr.[37] More importantly the role of the SS in the operation was the start of a process of rechannelling exterminationist/settlement colonising purposes into a bureaucratised system rather than a mass movement. Rather than unleash an attack upon Poland which would have strategically disastrous, anti-Semitism was employed as a foreign policy instrument, encouraging the Polish government to renounce the Minorities Protection Treaty, which gave its 10 per cent Jewish population (which was eventually to be about half of the 6 million Jews murdered by the Nazis) access to international forums. Thus Poland was distanced from its protector France.

The rapprochement between Poland and Germany created ongoing pressures for the German minority. Attempting on the one hand to conciliate the Nazi regime and on the other to free itself of German dangers, both elements of the Polish government's policy drove Germans toward the Young German Party, founded in Bielitz—the only town in Poland with a German majority in 1931—but rapidly spreading throughout Germans in the west of Poland. After the Non-Aggression Pact this organisation pledged its 'loyalty' to the Polish state. The Germans secured the status of Volksgruppe, a step up from being regarded only as Polish citizens of German nationality, and even government sponsorship of one of its leaders to the senate.[38] Internal conflict over anti-Semitism was both aggravated and used as a lever to prise space for Nazi organisation.

Having secured the destruction of Czechoslovakia in the

1938 Munich agreement, the Nazis incorporated the core area in 1939 (encouraging other nations such as Poland and Hungary to claim areas with ethnic minorities of their own) and then turned on Poland, having concluded a pact with the USSR to divide the country between them. Some thousands of Germans were killed by Poles before the German victory and in the aftermath 'ethnic self-defence' units were encouraged to take revenge. In these annexed territories the first settlement colonising exercises were set under way, being a prelude to the mass exterminations. Thus from Warthegau, an expanded version of the pre-war province of Posen, about 800,000 Poles and 400,000 Jews were displaced eastward to accommodate 400,000 Germans before the war with Russia in 1941.[39] This type of 'warfare', which escalated with well-known consequences, resulted in the expulsion of nearly all Germans from Czechoslovakia, Poland, East Prussia and substantial zones of pre-war Germany between 1945 and 1947. Governing everywhere on the principle of collective punishment and often outright exterminationism led to non-combatant deaths running between 10 and 20 million. The precedent set by Nazism, of settling national conflicts by 'resettlement', was then used by the victors to remove Germans bodily from eastern Europe.

Hannah Arendt's view of Imperialism as lawlessness threatening to strike back at the rule of law in the Imperial nation state is surely correct. And her picture of Imperial democracy as successful compartmentalisation of the empire away from the mother country is right. Fascism is the collapse of that compartmentalisation, the collapse of distinctions between the parts of the *imperium*. The metropolitan rule of law (and therefore democracy) requires two things: first, isolation of the domestic disturbers of tranquillity; second, a state monopoly of all coercive relationships with foreigners, aliens and colonial subjects. The imperial principle—that all members of the nation have a co-responsibility for its collective security—is compatible with democracy and rule of law at home only so long as the state monopolises both processes and they remain clearly separate. Fascisms seek all possibilities to break down the distinction between 'criminal' and 'foreigner' and to smear domestic 'criminal-aliens' as 'traitors'. In doing so they set up a process of reciprocal violence which allows them first to pose as 'auxiliaries' of the state and then to hijack it altogether. Their main tactic is to force people to decide whose violence they fear most, when they can no longer rely on the state to sustain order.

The aftermath of World War One permitted the big three to preserve their empires more or less intact, while it either broke up (in the German case) or thwarted the anticipated extension (in the Japanese and Italian cases) of the empires of the recent industrialising nations. Over-extended empire allowed the metropolitan power to reorganise trade relationships during the great depression within an already established circle of influence or control. But in the compressed empires any democratic consensus between export capital and popular class parties depended upon export performance into areas over which little political control could be exerted. In Japan and Germany, political and economic internationalisms were linked to a democratic economic expansionist strategy which was shipwrecked by the great depression. These levels of explanation might distinguish between the tendencies in the two kinds of empire towards fascism to be found at the level of military and industrial elites. But the kernel of the argument here is that even if all manner of elite interests are attracted to fascism, it is perhaps more important to ask why embryonic fascisms were there in the first place to be subsidised, petted and encouraged. Once again, albeit in somewhat different form, the compression of empire is important. It forced a choice between accepting the constraints imposed by the liberal Imperial powers and physically resisting them, which was in fact no choice at all. Accepting them meant accepting the limits of territorial acquisition imposed and relating to the rest of the world as nations among nations. The various liberal, clerical or socialist internationalisms which assumed these responsibilities did so in circumstances that placed them in sharp opposition to their own national egoisms. The collapse or absence of distant colonies was probably not very important. What was far more important was the loss or failure to extend political control over nearby zones of large-scale national populations. Ethnic frontier nationals and settlement colonists were both numerous and outwardly similar to ordinary metropolitans, in a way that the relatively limited and elitist personnel of orthodox economic exploitation colonies were not. Ordinary people in the metropolis could easily identify with ordinary citizens on the ethnic frontier. Consequently, any failure to secure the ethnic frontier could quite easily be represented as an act of treachery.

No one who has witnessed the transformation of the British image of the Falkland Islands in 1982 from insignificant far-flung possessions into a citadel of staunch and loyal British subjects need wonder about how Fiume or Posen were so transformed in 1918–20. On simple mimetic principle, because other nations attempted to grab them, they became exceedingly desirable. It may of course be argued that this kind of transformation is the skilful work of propagandists, but such an argument misses the point. There is something there to be 'propagandised' in the first place. The Imperial principle, that all citizens are co-responsible for each other, may seem trite except when it can be shown to have practical implications. For metropolitans these implications are mostly episodal, whereas for people in frontiers and settlement colonies they linger, rarely much below the surface, and are the names given to the chronic force fields. During the 1920s nationalist vigilantism against metropolitan 'traitors' (as anyone who accepted the post-war treaty constraints was branded) was spawned in Italy, Germany and Japan.[40] In Germany and Japan it escalated in the late 1920s with a programme of *Lebensraum* (popular settlement colonisation) at the time of the depression. In Italy fascism took power in 1922 without the necessity of economic collapse to link all the possible stands of 'external constraint' together.

If this argument is correct then it follows that ethnic and settlement frontier zones of the liberal Imperial democracies may have been kept at a distance from metropolitan political concerns only because these powers were dominant after 1918. I suggested earlier that had Britain lost the First World War it is just conceivable that a united Ireland might have been formed in the way that Czechoslovakia was formed in 1918–19. But the idea that all the ills of Ireland since 1920 stem from partition is clearly a myth. Because Ulster was never made a Fiume or a Posen, it became much easier to distance Northern Ireland from the mainstream of British politics. The idea that this would have been the case if Britain had lost it in 1918–20 is at least suspect. Whether it might have been transformed into a 'Sudetenland' cannot be known, but in so far as the difference between Britain and Germany rests on the outcome of the 1914–18 war, it is a distinct possibility that a united Ireland of 1920 might have had a renewed British difficulty in the 1930s much more serious than anything Éire actually experienced.

The System of Communal Deterrence

Unlike the 'lost' or refugee Germans who were a perpetual focal point for German nationalist attacks on metropolitan internationalisms during the inter-war period, frontier citizens of the Imperial democracies were largely insulated from metropolitan attention. The consensus that there were regional peculiarities cast a blanket over their 'peculiar' institutions and amounted in practice to leaving them largely free of metropolitan supervision. In the case of Northern Ireland a parliamentary convention developed not to discuss issues at Westminster which were the concern of the regional parliament at Stormont. In the case of Algeria, the colon influence in the Radical party was often used to spike parliamentary interest in Algeria (notably during the Popular Front era of 1936 when Algerian questions were raised in the metropolis). And in the US South, the pivotal position of southern Democrats in the congressional committee system enabled them to thwart legislation that was held to be contrary to 'southern traditions'.[1]

Northern Ireland's population of about 1.5 million was between 2 and 3 per cent of the UK population. The Unionists, about 1 million strong, were roughly 2 per cent of the UK population, a 65 per cent majority in Northern Ireland and between 20 and 25 per cent of the population of the whole of Ireland. The French Algerians, at about 1 million, were also about 2 per cent of the French population, but in Algeria itself they were around 12 per cent of the total, vastly outnumbered by Moslems who were French subjects. The US South, by contrast, contained a quarter of the US

population in the eleven states. Two million whites (just over
one per cent of the US population) lived in counties with black
majorities. Ten million whites lived in counties with black
populations of more than 30 per cent. In 1910, 91 per cent of
American blacks lived in the South; by 1950 that figure had
dropped to 68 per cent. No southern state except Mississippi
had a black majority throughout much of the twentieth
century.[2]

In the case of Northern Ireland, devolving responsibilities
to the unionists while loosening the restraints upon how those
responsibilities should be exercised meant that the unionists
could easily be blamed if things went wrong. This distancing
helped to foster the self-identification of Protestants as Protestants rather than as British—and to feed notions of 'conditional loyalty' to Britain only so long as Britain supported the
union.

The practices of segregationism and disenfranchisement in
the US South were proclaimed as expressions of 'states'
rights'. In much of the South, the confederate flags flew in
places where the stars and stripes would fly in the North. Here
no credible claim has been or probably could be raised to the
territory of any southern state by external powers (unless by
Mexico to the south-western states); yet the distance between
the metropolis and frontier was expressed during the 1950s
when confederate notions of conditional loyalty such as
'nullification' and 'interposition' were raised against the
judgments of the federal Supreme Court.

In Algeria, where the Europeans were not a majority,
except in some of the coastal cities, no comparable distancing
process was possible after the failure of the Blum-Viollette
proposals in 1936-7 which would otherwise have increased the
likelihood of resorting to it. Instead Algeria was drawn more
deeply into French politics and contributed to their reshaping
in 1958-62. The French Algerian concept of conditional
loyalty found expression in the uprising of Algeria in 1958; one
of its instigators spoke of the 'inviolable principle of French
kinship in Algeria which was part and parcel of the French
constitution' and any policy departure from this violated an
'unwritten law'.[3]

French, Protestant and white predominance in each society

was upheld primarily by institutions of local government and control over the law, order and judicial apparatus. In the US South the disenfranchisement of blacks deprived them of any control over local government or justice. In predominantly white areas it could be used to obstruct the development of black residence and economic activities—to insulate white society from any kind of black competition. And in black plantation counties it could be used by small white minorities of plantation owners and their retainers as an instrument of control over their black labour forces. In Algeria the *communes de plein exercice* entrenched European municipal majorities, regardless of the size of the Moslem populations within them. Although, in the twentieth century, Moslem representation was gradually increased and the Moslem representatives were eventually allowed to take part in the election of mayors, these institutions, like those of the US South, allowed for both exclusion and subordination of Moslems simultaneously. The settlement colonial contradiction between insulating citizens from native competitive pressures and exploiting native labour was bridged by local government systems in both situations.

In Northern Ireland the peculiar institutions established after 1920 were designed to secure control over areas with nationalist majorities. The gerrymandered local government institutions replaced commissioners who had been put in to run nationalist councils that did not recognise Northern Ireland. The mechanism depended on gerrymandering electoral boundaries to convert Catholic electoral majorities into Unionist majorities on local councils. Areas with very large Catholic majorities could not be organised in this way and some Nationalist councils remained. Others had to be occasionally reorganised by the Unionist regional government with its large absolute majority in the Stormont parliament.[4] Thus while local government facilitated exclusivism— discrimination in employment policies and later housing allocations—it created no opportunities for super-exploit- ation of Catholic labour. The difference between ethnic frontiers (Northern Ireland) and settlement colonial frontiers (the Deep South and Algeria) reappeared in their local government institutions. The old Dublin Castle controlled police force (the RIC) was replaced by the 90 per cent Protestant RUC controlled by Stormont. Although a third of its places were reserved for Catholics, the highest quoted Catholic membership figure was 17 per cent in 1936.[5] The Special Constabulary recruited during 1920-22 from the Protestant population at large (the B Specials) was preserved as a permanent reserve force. Extraordinary powers and extraordinary rights to judge the occasions for the use of those powers were granted to the Minister of Home Affairs by the Special Powers Act.

None of these societies could ever claim to have secured a better form of co-existence than one of tranquillised or ritualised deterrence. This point has to be plainly stated as a starting point if we are going to argue that tranquil co-existence is a better mode of co-existence than convulsive violence. Only then is it possible to see how much effort may have been put into the work of ensuring that convulsive violence did not occur. Most readers will say that that was not enough. I shall not argue with that because many moderate and progressive citizens involved in these efforts say that themselves. What they were only sometimes able to do was to say so publicly, for reasons which will, I hope, become apparent. Their influence has tended to be visible only during periods of tranquillity. In times of ethnic confrontation they are visible either as isolated individual voices or they are in varying degrees concealed from view.

There is an important point at stake in developing this perspective. If societies of communal deterrence are so intrinsically volatile, the chronic coercive forces within them lead to one of two alternative visions. Either the dominant populations tend to be regarded as an intrinsically deformed section of the human race somehow different from the rest of the world or the outwardly barbarous developments that occur in these societies will be used to prove that really the whole of the human race is intrinsically barbarous. My argument is that the first chapters of this book would, if offered only these choices, tend toward the second. But the consequences of treating the second argument loosely and without a recognition of what it implies for all of us are illustrated by Robert Ardrey's *Territorial Imperative*. Ardrey holds that man is instinctively a territorial creature. The territorial instinct is innate, which means that it is somehow indelibly printed on us whether we like it, recognise it or not. Ardrey delights in attacking the 'academic monopoly which substituted high mindedness for higher learning'. 'In all the rich catalogue of human hypocrisy it is difficult to find anything to compare with that dainty of dainties, that sugared delicacy, the belief that people don't like war.' It is not so much the first function of territory—the space in which we find security—that makes Ardrey interesting, but rather its second function: 'In primate societies the biological nation as a guardian of security has perhaps been too perfect, for it has sacrificed stimulation, the second of territory's psychological functions. The fun has gone out of the border.'[6] This echoes Rebecca West's description of the role of the Christian school teachers in Macedonia, where the Western powers forced the Turkish empire to permit the establishment of schools with foreign staff for their Christian subjects. The competition between Serbian, Greek and Bulgarian schools and school-teachers was such that 'a number of the schoolmasters and schoolmistresses in these competitive establishments were shot or were not shot only because they shot first . . . The teacher is often a hero and a fanatic as well as a servant of the mind.'[7] In the inter-war period Serbian domination in Macedonia was matched by the Bulgarian terrorist group IMRO which, for a time, generated a virtual fascism in Bulgaria itself.

'I am a playwright', says Ardrey, 'and for what a play is all about I look to what is said when a curtain falls.' While the last paragraph of his work extols the place of our own, the penultimate includes the following: 'We are predators, of course, and from time to time we shall go out looting and raping and raising general havoc in the surrounding country-side. There will be reprisals, naturally. And that is another reason why it will be so good to have a place to stand, some place to regard as ours.'[8]

Ardrey does not appear to be at all alarmed by his conclusion. He seems to believe that it is possible to reconcile this euology of barbarism with the preservation of some kind of civilisation. Thus he criticises Konrad Lorenz' view that only demagogues have a 'certain working knowledge' of the innate process of behaviour on the grounds that even they do not understand it in other nations. 'The record of the Second World War suggests total ignorance on the part of the intruders as to how defenders were likely to behave.' And warfare arises from 'failure of an intruding power correctly to estimate the defensive resources of a territorial defender.'[9] Outwardly this looks like a clever territorialist riposte to 'intruding' demagogues but actually a cursory reading of *Mein Kampf* suggests it miscarries—the whole machinery of extermination was a *gamble* to create a *Lebensraum* that would not need to be perpetually defended against those 'intruded' upon because it would be covered with the very settler/farmers who are so highly esteemed by many kinds of frontier 'stimulationists' (including Ardrey) as preservers of biological nations.[10] Furthermore Ardrey seems to forget that from a German point of view—and that cannot need to be justified in Ardrey's terminology as more than a 'biological' sense of self-preservation—the 1918 boundaries were a 'territorial' intrusion of massive proportions. Ardrey's eulogy of border stimulation is bad news for anyone who actually lives in a mixed nationality or ethnic zone who has ever *tried* to make life approximate to anything other than savagery. Did the Germans of these zones all live down to Ardrey's standards of innate behaviour?

The 'democratic third' of Bohemian Germans who stood by Czechoslovakia in 1935-8 resisted these 'stimulating' impulses and did not treat 'looting, raping and raising general havoc' as an instinct they had any intention of indulging. They resisted even the innocuous sounding noises about 'local autonomy' because they saw where these would take them. Hitler had said of democrats, international socialists, pacifists etc. that 'he . . . will in the presence of any menace to his people, be it ever so grave an unjust, always (in so far as he is a German) seek after the objective right and *never from pure instinct of self-preservation* join the ranks of his herd and fight with them'.[11] I cite this particular authority to make the point that even the powers of darkness themselves know that they have principled opponents amongst their own 'herd' even when that part of the herd is already on a 'border'.

The danger with Ardrey's approach is that he is not just overthrowing certain utopianisms, he is doing something else as well. There are many situations in which the strength of force fields may be so great that no single 'remedy' can be found by those who seek to avert disasters. The Bohemian German 'democratic third' were certainly stuck in such a situation. It is one thing to say that restraining forces seem to be ineffective. But it is quite another to suggest that they don't exist. It is possible that people he charges with substituting 'high mindedness for higher learning' may have a sound grasp of the simple truths that it is easier to give voice to in the world of sacred metropolitan order than in the middle of territorialist convulsion. If the coercive power of chronic territorial force fields is recognised, it cannot be *celebrated* without corroding the merciful existence of sanctuaries of the rule of law in the metropolis. For all the hypocrisy that may be involved in preserving them, they are at least a space in which people can publicly proclaim values, which they may not live up to but which may none the less act as restraints upon what they will tolerate in practice. Hypocritical restraints do not cease to be restraints simply because they are somewhat hypocritical. If proof were needed of this then it is provided by radical nationalist conservatism and eventually Nazism in Germany. Ernst Juenger's 'better be a criminal than a bourgeois' or Hermann Goering's 'when I hear the world culture, I reach for my revolver' were rather concise statements of opposition to bourgeois cultural order.

To get the impact of hypocritical restraint into perspective, in Chapters 2, 3 and 4 we saw how the citizen's metropolitan state acted as a pivot in the crystallisation of ethnic/national conflicts, even when it did not act as a purely partisan force on the side of its citizens. The metropolitan-frontier linkage was therefore both a cause of antagonism—allowing the system of communal deterrence to accumulate malignancy—and a restraint, even if a feeble one, upon the most lethal forces within it. That was so until liberal imperialist democracy collapsed at the metropolitan centre and was replaced by fascism.

In Chapter 2 I argued that throughout the nineteenth century there was a tendency for ethnic frontier antagonisms both to become sharper and at the same time to allow citizen and native blocs to increasingly reciprocate each other's political strategies and forms of communal social organisation. In Chapter 3 I argued that settler citizen antagonism towards natives was protecting concrete economic differences between them and at the same time attempting to check their own displacement by more exploitable native labour. Bearing in mind that the ethnic frontiers were once upon a time of settlement origin, we could treat them all as sub-species of the same time of development—ones in which mass settlement prevented the development of any simple equation of class and ethnic identity and where the mass citizen settlement acquired an independent influence or power of its own. If all such societies were then placed on a scale, the major differences would be between ethnic frontiers, where the levels of material subsistence were broadly the same for both plebeian citizens and for natives, and settlement colonial frontiers where they were sharply differentiated. Three other scales of difference would be associated with this. In the first case, at one extreme a qualitative and more or less general privilege of citizens would be protected; while at the other end would be a system of petty discrimination whose 'benefits' might not in fact be general to all citizens. In the second case, at one extreme the position of settlers could only be protected by formal institutional means or by a *de facto* right to resort to violence without fear of reprisal whereas at the other, extreme territorialism could be a relatively reciprocal strategy of citizen and native. In the third case, at one extreme the settler position could only be defended ideologically by overt violation of democratic principles (of head counting and rule of law) while at the other extreme the outward letter of democratic law would not need to be severely violated.

But even in the case of ethnic frontiers there was a limit to development of simple reciprocal opposition. That limit was expressed in defiance actions which obliged the metropolitan power to recognise that its own sovereignty rested upon the tolerance of the citizen population. Leaving aside the confusion in the case of Bohemia where Austrian central state power could not accept any such claim without risk to its authority over other areas (the creative confusion multinational social democracy was able to exploit), the defiance actions drew an important line through the histories of these societies by killing the hope that the metropolitan state might be neutral between ethnic blocs. The Algerian case may perhaps illustrate the rule. The 1890s defiance action targeted against Algerian Jews was broken by metropolitan power, thus ensuring that institutional obstacles to Jewish assimilation were defeated. It was only in the 1930s that defiance action was targeted against Moslem assimilationist aspirations. Up to that point, even though the scale of economic privilege of urban Europeans over the mass of Moslems was enormous, the political currents in European politics were not so obviously preoccupied with fear of Moslem power and influence as were those of southern white or Northern Ireland unionist politics with blacks or Catholics respectively. Only by the 1930s were urban Moslems in a position to make their political presence strongly felt. In other words defiance actions tend to uproot the cohesion of institutional order itself and that uprooting has political consequences of its own that cannot be reduced to a simple listing of citizen 'interests' as the explanation for their political solidarity. This possibility, it should be noticed, is more likely to occur the more actual differences between citizens and native are being corroded. It implies the crystallisation of direct and popular antagonisms between citizen and native population which state power can no longer even pretend to mediate independently.

What we must now consider is how the rivalries between plebeian citizens (whether in ethnic or settlement colonial frontiers) and their native counterparts relate to Girard's theories of mimetic Desire. Within the framework of cultural order desires are focused upon transcendental or culturally designated models with whom no rivalry is possible because they are out of reach. This Girard calls external mediation of desires. In his analysis of literature, Girard shows how mimesis of models who are within reach leads to rivalries that are no longer about objects external to the desiring subjects. If initially the 'disciple' wants what he perceives his nearby 'model' to have, his success or near-success in securing it generates a mimetic build-up in which the original object of desire disappears from view and the rivalry is about the person of the other. In its extreme form one rival has only to desire something to encounter the other, also desiring it, as an obstacle. This is internal mediation of desire.[12] Eventually the differences between the antagonists are corroded as the cultural, religious and legal restraints upon the rivalry are eaten away. At the vanishing point the antagonists are the same, the restraints upon their rivalry dissolved. Only violence remains between them. This process only looks irrational to someone at a distance from it. Seen from within, each escalation of rivalry generates excellent reasons for the next escalation. Violence always generates reasons for itself.

We can cite contemporary illustrations from Northern Ireland. The demand of the Catholics in Derry for an end to gerrymandering of local government boundaries was about something very concrete. It also attracted a far from insignificant amount of Protestant support. The demand was based upon straightforward transcendental principles of justice. After more than ten years of violence the turbulence generated by disputes about the name of the city—whether it should be called Derry (as nationalists want) or Londonderry (as unionists want)—has stirred up a conflict which is about nothing and everything at the same time. If there were no other sources of antagonism, the name of the council would be of no consequence. But the practical implication of the name is that it has become a means of expressing an antagonism that has more 'causes'/'reasons' than any man or woman could any longer count. It pressures people to take sides every time they need to mention the name of the city, and allows them to be accused of taking sides on a vast array of collateral issues. A heated argument about this question that came to blows could be an example of internal mediation. The desire involved is simply a negative reflection of the desire of the opponent. Endless discussion about the rights and wrongs of the issue could settle nothing except one's sympathies.

Much of the point of Girard's analysis is to show how cultures both conceal and prevent these dangers at the same time. They must conceal in order to prevent and they must prevent in order to conceal. Epidemics of internal mediation that he calls sacrificial crises are retrospectively hidden from view when a scapegoat is targeted; all violence is redirected against him/her/it and the expulsion of the scapegoat is reinterpreted in Myth.

The antagonism between plebeian citizens and natives in frontier zones probably comes closer to illustrating this process than any other chronic social disorder. For here after the end of the settlement colonising process the objective differences between plebeian citizen and native tended to dimnish, while the process of corroding the differences tends to increase rather than liquidate antagonism. Most settlement colonial structures which do not lead to the extermination of the native population but which generate the hybrid of popular settlement and the economic exploitation of cheap native labour tend to decay as the second process limits the first. The end of these structures has the appearance at least of a 'dialectical' outcome—imperialism generating an opponent that overthrows it—and conceals the pure antagonism which may be part of the story (as in the case of Algeria). In telling the history as a dialectical history, the moments of reciprocity or equality in antagonism are eventually concealed from view by the effective scapegoat of the settlers who can—with a good conscience, perhaps—be called the source of the previous disorder. What interests me here is the problem of living in a world of antagonism.

Once state power cannot monopolise coercive relationships between itself and a native population, the whole system is one of threatened violence in which the state is a feeble pivot between its ostensible supporters (including vigilante sections of the citizen population) and the natives. This has debilitating consequences for sections of moderate and progressive citizens, because antagonism becomes endemic.

Antagonism can be said to be endemic when ethnic communities come to experience each other through the most threatening and aggravated acts of the 'other'. Ideologies of ethnic supremacy are perceptions of the 'other' as a conspiracy against which eternal vigilance is required; they are related to deterrence or vigilance practices which they reinforce and by which they are reinforced. One of the problems in this chapter is to explain how it comes to pass that these (often) minoritarian beliefs become representative, systematically limiting, concealing or reducing the significance of less antagonistic forms of intercommunal communication. When antagonistic relationships between ethnic blocs are popularised, tranquillity is poised on something of a hair trigger and all changes are subject to a tacit 'troublemaker veto'. The 'troublemaker' of the dominant society is one who can be kept under control and perhaps criminalised 'at the moment', but who might attract wider sympathy and support if certain things are allowed to happen. This veto tacitly underlies much of the political behaviour of the dominant society. Some pronounce it as a thinly veiled threat, some allude to it as a pretext for defending the *status quo*, some honestly fear it and calculate that no change is worth the threatened disturbance, some deeply resent it; but it is never taken lightly. The possible sources of 'trouble' can rarely be clearly located as particular individuals or interests. Dominant interests can manipulate this threat to their advantage though it exists in spite of them. But the troublemaker veto figures in one way or another in most political statements from the dominant society. 'Extremists' relish it and 'moderates' often deplore it. Reason is not wanting in these statements: in the case of moderates it is rarely inferior to what passes for reason in metropolitan political discourse. As Martin Luther King put it, 'Liberalism failed to show that reason by itself is little more than an instrument to justify man's defensive ways of thinking.'[13] These societies are a radical illustration of that general truth in a context of thinly concealed possibilities for chaos.

From the standpoint of the dominated society the operation of this troublemaker veto looks totally different. Those who pronounce thinly veiled threats seem to make the running and the rest seem to be simply 'led', even when they are given credit for benign intent. Excluded from power, sections of the dominated society in their turn see an evil system. Everything that happens in the society, that either does or might malignantly affect the dominated, is part of a conspiracy against them of which the dominant society (or the greater part of it) is guilty—if only in the sense of being gullible supporters of it. Both visions are expressions of representative violence. Supremacisms diagnose rebellion everywhere and the ideologies of rebellion can become their mirror image;

then both tend only to see the most malignant features of the 'other' and to hold the whole of the 'other' in some degree collectively responsible for the worst things done in their name. Vigilance of power perpetually generates the symptoms of rebellion it purportedly guards against; while rebellion on the principle of collective responsibility validates the anxieties of the dominant.

Given the nature of the troublemaker veto, which restrains the progressive elements of the dominant society and makes the expectation of change at best 'gradualist', it is obvious that the circle cannot be broken by the dominant themselves. Progressive elements in the dominant society tend to speak to their own people first, because they are the people with electoral veto over power. But tranquillity produced by communal deterrence is a screen in the way of seeing the problems. If the dominated have acquiesced, they do not appear to be suffering from any urgent suffering. If a few protest, they look like 'troublemakers'. But a massive protest looks like rebellion and is seen first and foremost as a threat.

It is often argued that dominant societies support their own monopoly of power to protect privileges or because they are suffused with petty meanness or bigotry. But if we are looking for the universal element, the thing which actually determines who is dominant and who is dominated, there is really only one privilege—the knowledge that the law is 'our law'. To explain to metropolitan readers why this privilege is so important, it is necessary to remind them that most of them share it and many take it for granted with a good conscience. If they themselves are with scapegoats of metropolitan society—the people who have experienced the claims of institutional order as a hypocrisy—and together with them bring strength and hope to alleviate sufferings, then they will know that it is a mercy that scapegoats do not take vengeance on the rest of society for their suffering, with all the threats of cyclical violence that this might entail. If they deny that there are such scapegoats and take pride in the liberality of their society, their position is only accidentally different from that of people in other situations who think it normal that the law should be 'our' law, meaning 'our' protection against anything we might want to be protected against, such as the Oran colon who said in 1960, 'Be logical, if you have trouble with an Arab do you expect an Arab policeman to defend you?'[14] Whichever way we look at it, we tend not to hold ourselves responsible for injustices done by others from which we benefit indirectly and at several removes—even if we recognise some kind of responsibility when we see it. The barrier to empathy is that we do not feel injustices we have not ourselves borne. (This is not only a caution to readers. It is the author's confession and caution to himself.) We are ourselves and so long as ethnic experiences really are different, differences are real.

By 1955 in urban Algeria, European factory workers were about 25 per cent of Europeans employed and their average income was more than double that of the Moslem factory workers, who were 27 per cent of urban Moslems employed. Even excluding the 25 per cent to 33 per cent of Moslems in chronic underemployment, the overall urban Moslem average income was a quarter of that of the European average. The European factory workers who (apart from a very small 3 per cent of domestic servants) were at the bottom of the European income range were none the less earning more than all but the top 10 per cent of employed Moslems (executives and civil servants). But until the 1950s substantial numbers of Europeans voted for parties of left.[15]

Albert Memmi argued that there is no such thing as a colonial who is not a privileged coloniser. In fact, the degree of economic equality between European and Moslem in North Africa was so striking that this point appears at first sight to allow minor exceptions and to be a simple reflection of economic realities. But he pursues particularly the theme that the small coloniser is an 'obstinate defender of colonial privileges'. He dismisses the idea that this might be an 'expression of anxiety by a minority living in the midst of a hostile majority' with the argument that, 'During the peak of the colonial process, protected by the police, the army and an air force always ready to step in, Europeans in the colonies were not sufficiently afraid to explain such unanimity'.

But as Berque says, it was perhaps precisely when they did feel secure that the ' "little men" [felt] themselves in opposition to the "big men" [and] often took up native causes, played an active part in the left-wing politics, put liberal theses into practice'.[16]

The Europeans were heavily concentrated in the towns and cities. The European agricultural population fell from 211,000 in 1911 to 125,000 in 1948 and 93,000 in 1954 on the eve of the rebellion. In the towns 'they found the conditions which where closest to those of their country of origin' (Benatia). Yet between 1926 and 1936 the Moslem population of Algiers rose by 21,000 (taking it from 26 per cent to 31 per cent of the total) and the European population by only 10,000. It appears that sanitation laws were used as pretext/reasons to obstruct the creation of a Moslem cemetery; that Moslem sectors were not provided with adequate schools; and that in the 1930s, the navvies employed on the municipal embankment project included only one-fifth Moslems, receiving about two- thirds of the wage levels paid to European navvies.[17]

The tranquillity of the 1930s owed something to the fact that urban Moslems did not overtly challenge French power. Berque speaks of policemen patrolling the Moslem Casbah in pairs who 'dealt out lashes before words and *no-one had dared to protest*'. If Europeans in general were shielded from these experiences, and yet were aware, if not of them, then at least of Moslem feeling about the *status quo*, that may be part of the anxiety of 'even the most tranquil and self-confident citizens', of their sense of 'having incurred the resentment and wounded pride of the other'. As Berque puts it, even where contacts existed as between school friends or loyalties between men or 'even groups of men', 'something subsisted which was neither religious reticence, nor impotent anger nor watchful vio-lence'.[18]

At this stage the rising Moslem presence seems to have left Europeans able to define the problems it gave rise to. A conservative senator declared that he was in favour of friendly relations with the natives but asked them to understand the situation and consider that it was 'indispensable that the French element conserve unceasingly its preponderance'. But the socialists and communists, who had oscillated between supporting eventual self-government and opposing the revival of Arab nationalism, swung in 1934 towards support for a single electoral college with a much expanding Moslem franchise. Spurred in part by the revival of anti-Semitism in both metropolitan France and Algeria, the sense of urgency may have been to prevent fascist efforts to exploit Moslem anti-Semitism after the pogrom in Constantine. But another aspect of this switch was an awareness that moves toward equality of citizenship and integrationism with France were necessary to head off the rise of Arab nationalism.[19] They combined integrationism with demands for the loosening of controls on migrant labour and the legislation of minimum wages for agricultural workers. In the urban context they stressed the importance of equal pay for equal work. In other words they sought to accelerate the assimilation of French educated Moslems without loss of Islamic status and at the same time, by attacking rural vested interests in Moslem underemployment, to raise the living standards of Moslem labour and thereby the possibilities of an equal pay for equal work solidarity between European and Moslem labour—something that would become more difficult to sustain when urban Moslem underemployment grew. No doubt at the time it must have looked like a credible basis for a compact since it was much more generous to Moslems than mainline colon politics.

The pressures towards independence came from two sources. Moslem migrant labour, which had been obstructed until 1913 by rural colon interests fearful of labour shortages and the impact of migrant income remittance on rural Moslem society, reached about 100,000 by 1920. Often on the receiving end of metropolitan labour hostility, they were organised in the PPA, a Moslem separatist movement which broke away from the French Communist party. This organisation rejected integration entirely and was no doubt the current that Euro-leftists sought to pre-empt. The 'Ulama by contrast were the Moslem reaction to the equation of Frenchness and modernity. The integration of Islam and the modern world, affirming an Islamic history and culture of Algeria, building up Islamic schools and cultural institutions was essentially similar to organic work in the ethnic frontiers.

The tactical attitude of the 'Ulama towards the events of the 1935–7 period was shaped by the line-up of domestic French politics. When the Popular Front proposal to expand the Moslem electorate in the existing electoral college was announced, opinion in Algeria became increasingly polarised between supporters of the single college of the Blum-Violette scheme (Moslems and some of the European left) and those of an alternative second Moslem college (the majority of Europeans). All but one of the deputies ended up opposing the Blum-Violette scheme and it was buried by a threatened strike of European mayors. Unlike 1898, the defiance action of 1937 worked.[20]

In its aftermath the government tightened the screws on the PPA, a measure which the communists relished, hoping to gain members from among its rival's supporters. Albert Camus, who broke with the communists in this period, criticised them for failing to see how the social evolution of the Moslems under colonialism *'lacked* cohesion and *risked* developing into a radical nationalism'.[21] This pre-emptive concern for justice is an ongoing ambiguity affecting dominant societies generally. It seems possible to pre-empt the anger of the dominated by taking the initiative, but the arguments for doing so that are addressed to the dominant society are unavoidably paternalistic when viewed from the standpoint of the dominated.

The subsequent growth of the Moslem urban populations exposed clearly the colonial character of Algerian society as a whole. It ended the illusion that colonialism could be reformed by attacking the power of rural colon agricultural interests. Obviously this placed European urban workers in a much more defensive position. The more established the Moslem presence in cities and the more educated Moslems there were to compete for hitherto European occupations, the stronger the impulse to defend European occupational boundaries. Whereas in orthodox colonial structures, many of the skilled and white-collar occupations were largely filled by colonised peoples, in Algeria the European presence became in this period both the model of what was possible and the obstacle to securing it. From Oran in 1960, Bourdieu reports a Moslem perception thus:'The European is favoured here. For us, unemployment is natural. For a European it is a scandal no-one can tolerate—the authorities couldn't nor could other Europeans. Every effort is made to find something for him;

they discover he has skills and qualifications; even if he hasn't got any they find some. And once he has been put in a job, he always turns out at least a little bit higher placed than all the Moslems . . . that's what string pulling can do and yet you never know who pulled the string: everyone did.'[22]

Bourdieu shows how poor Moslems were stuck in a world of underemployment without educational or occupational qualifications, hoping for the chance of irregular, capriciously regulated, low paid work. For them, the colonial world was a universe dominated by a malignant, all-powerful will: 'What is perceived is not discrimination but the racialist, not exploitation but the exploiter, not even the boss but the Spanish foreman.' Unemployment is understood as 'the work of a sort of evil, hidden god'. And 'the frequency and emotional intensity with which "string pulling" is referred to always in the vaguest possible terms, sometimes without any reference to a situation concretely experienced, shows clearly that, for the most underprivileged, it is a datum of mythic reason as much as of experience.' The European seemed to be in some way related to a power system that was closed to subproletarian Moslems. Whether they held all Europeans responsible for this or not, the thwarted desire was defined by what the Europeans had. Fanon's theory of violence asserts that fatalism and day-dreaming or resignation in the face of colonialism can only be overcome by striking out against it. But who embodies it?

The colonial system is experienced as violence, a context in which everything is a question of 'them' and 'us', so 'the good is quite simply that which is "evil" for them (the settlers)'. 'There is no native who does not dream at least once a day of setting himself up in the settler's place.' Bourdieu's observations show that this is not limited to rural labourers dreaming of taking over colon estates; it is also the sub-proletarian dream of becoming a regularly employed worker as the mass of Europeans are. 'There isn't any work because there are too many foreigners'.[23]

It cannot be an accident that Fanon's conception of violence is more popular amongst dominated peoples in largely Europeanised milieux (whether colonial or otherwise) than in the areas of the thinly settled colonial world. The settler personalises the alien order and—even if many did not resort to capricious violence—settler vigilance taught the natives that power and self-assertion were the properties of those who could successfully inflict violence (Girard's Kudos). Fanon argues that the natives, fearful of responding against the settler, were violent towards each other—and that 'terrifying myths' and superstitions of religions which condemned natives to resignation and day-dreaming were the means of containing these tendencies. To kill a settler was to both kill the enemy and to liberate the native: 'All the new revolutionary assurance of the native stems from this discovery (that he is a man just like a settler). For if, in fact, my life is worth as much as the settler's, his glance no longer shrivels me up or freezes me.'[24]

The reason why Fanon's theory of violence has attracted so much attention is that it makes a virtue out of the cyclical violence that follows. Fanon observes that the violence of the native will bring forth reprisals and generate a cycle of further violence which will be 'more terrible in proportion to the size of the implantation from the mother country' (i.e., the relative size of settler to native population). It is true that Fanon argues that settlers who do not join in the 'guilty hysteria' induced by native violence 'disarm the general hatred that the native feels towards the foreign settlement'. But what did this amount to in practice? It would have been necessary for settlers to detach themselves *visibly* from the generalised defensiveness of other settlers. Even the more pacific settlers may quite realistically have judged that their own survival after 1955 was the accidental result of not being in the wrong place at the wrong time. A revolutionary violence based on the principle that the 'good is that which is evil for them' can only burn itself out when 'they' are all expelled—except those settlers who carried their opposition to the *status quo* to the point where they risked everything and could be held up as the standard by which the rest were judged. When Fanon spoke of 'the burial [of the colonial zone] in the depth of the earth or its expulsion from the country', this was no figure of speech.[25] His view of liberating violence probably comes closer than any other contemporary political formula to the sacrificial chaos in Girard's analysis of the origins of cultural order. All settlers who react to anti-settler violence with 'guilty hysteria' are seen to be guilty of the crimes of colonialism and its Evil Intent. The expulsion of the settler against whom all violence has been directed expels the source of Evil. The chaos ends and brings peace.

The colons of Algeria were trapped in such a circle and it was this—not any specifically colonial privilege—that distinguished them from metropolitan French people. On this point there was tacit agreement between Jean Paul Sartre, who supported the FLN war of independence, and Albert Camus, himself a French Algerian, who opposed it.

'With us,' said Sartre, 'to be a man is to be an accomplice of colonialism, since all of us *without exception* have profited by colonial exploitation.' And as Camus puts it, 'If some Frenchmen consider that, as a result of colonising, France is in a state of sin historically, they don't have to point to the French in Algeria as scapegoats; they must offer up themselves in expiation.' Indeed the benefits of the economic exploitation of Algeria were diffused by 'unequal exchange' and most French people in Algeria lived at slightly lower standards of living than their metropolitan counterparts. Sartre spoke of de Gaulle as the 'Grand Magician whose business it is to keep us all in the dark at all costs',[26] which is exactly what he did with perhaps greater success than Sartre anticipated. For all the awareness of French co-responsibility with the colons, their exodus was the only possible outcome of the collision of antagonistic intents which reduced all issues to one. This was concealed from view right up to the moment it became irreversible.

The textile mill villages of the Carolinas are perhaps a classic example of capitalism 'dividing and ruling'. They excluded blacks and employed a non-unionised labour force of whites from farms that were under pressure of bankruptcy, tenancy and foreclosure. At the wage levels payable, these mills were around the turn of the century part of a shift of the textile industry from the north-eastern to the south-eastern states. Cell says that, if the mill owners behaved like paternalistic planters, that is no accident. Many of them were planters and the location of the mills on the Piedmont was an intentional device to prevent the mills acting as alternative employment for their black agricultural labour forces. A southern conservative editor, William Watts Ball, spoke in 1910 of a possible 'complete abandonment of the farms [in South Carolina] to the Negro directed by landlords and overseers'. 'Whites failing to compete with the Negro on the farms on account of the latter's low and often depraved state of living, have been driven to flee to manufacturing towns as cities of refuge and there they have segregated themselves.' But he also noticed that in the preceding thirty years there had been a rapid dwindling of Negro carpenters, craftsmen, masons, joiners and bricklayers—a clear sign, though he does not say it, that segregationism was assisting their displacement by whites. Unlike Algerian Moslems in urban areas, blacks were experiencing a reversal rather than encountering obstacles to a tentative entry.[27]

The admittedly extreme case of Wilmington, North Carolina, illustrates what new pressures were rising in the early twentieth century. During the 1898 *coup d'état*, professional and skilled blacks were driven from the town. The climate of intimidation was such that the Democratic legislature in 1899 passed a Vagrancy Act for Wilmington to get black labourers back to work for white employers. Yet at the same time it repealed an 1891 law passed at the behest of black belt plantation interests to prohibit the activities of labour recruiters. A representative from a white Appalachian mountain district said that he 'didn't care if all the Negroes left the state'. The higher the level of coercion that could be applied to blacks the easier it became simultaneously to remove them as a competetive force and a self-organised presence and at the same time to corral them as a subordinated labour force in particular economic sectors. The intra-white conflicts over disenfranchisement proposals appear to have been something like a race to initiate an arrangement beneficial to the initiators. Thus when the planter-inspired measure included the literacy test, it was denounced by some Populists both because it would exclude some ordinary whites (to the advantage of propertied interests) and because it would not affect the 'most vicious, troublesome and obnoxious class of Negroes'.[28]

In the early 1890s, Wilmington had had a fusion arrangement between Democrats (white) and Republicans (black). When the Republican-Populist regime came to power at state level in 1896 the local government system was reorganised so that three out of five of its elected aldermen were black and these were supplemented by five aldermen appointed by the Republican governor. The five appointees and two of the blacks elected a mayor while the elected whites and one of the blacks elected a rival mayor and the case was disputed in the courts. As the centre of a well-organised black community, impatient with the cautious approach of the white Republican governor to black office-holding and educational interests, Wilmington provided the focal point for agitation about black 'control'. In the 1897 climate, Populists and Democrats were accusing each other of using the black vote, both having previously sought and tolerated arrangements in which blacks were junior partners. Wilmington was described as a 'Mecca for Negroes' where white artisans were being displaced and black policemen were maltreating white people. When the black editor of the *Wilmington Record* replied to Rebecca Fulton's defence of lynching as a necessary deterrent to black rapists, all manner of allegations were raised about how the blacks were intent upon repealing laws against mixed accommodations and intermarriage. The *Atlanta Constitution* claimed that black leaders had a plan to secure control of North Carolina and to colonise it by drawing blacks from all over the South to create the 'refuge of their people in America'. Oblivious to all contrary evidence, 'such intentions might be publicly denied,[but] there was no doubt of their truth'.[29]

In the South after 1900, lynching apologists always argued that it was a necessary deterrent to black rapists. And in later years when desegregation controversies were stirred up, pamphleteers and propagandists would use lurid visions of desegregation leading to forcible interracial sexual relations and assaults upon white womanhood.[30] It was almost as though they believed that the driving force behind black demands for equality was a lust for white women. Yet a very high proportion of American blacks have white ancestors, a legacy of the power of planters over slave women, and even during the segregationist era it was not uncommon for white men to have sexual relations with black women, covering the whole range between prostitution and *de facto* marriages. At the same time, black men lived in fear of proximity to white women which could lead to accusations of rape and to summary lynching. If lynching had no other purpose than to draw black men's attention to the contrast between white men's kudos in this sphere and the massive risks to themselves if they attempted to rival them, it would have had that effect at least.[31] In the 1960s, Eldridge Cleaver described his own motives for raping a white woman—which he declared later was an attack upon humanity and which he wholly repudiated—as an act of insurrection against white men's laws. 'Somehow I arrived at the conclusion that, as a matter of principle, it was of paramount importance to me to have an antagonistic ruthless attitude toward white women.'[32] If, as Girard says, all Desire is mimetic and violence used to defend something from a rival teaches us both what it is that is supremely desirable (because it is defended by violence) and that violence is the way to get it, lynching must have created the temptation described by Cleaver and which white supremacists professed to diagnose as the driving purpose behind black desires for social equality. Furthermore, once a conspiracy theory has been propounded which allows blacks no way to disprove their intent to 'mongrelise' the white race, any action of a black that gives a hint of such intent will persuade those who keep up a perpetual state of vigilance that, were it not for their own vigilance, all blacks would respond as Eldridge Cleaver had done. In this conspiracy theory, opponents of segregation became the political wing of violent 'race mongrelisers'. A system of power relations that tolerated this kind of physical vigilance would have effectively devolved its powers over blacks to the most virulent elements of all classes of white society.

In the Mississippi river and Delta counties, subsequently to witness some of the worst scenes of violence in the 1960s, planters used threats and actual violence to control their black labour forces. But they protected 'their' blacks from mobs and avoided having them jailed or otherwise being made unavailable for work. Some restrained temptations to be coercive because their reputations amongst blacks could be important during periods of labour shortage. In much of the South, planters impeded industrialisation because they feared its effects on both labour supply and wages.[33] The successful efforts of a local chamber of commerce in southern Mississippi to get a northern owned planning mill to reduce its wage levels for its predominantly black labour force ensured that thereafter the mill preferred black labour. A lower class of white mill and factory workers had been growing since the beginning of the century. In the depression after 1929, whites secured employment in hitherto black sectors such as municipal services; some made efforts to displace black railway firemen (by murdering them); and others attempted to intimidate blacks off a plantation. A case was reported of blacks on one plantation burning a white tenant's cabin to force the landlord to exclude white tenants. The plantation owners themselves, however, did not like white tenants and wanted them out of the county. 'I wouldn't have one on my place,' said one. And another said of white sawmill workers: 'They are the kind who drink and gamble with the Negroes and sleep with their women and then if anything happens they want to kill all the Negroes.'[34]

The main problem white tenants posed for planters was that they tended to be more assertive than blacks, because they were not so powerless. They had to be forced to behave like blacks or got out of the way to prevent their example from spreading. This rather than the idea that whites were too 'status conscious' or proud of their 'racial superiority' to do 'nigger work' looks like the reason for the virtual exclusion of white rural tenants in these areas. Of South Carolina, William W. Ball said: 'There is no denying the plain fact that a great proportion of the white people hold in the back of their heads the right to visit summary punishment on Negroes for certain crimes—a right which the more lawless class asserts as to numerous crimes and misdemeanours . . . Every decent white man and woman maintains and exercises a right of treating all Negroes as inferiors.'[35]

Evidence about poor white attitudes towards blacks is, not surprisingly, contradictory. The environment they lived in created an opportunity to take aggressive action against blacks with a low risk of reprisal, except in some situations where such actions interfered with planter prerogatives.[36] At the same time they faced a *de facto* interdependence (the basis of paternalism) between planters and their black labour forces, because of the planters' preference for black labour. The poor whites' reputation as 'lazy' and 'vicious' suited planters very well, lending substance to the claims of paternalism. And for blacks without any form of defence, the knowledge that any white man could attack them with impunity was adequate ground for reckoning many white men possible threats.

In Powdermaker's account the poor whites were the most hostile to blacks acting as an agent for the white race 'taking actions and expressing sentiments to which [white] society as a whole is not ready to commit itself.' In Davis and Gardner's account, this agent role was placed upon lower middle-class whites, while they found lower-class whites often developed friendly relations with blacks amongst whom they lived. The solution to this apparent dispute seems to be that, in general, whites were kept at as much of a distance as possible and in ignorance of what it felt like to be black. 'Since so much of the Negro's trouble is due to the white man's fears, it pays to keep him feeling safe.' Thus whites who had in fact no human and friendly contact with blacks were effectively represented towards them by the worst things that emanated from the classes of whites to which they belonged. As poor whites could not criminalise the violence emanating from their own community, whereas dominant whites could prevent lynchings of blacks they chose to recognise as well behaved or peaceful, routine restraining forces upon anti-black violence seemed to come from upper-class whites whereas routine threat emananted from lower-class whites.[37]

Segregationism was a mechanism for preserving the drastic inequality of the force possibilities available to whites, while restraining them from spawning a perpetual chaos.[38] The practices of white supremacist vigilance left blacks no space to prove that any desire for equality was anything other than a violence (to 'mongrelise' the races). The impossibility of criminalising these vigilance practices was the impossibility of criminalising such ideas, creating the space in which all variants upon them were an expression of freedom of speech and opinion. 'Troublemakers' could be kept under control only if the inequality of the races was upheld in law, so that blacks acquiescing in such claims could be seen to be peaceable and therefore not acceptable targets for vigilance. Much of the sincere conscientiousness of southern segregationists is only comprehensible if we look at their vociferous opposition to inter-racial sexuality and liquor in this light. 'Our people, our white men with their black concubines, are destroying the integrity of the Negro race, raising up a menace to the white race . . . and preparing the way . . . for a death struggle for racial supremacy.' There is tacit recognition that if white men did excite black anger, by doing what they proclaimed their right to punish black men for doing, violence might sprawl out of control.[39] From this angle segregationism and separation of the races was a way of making tranquil coexistence possible. The free-floating right of white men to punish blacks had to be contained and restricted to upholding the lines of the segregationist system, rather than being a licensed method of settling any and every issue any white man chose to use it for. Only in such ways could institutionalised violence acquire a good conscience and call itself white civilisation.

In 1940 William Watts Ball commented on the improvement in southern race relations—there were no reported lynchings that year—that resulted from increased separation between the races. 'In those bad old days when lynching was common there was also a kinder relation between some of the whites and blacks than now exists. A respectable white man usually had Negroes who were his friends or dependents, who came to him in trouble . . . that relationship has almost disappeared.'[40] A clearer connection between the savagery of lynching and the paternalist system would be difficult to establish. So long as planter paternalism was the key restraining force upon white violence, its preference for dependent blacks perpetually regenerated the impulse to white plebeian expulsionism, so that poor whites were involuntarily 'represented' by the most virulent of their own kind and the influence of the peaceable amongst them was far more diminutive than their possible numbers.

Organisations of class solidarity cut through this form of representation. When the Agricultural Adjustment Administration (AAA) schemes during the 1930s Depression led to the displacement of many sharecroppers, black and white, the Southern Tenant Farmers Union, formed to protect tenant rights, was explicity interracial. 'Black people couldn't do it on their own without inviting racial slaughter.' Whites who joined both shared and diminished the risks.[41] One of the focal points for the Southern Tenant Farmers Union in the 1930s was Poinsett County, Arkansas, where the deputy sheriff became a socialist and took an important post in the movement. Huey Long and some of the pro-New Deal currents in southern politics, despite their proclaimed support for white supremacy, tacitly facilitated black voter registration to strengthen their own hand. Once blacks could withdraw the support they were being called upon to give, they had some capacity to influence the system that ruled over them until or unless sufficient white vigilantism could be orchestrated to disenfranchise them again.[42]

Booker T. Washington's accommodationist philosophy, despite its outward show of accepting white supremacy, was inwardly an injunction to recognise the facts of power. The professional and commercial strata of black society were obliged to tread cautiously to preserve and expand the capacity of blacks for self-organisation. Within the segregationist system they were trammelled by the power of school boards and other instruments of white control and their economic power was limited. Developing race pride broke the temptation to regard 'whiteness' and value as identical. Significantly, in the plantation counties education seemed to be almost self-defeating—the educated blacks could find no outlets for their skills and tended to migrate northwards. Tony Dunbar noticed how local civil rights organisations got off the ground in the 1960s not so much through clergy, teachers or professionals taking initiatives as through the activities of small black owner-occupying farmers.[43] The very appearance of such a group depended on the decay of the plantation system itself which did not begin in the Mississippi Delta until the 1960s.

However, even if segregationism was allowed to ritualise itself and appear as a normal, 'traditional' thing and to strengthen somewhat the restraints against capricious violence, overt challenge brought out the violence within it into the open. Black challenges were seen as troublemaking which whites knew would be responded to by white 'troublemakers'. Martin Luther King's philosophy of non-violence differs most emphatically from Fanon's view of 'liberating violence' in its view of the oppressor. King said that many segregationists were sincere people and the oppression was a product not only of sin but of conscientious blindness. Love—agape—was not a sentimental thing. Forgiving one's enemies meant 'that the evil deed is no longer a mental block impeding a new relationship'. The viciousness and evilness of an enemy's acts 'are not quite representative of all that he is'. And to the bitterest opponents, 'We shall match your capacity to inflict suffering by our capacity to endure. We shall meet physical force with soul force. We cannot in all good conscience obey your unjust laws because non-co-operation with evil is as much a moral obligation as is co-operation with good.'[44] Where 'liberating violence' struck an enemy and the circle of violence created absolute enemy relationships, meeting violence with non-violence deprived the oppressor of the justification for his own violence and brought him face to face with his own role in the system.

The space of forgiveness was also a space for repentance. The whole internal logic of segregationism—that it was 'traditional', that it was gradually being ameliorated, that accepting it was essential to control white troublemakers—all stood exposed when the violence created by the challenge to segregationism was only the violence of its supporters. Non-violence was a refusal to respond mimetically to the violence of the system, to avoid allowing challenge to appear as a 'law and order' problem which would be used to justify the system itself.

For King, the ultimate objective was to secure a society in which blacks and whites coexisted as equals. And although breaking down segregationist laws was essential, because the law shapes peoples' habits, no reconciliation was possible unless and until blacks and whites would fulfil unenforceable obligations to each other.[45] Fanon's 'liberating violence' bound the knot of collective responsibility tighter, King's non-violence set about loosening it.

There were many in Algeria whose practice was much

closer to King's position, insofar as they did not treat the generality of Europeans as collectively guilty. But in the circle of violence they were concealed from view. Conversely, there were blacks in America who were drawn to Fanon. James Forman in 1967 interpreted Fanon thus: 'Any colonised people are exploited people. But all exploited people are not colonised . . . When Fanon says we must stretch Marxist analysis when we look at colonial situations, he is referring to [the condition in which exploited US whites form part of the colonising group] even though he didn't explain it.' Eldridge Cleaver said of Fanon that he teaches colonial subjects it is 'perfectly normal for colonial subjects to want to rise up and cut off the heads of the slave drivers.'[46] But however attractive Fanon became as a legitimiser of the temptation to mimetic violence, the politically most significant fact is that it was never acted upon by blacks during the civil rights campaign in the South.

The relationship between Northern Ireland and the two other societies will elude us if we insist upon starting from the economic 'privileges' of Protestants, whites and colons. We will face the paradox that when colons were in their most economically privileged condition they were also at their most politically 'liberal'. We will face the absurdity that there were privileged planters restraining the vigilance of poor whites. None of this makes any sense unless we underline the one thing that all of these societies (including Algeria from 1938 probably and from 1945 certainly) shared. Relationships of antagonism were structural; the corrosion of institutional order preserves antagonism as a possibility, in spite of efforts to attenuate it by civility, good neighbourliness or benign manifestations of good feeling.

Vigilance, as we saw in the US South, does not require a real rebellion to justify itself. The knowledge that in the last encounter its own violence was triumphant generates the fear of revenge. Vigilance diagnoses an all-embracing rebellious intent in signs of self-confidence that are incompatible with its conception of the blacks' place. To define blacks' place it had to establish their lack of power by force and chronically to pre-empt the role of normal law. The process of restraint—segregationism—so long as it could not criminalise vigilance practices created a space in which 'theories' or 'ideologies' of black inferiority could be accorded the status of expressions of freedom of opinion while opposition to segregation could be represented as the political expression of incipient black violence.

In Northern Ireland nationalist violence was no fiction and the successful legacy of organic work—itself an expression of power—put definite limits on vigilant efforts to define Catholics' place. But here again vigilance, even if it could be restrained, could never be criminalised. To say that it was more 'justified' is only to say that the violence of Northern Ireland had been and remained a more reciprocal possibility and that vigilance did not and could not create a generalised social subordination of Catholics. But in the absence of sacred order, of which the non-criminal character of vigilance practices is only the most obvious manifestation, vigilance is its own world. Its capacity to identify conspiracy arises from its conviction that, but for itself, all the most trivial signs of native restlessness would erupt into violence. The malignant unity between all of these three situations is quite simply that antagonism is itself before it is any of the interests it has been fashioned to serve. When antagonism expresses a drastically unequal relationship it looks instrumental. The less unequal it becomes the more its reciprocal character enables it endlessly to regenerate reasons for itself. That was the core of chapter two on ethnic frontiers and it remains to explain here in more detail how antagonisms regenerate themselves in spite of efforts to attenuate them, and belief that they are being attenuated, when the 'interests' shielded behind them are neither deep nor universal to the dominant population.

Catholics in Northern Ireland, like other native nationalists in ethnic frontiers, but unlike blacks in the US South or Moslems in Algeria, were not placed in a position of social subordination, obliged to defer to Protestants. Their society was internally self-organised, freeing them from many kinds of communal dependence upon unionists in the spheres of education, professional services, retail trade, entertainment etc. Its self-confidence after 1920 depended on the Catholic state next door, as it had previously depended on pan-Catholicism. Seamus Brady describes his youth in Derry in the 1920s and 30s when men 'were sent to prison for *daring* to whistle the national anthem of the Republic within the hearing of a policeman'.[47] 'The environment in which we were reared was one of defiant hope, clinging to the Irish ways, learning the Irish language, Irish songs, Irish dances, playing Gaelic games, and looking all the while to Eamon de Valera and the south of Ireland for deliverance.' Especially in the southern and western areas of Northern Ireland, the failure of the Boundary Commission of 1925 to adjust the border left them under the gerrymandered local authorities, one of whose original purposes had been to weaken any case for such adjustment. The issue of politics was the 'border' but bound up with that question was every expedient and malpractice that was invented to protect it. Each of these expedients was defended by the charge of Catholic disloyalty.

There is nothing 'inherently' or 'genetically' Irish about this. In post-1920 Yugoslavia, within its overwhelmingly Serbo-Croat speaking majority, there were three religions, at least two of which called themselves nationalities. The Catholic Croats saw the Orthodox Serbs' hegemony as a Serbian domination, simply extending the rule of pre-war Serbia over the ex-provinces of the Austro-Hungarian empire. The non-co-operation of the Croatian Peasant party in the early years—holding out for a federal autonomy for Croatia—ensured that institutional Serbian dominance (notably of the gendarmerie and the military) remained and was reinforced. The Serbian poet and Croat mathematics lecturer recorded by Rebecca West in 1937 argued with each other about Serb domination. The Croat asked why there were not more Croat officials, to which the Serb replied that the Croats were not loyal (which most of them were not). 'And how,' asked the Croat, 'could we be expected to be loyal when treated like that?' to which the Serb replied 'How can we treat you differently until you are loyal?' The Serb's conclusion was that 'what is so horrible in this conversation is that you are never wrong, but I am always right, and we could go on talking like this for ever, till the clever way you are never wrong brought death upon us.' 'Some have died already,' replied the Croat. Later on, speaking alone in the absence of the Serb, he said 'Nothing here has any form. Movements that seem obvious to me when I am in Paris or London become completely inconceivable when I am here in Zagreb. Nothing matters except the Croat-Serb situation. And that, I own, never seems to get any further.'[48] This sums up the spirit of much that went on in Northern Ireland also.

After 1920 when Unionist power was entrenched in the North and its primary political imperative was to maximise the ratio of Protestant to Catholic electors everywhere, the worst Unionist orators implied that Catholic emigration was a positive good and were unashamed to declare that the local councils should be used to secure Protestant numbers. Between 1937 and 1961, Catholics were 92,000 of the 159,000 emigrants; between 1961-71, they were 44,500 of 69,000 emigrants—a per capita propensity almost three times that of Protestants.[49] What matters here is not that natural causes (such as higher birth rates, higher dependence on marginal farms) may account for a large part of this but that there were numerous signs that this was regarded by unionists as a good thing. Some, while celebrating these tendencies, virtually embraced responsibility for them. Such statements as that of E.C. Ferguson MP, who asked the annual Unionist convention in Enniskillen in 1948 'to authorise their executive to adopt whatever plans and take whatever steps, however drastic, to wipe out this Nationalist majority' [in Fermanagh] were rarely overtly contradicted by more restrained unionists. In this period, for example, the Anti-Partition League was organising a major diplomatic and electoral offensive against the continued existence of partition. Unionist ranks were not likely to split in the face of a campaign which generated hyperbolic utterances like that of the Fermanagh Nationalist MP Cahir Healy. He had twice been interned without trial. And he told the Unionists at Stormont: 'This House is not going to determine when partition will end. The Irish people and Westminster will determine that question and when that hour comes they will not give a tinker's curse what you think about it.'[50]

In the late nineteenth century and early twentieth century the countryside of rural and small town Ulster, like the southern Piedmont of the USA, was dotted with textile mills. In the pre-1885 period many of the linen manufacturers were

Liberals and the Linen Merchants Association supported the Unionist cause because it feared that home rule would impede access to British empire markets and disrupt business confidence.[51] But those whose support for the union was expressed in this economistic form rapidly lost the political initiative in the 1880s to those who took the leadership of popular unionism. The pressures of territorialist antagonism increased after the introduction of elective local government in 1898 and more especially during the post-1912 period when the mass of the Protestant population was being organised into the Ulster Volunteer Force, raised to resist home rule. The Clark mill at Castledawson may not be representative, but here the proprietor family provided successive commanders of the B Specials and many of their employees were enrolled in its ranks.[52] If this instance is a case of an inter-class political unity dominated by the employer class, a major difference between this situation and that of the southern Piedmont is the small- and middle-sized owner occupied farming society encircling it.

Irish landlords had never been directly involved in agricultural production and although the *de jure* insecurity of their tenants inhibited their powers of political self-organisation (before the 1872 Ballot Act and the 1870 and 1881 Land Acts), they enjoyed a relatively high *de facto* economic independence. The Land Acts of 1885 and 1903 eventually turned them into owner occupying farmers. The pattern of farm holdings to this day reflects the pattern of the original plantations of the seventeenth century. Large tracts of the hinterland of Coleraine, most of north Down and nearly all of Co. Antrim were overwhelmingly Protestant. Further west, in much of Co. Derry, most of Co. Tyrone and mid Armagh there was a tendency for Protestants to be more heavily concentrated in lowlands and Catholics on higher ground. Mountainous districts, notably the northern glens of Antrim, the Sperrins, the Mournes, the Fews and the areas which were once marshlands round Lough Neagh (Aghagallon, Coalisland, Toomebridge) contain very high percentages of Catholics. So, while the Land Acts created a large class of owner occupying farmers, the Catholics have been disproportionately represented amongst the more marginal hill farmers.

As Northern Irish farms have been small by English standards, they have tended to be able to absorb only a part of the
family labour and have therefore been the source of much
migrant and emigrant labour.[53]

The economic contrast between the inner Ulster area and
the rest of Ireland was already growing before the Great
Famine of 1845-50. Factory industry was concentrated in
Belfast and the handloom weaving industry had contracted
into its then largely Protestant hinterland area. The Famine
was mitigated (except in 1847 when food prices rose to
astronomical levels) by the income of weavers. This not only
reduced the level of popular distress: it sustained landlord
income and enabled landlords to react more positively to the
distress that did appear, it prevented the institutions of local
government from falling into a cycle of attempting to support
a high proportion of their populations out of a rising local
taxation on those who were struggling to keep above desti-
tution themselves. Local institutions and landlords emerged
with much better credit than elsewhere. While this attracted
some notice at the time, its potential divisiveness grew as it
was reinterpereted in the 1870s. The ongoing emigratory
pressures which were everywhere a consequence of efforts to
prevent further subdivision or secure consolidation of
holdings, began to generalise themselves in the North after the
collapse of the flax boom in 1867. The Catholic clerical *Ulster
Examiner*, in the process of shifting toward a home rule
position, said of the prosperity of the middle rank of farmers
that this could not be judged a 'national achievement' while
emigration was depopulating the countrty. Just as the Famine
came to be seen by nationalists as the start of a deliberate
effort to scatter the Irish race, unionists came to represent the
different experience of North as proof of Protestant industry
and achievement. These ethnic reinterpretations of the
Famine rubbed away the confused edges of shared experience,
and the emigration question ceased to be the common experience that had held together the Land League-Liberal
agitation of 1880-81.[54] Once Unionist power was established
in 1920 differential emigration rates became a maliganant
political focal point.

In Belfast in the 1870s, before the massive growth in skilled engineering and shipbuilding employment, Catholics made up something like 25 per cent of the skilled labour force, heavily concentrated in construction. They also comprised about 40 per cent of the general and unskilled male workers. [55] The post-1870 engineering expansion occurred when the scale and intensity of sectarian rioting increased and produced sharper territorial boundaries than heretofore. The Catholic percentage of Belfast's population peaked in the 1860s and thereafter the Catholic population grew at a slower rate than the city itself. In 1901, the Hepburn and Collins survey shows that of male household heads 13 per cent of both Protestant and Catholics were professionals, managers, businessmen or higher public servants. The lower white collar classes included 12 per cent of non-Catholics and 8 per cent of Catholic heads. The skilled manual workers included 35 per cent of non-Catholic and 31 per cent of Catholic heads. But the semi-skilled and unskilled manual workers included 36 per cent of non-Catholics and 44 per cent of Catholic male household heads. Furthermore, a larger number of Catholic than non-Catholic households had women heads. Within these aggregates, the greatest contrasts were found in engineering and shipbuilding—16 per cent of non-Catholics and 9 per cent of Catholics—and in general labouring 14 per cent of non-Catholics and 22 per cent of Catholics. The expulsions from the engineering and shipbuilding industries in 1920 almost certainly sharpened this asymmetry. Also, the outward similarity of the professional strata sizes conceals the fact that much of the Catholic professional strata were engaged in teaching and other services specific to their own community, whereas the control of industry and finance has been largely in Protestant hands.[56] The implied equalities of status were not matched by equalities of economic power. Overall Catholics have been heavily under-represented in the well-organised and highly paid sectors of skilled manual labour and in the direction and ownership of larger industrial companies. They have been more chronically and severely subjected to under-employment and more dependent on construction and agriculture and—although figures can only be inferred from differential emigration rates and local observation—on migrant labour.

Unlike the black educational system of the US South, the Catholic education system has remained firmly under the control of the Catholic clergy, providing the Catholic white collar sector with most of its strength. Clerical anxiety about the future of the educational system was an important reason for upholding the old style Nationalist party—wiped out by Sinn Féin electorally in the rest of Ireland in 1918. Once it became clear that the Free State government would not and could not honour its original pledge to finance northern Catholic schools, abstentionism in Stormont and Westminster arenas became positively dangerous. Despite the very strong pressures of the Protestant churches, the Orange Order and other popular Protestant organisations to 'protestantise' the state educational system, the Northern Ireland government's treatment of Catholic school financing differed sharply from southern states' financing of black schools. This is one area of Unionist government policy in which some of its strongest critics give it credit.[57]

Bew, Gibbon and Patterson argue that in the inter-war period the Unionist government's actions reflected tension within it between a dominant populist strategy—ensuring the consolidation of Protestant support by being highly responsive to specifically Protestant groups and organisations, often involving commitments of public expenditure in an *ad hoc* and demagogical manner—and a minor anti-populist strategy. The anti-populists constituted a system of restraint, favouring normal bureaucratic standards of administration, frowning upon overt pan-Protestantism, and tending to uphold conservative standards of financial rectitude. The anti-populists were closer to metropolitan British political concerns and acted as a check upon the excesses of populist unionism. The ultimate danger to the Stormont system perceived by anti-populists was that the northern nationalist opposition, the southern government and the British government should ever develop a common interventionist approach to the North.[58] Given the accommodative arrangement evolved between the British government and the Catholic hierarchy in the field of education before 1920, here more than anywhere was anti-populist restraint essential to preserve any kind of internal accommodation after the establishment of Stormont. For example, popular Unionist opposition to a government measure to increase aid to Catholic schools in 1947 was resisted; to deflect the opposition, the minister Col. Hall-Thompson, was obliged to act as a scapegoat after the measure had been passed.[59] Resigning from the government, he was defeated by an independent Unionist in the next general election.

At its worst in the 1930s, government ministers in Northern Ireland delivered public speeches encouraging and legitimising systematic discrimination against Catholics. While these speeches were part of a campaign to break up a non-sectarian movement in Belfast (the Unemployed Relief Committee) it cannot be an accident that they were made during a period when relations between the British and Irish governments were antagonised by the Anglo-Irish trade war. Only in these circumstances would the risks against which anti-populists warned populist unionism have seemed negligible. The future prime minister Lord Brookeborough called on Protestant employers to employ Protestants because 'Catholics were getting in everywhere'. But he also said that he knew the great difficulty they had getting suitable Protestant labour and that he (presumably unlike others) could speak freely on the matter because he hadn't 'any Catholics around his place'.[60]

In 1931-2 the impact of the Depression on both local industry and distant migrant labour opportunities generated a net inflow of 4000 into agricultural employment. In 1935 there was extensive rioting and displacement of Catholics from residential and occupational space. [61] In the absence of specific institutional devices to permit Protestant labour to command higher wage rates than Catholic labour, there would have been limits to how far this policy could have been pursued (assuming required levels of employer zealotry) without creating opportunities for other employers, motivated by simple economic self-interest, to seek out Catholic labour. Brookeborough's speech is important, whatever notice private employers *may* or may not have taken of it, because it gave expression at the highest level to the intent of unionist power. It remained 'representative' for Catholics because it was not repudiated. Although he didn't say it in his speech, he had 'no Catholics about his place' because the police had told him of an IRA plot to kidnap his sons. It supposedly involved his Catholic estate workers, whom he then dismissed. He told me that this was his main reason for making the speech and, if so, it indicates a great deal about the consequence of the Protestant power monopoly. That an anticipated incident of this kind should be made the occasion for what amounted to a governmental sanction for generalised discrimination casts a revealing light on the precarious position of Catholics within the North of Ireland, whenever the possibility of a combined British, Free State and northern Nationalist alignment—of the kind anti-populists warned against—was at its least likely. Although British troops were called to quell the 1935 riots, the British government did not visibly censure Stormont.[62]

Exploration into the motives of anti-populists amongst Unionists might show either that they were simply more devious and cautious and that their opposition to populist excesses was purely strategic; or it might show that they used strategic arguments about the possible consequences of excesses to anchor what they considered to be principles of justice. It will, I hope, by now be obvious that these kinds of uncertainty of motive are part of the reality of communal deterrence relationships. Benign tendencies in these societies, whether a reflection of abstract amity or a calculation of the dangers of unbridled sectarianism, are strengthened by an awareness of a constellation of countervailing powers acting as a restraint. When that constellation of powers was enfeebled in the 1932-38 period its restraining power was cancelled. In other words the capacity of moderate unionists to make their presence and influence felt depended upon a wider power relationship over which they themselves had limited influence. And this was necessarily the case because Catholics had no direct means of influencing intra-unionist disputes. Thus, the capacity of moderate unionists to fashion any accommodation with Catholics depended on recognising the implicit power behind them, not as a threat, but as the basis upon which an approximation to equal co-existence could be recognised— finding a form of peaceful coexistence respecting mutual capacities to deter.

This form of coexistence resembled that of tranquillised

segregation. Greensboro, North Carolina, prided itself on its progressive business image. It could do so because blacks acquiesed or appeared to acquiesce and the whites curbed the more overtly supremacist claim of segregationism.[63] Implicitly the blacks' power was the power to upset this progressive image. In Northern Ireland the main difference was that the powers being recognised were a closer approximation to equality, even though it could only be a deformed approximation given the solid control of unionism over the institutional apparatus.

We must now explore this issue at the base of the society. Protestant supremacism defined refusal of compliance with the state as a violence and tacit support for the IRA. In its more hyperbolic forms it identified Catholics as a whole with a conspiracy against Protestantism. 'Popery is something more than a religious system: it is a political system also. It is a religio-political system for the enslavement of the body and soul of man and it cannot be met by any mere religious system or any mere political system. It must be opposed by such a combination as the Orange Society, based upon religion and carrying over into the politics of the day' (William Johnston, 1861, subsequently MP for Belfast 1868-78). In this vision Orangeism is the Protestant response to Catholic organic work. The fundamental premise is that 'they all knew that the Roman Catholics of Ireland obeyed their priests in everything'. So how was obvious disobedience to priests, notably armed insurrectionary movements, explained? 'They had been told that the Fenian organisation had been denounced by the priests; and why, if they were so obedient in everything, were they so disobedient in this? Either the people of the Church of Rome had showed disobedience to the priests or else the priests were not in earnest' (prominent Johnston supporter in the 1868 election). In other words, all Catholics are under clerical control in political as well as religious affairs (the ones who pretend otherwise are not believed, unless they have secured ostracisation by becoming unionists) and all manifestations of the Irish nationalism are part of a centrally co-ordinated plan run by the Catholic Church. Outward differences of opinion are a decoy.[64]

The legacy of the formation of the Northern Ireland state in the civil war of the 1920s provided this perspective with 'proofs' of itself. In many areas the conflict between the B Specials and the IRA was essentially between the two communities and has left massive bitternesses behind. When Catholic clergy or Nationalist politicians combined their denunciations of IRA violence with a recognition of provocation or a statement to the effect that the end is justified but the means are evil, this kind of apparently less than total condemnation was held to prove that the condemnation was only tactical and concealed secret agreement of all Catholics with violent insurrection.

Such conspiracy theories are parasitical upon Protestant evangelical theology. Fundamentalism holds the Bible to be the Word of God and all currents which deny its literal truth are 'deadly because of their false view of the scriptures'. It is at odds with most forms of orthodox Protestantism and sees in the Roman Catholic church a direct wordly mediation between God and man by the priesthood. It reconciles its hostility to Catholicism with Christian precepts, by 'loving and praying for Catholics' that they may see the error of their ways but 'hating Roman Catholicism'. If ever this attitude toward Catholicism is shorn of its core of faith, it translates into a religious supremacism. We have access to God which they do not have. We are free, they are enslaved to the antichrist (the Pope). The relationship between these two possible implications of fundamentalism was once summed up by Peter Robinson, now the deputy leader of the Democratic Unionist Party, when he said of its leader Rev Dr Ian Paisley, 'As a gospel preacher Dr Paisley must be held in the highest esteem, but it is in his exposure of the evils of Romish worship that he receives much attention.'[65]

These kinds of beliefs were only questionably representative of unionists fifteen years ago, if by representative is meant that majorities or overwhelming numbers 'believed' them. But their potential representative power did not depend on this. They gave clear self-righteous expression to fears and antagonisms which many would have expressed much more equivocally. In the same way that even tranquillised force relationships destroyed real communication in the US South, so that blacks developed the habit of saying what they thought whites wanted to hear, tranquillised force relationships in the North of Ireland erected another kind of barrier appropriate to the more equal relationship between Protestants and Catholics. Rosemary Harris studied a border area in the 1950s and 1960s. Here 'nothing convinces that the priest is a moderating influence'. Many Protestants saw him as 'the political extremist'. In the lowlands Protestant farms predominated, but the further up the hills the farms became more Catholic. The Protestant hill farmers who shared farming tasks with their Catholic neighbours and related to them as equals were almost all members of the B Specials and reckoned that their capacity to hold onto their farms had in the past depended on the B men and might do so again. (In this area today IRA murders of UDR men on isolated farms occur often.) A precondition of friendly relationships was the systematic avoidance of any topic of conversation that might touch politics or religion and the concealment of everything that in fact divided them. If this civility was the foundation of 'good' relationships, it is easy to see how they might in fact be represented towards each other in matters political and religious by 'bad' relationships. The only clear-cut communication Catholics would have heard would have been the political expressions of the leaders these unionists voted for or followed on 12th July demonstrations—or the occasional abusive or violent exchanges that punctuated the normal routine of civility. The mutual threat relationship acted as a filter. All the benign tendencies to be good neighbours, to treat others as you would be treated yourself; all the small or large gestures of intercommunal goodwill that may or may not have been made were inarticulate, because the fundamental source of division was too dangerous to talk about. Civility meant pessimistically anticipating that discussion of such questions would degenerate into a cycle of self-justificatory exchanges, which would get nowhere except bad tempers. Civility seems to have magnified social distance and made it somewhat less convulsive than it might have been; but it left both communities to be 'represented' toward the other by the more aggressive elements of their own kind that could secure 'representative' qualities. In other words, all the ambivalent feelings, like that of a B Special who said, 'Sure what's the difference between us anyway, excepting we go out and demonstrate and get drunk on different dates', would have been concealed from view. The same goes for the whole fabric of internal restraint, whether expressed by the disciplinary function of the Orange Order over 'wild men' or the religious ministers who joined it in order to exert restraining influence over it.[66]

Orangeism, with its parades and ritual, was a system of communal deterrence. On the one hand it perpetually legitimised 'vigilance' and on the other it sought to discipline it and keep 'wild men' under control.[67] It justified all measures that were routinely taken to keep Northern Ireland 'Protestant', such as preferential employment of Protestants and caution in the allocation of public authority houses to Catholics, which might upset political control. But with all other means of communication blocked by civility, the worst things said and done in its name which were not also repudiated by it presented Catholics with the contrast between the civility of Protestants in everyday life and these collective expressions. The extent of intercommunal goodwill could only be demonstrated by symbols whose depth of meaning could not be assessed: Orange marches avoiding Catholic areas; stopping their drumming when they passed Catholic chapels or hearing restraining speeches that stressed Christian duties to neighbours rather than the need for 'vigilance'; accepting the right of Hibernians to march outside 'Catholic territory' or making gentlemen's agreements to let Catholic councillors distribute public sector houses in their own wards where they might safely be built and let to Catholics without disrupting electoral geometry.

But by no means did these kinds of benign symbols prevail everywhere. The now well-known Tunnel of Portadown has become the scene of much violence. In the late 1860s and early 1870s efforts to march through this area often created confrontations with the police. On one such occasion in 1873 the disorder spread backwards into the town centre and interrupted market day[68]. Significantly, the leading inhabitants of the town blamed not the marches (although they were not all sympathetic to them) but the police. In this way they helped to assert tacitly that tranquillity depended on letting such marches take place. The sincerity of present-day Orangemen who believe that the march is a traditional and peaceful expression of a legal right depends on the fact that for a long period of time it passed off without disturbance. But once challenged, all the various different strands of justification of this practice—that it is not a vigilance practice only a tradition,that past Catholic acquiescence proved its acceptability and legitimacy, or that it is a vigilance practice and must be maintained—may converge on the same point. Communal deterrence practices may ritualise and conceal their origins in vigilance. In this way they may become restrained and compatible with civility in day-to-day relationships. But challenge is likely to allow the whole to be 'represented' by its most virulent part.

The same goes in a far more obvious way for the forces of the law, especially seriously for those which are subject to the least disciplined superior control. During IRA emergencies— and indeed on many other occasions also—the B Specials were mobilised. In effect one community would police the other. 'Those whom the hill-Protestants had to fear were some of those with whom they had the closest of neighbourly and apparently friendly contacts.' While neither Protestant nor Catholic showed much affection for the police, the B Specials were clearly regarded as a Protestant organisation. Harris tells of B patrols that ordered car passengers they regarded as cheeky to get out of their car and take off their shoes; and of an instance in which a B man's use of an occasion of duty to continue a personal quarrel with a Catholic led to a police prosecution of the B man. His acquittal became a cause for great celebration amongst the local B men.[69] The very existence of the B Specials, whatever their role in preserving security, institutionalised the mimetic temptation that had attracted Patrick Pearse, the founder of modern republicanism, to the Ulster Volunteers: 'Personally, I think the Orangeman with a rifle a much less ridiculous figure than the Nationalist without one . . . in suffering ourselves to be disarmed we in effect abrogate our manhood.'[70]

So far I have treated civility as a screen between opposed views of the world in zones of contestation. But what was true for zones of contestation was only different in degree in other areas such as the more cosmopolitan atmosphere of the Belfast suburbs. Robin Boyd, director of the Irish School of Ecumenics, himself a northern Presbyterian, sounds a note that I have heard uttered with equal sincerity by many northern unionists (and unionist supporters of the Alliance Party): 'Looking back today one can see the sickening failure of Ulster Protestantism throughout these 50 years of Stormont rule; the failure to share our rights and freedoms with our Roman Catholic fellow citizens; our failure even to know anything much about their problems, their alienation, their sense of exclusion in their own country which was also ours. We simply did not know. We were not encouraged to know. I had left Ireland before I made my first real Roman Catholic friend. My parents would never let us speak a word against Roman Catholics; but we never met any. Young people growing up in a middle-class Belfast suburb simply didn't know that was happening.'[71]

There are many moderate unionists who see in the Irish Republic nothing except an irredentist claim to know what they feel is their country. They point to the pre-eminence of the Roman Catholic church within it and its role in shaping civil law. They point to its relative economic inferiority to the North and say what could they possibly want to do with that state? Pressed on the injustices of Unionist rule they will point out that the Northern state was besieged from its birth and that the nationalists withheld consent from it, drawing the conclusion that these evils were relational rather than one-sided. And from their own experience they observe that the main effect of nationalism was to allow the more bigoted strands of unionism to prevail over the more moderate. Whether or not that moderation extends to understanding anything of the experience of exclusion that keeps nationalism alive or not is another question. The clergyman who said that until he read the 1969 Cameron report he thought discrimination was simply a nationalist propaganda word speaks volumes about how civility acted as a barrier to empathy.[72]

Knowledge of discriminatory intent that is independent of actual experience of discrimnation against oneself is what Bourdieu called in the Algerian context a 'datum of mythic reasoning'. It is only necessary to consider that domination is made tolerable by avoidance of its humiliations to see how such 'mythic reasoning' is generated. When discrimination possibilities are known to exist, that knowledge is not compensated by being told that they are not absolute; least of all if the one who says so is in no danger of being discriminated against himself. Patrick Shea, a very rare example of a senior Catholic civil servant in Northern Ireland, describes the lack of enthusiasm he encountered in his school environment for his intended career (at this period Seamus Brady described how the Catholic school system was orientated toward careers in the civil service in the Free State). Subsequently, Shea encountered both discriminatory obstacles and Protestants who not only disapproved of such obstacles but helped him to defeat them. But the striking thing about his account is that these non-sectarian Protestants were obliged to contend with forces of bigotry at a very high level.[73] The more general Catholic avoidance of such obstacles as Shea encountered is easy to understand. An Englishman who came to the North to manage a company told me how on one occasion he directly employed a worker for a specific job who happened to be a Catholic. Some strange looks were made at him by a few workers but nothing was said. A short time later a priest arrived with a list of workers he said were looking for work. Unwittingly, he had broken a long-standing convention that this company did not employ Catholics. Most of the Protestant workers seemed quite unperturbed and some indicated positive approval. The *de facto* exclusion of Catholics had been established decades before.

Richard Rose (1968), Eddie Moxon-Browne (1978) and Sarah Nelson have looked at the question of how far Protestants recognised the existence of discrimination against Catholics. Rose found that (before the civil rights campaign of 1967–9) 74 per cent of Protestants didn't believe that Catholics were discriminated against, and of the 19 per cent who believed they were, only one-fifth (4 per cent) had personal knowledge of it. Eddie Moxon-Browne says that the contention that anti-Catholic discrimination was a major cause of the troubles produced one of the highest inter-sectarian disagreements revealed in his 1978 survey. Sarah Nelson who conducted lengthy interviews with Protestants in the late

1960s and early 1970s said that the subject aroused inter-
viewees to great heights of indignation and caused them to
justify at great length practices which appeared discriminatory. The main line of defence for these practices was the fear
of numerical takeover. What rankled most was that the civil
rights protests were felt as an accusation against them.[74]

In 1958 Desmond Fennell, in a series of articles on
Northern Catholics, described their political situation as
'chaotic'. His series showed up a multiplicity of strands in
Catholic politics. 'If nationalist means a person who believes
in a more or less vague way that Ireland shall be one, then it is
true that most Catholics are nationalists.' He met all kinds of
variants on this theme. The few nationalist councils were
usually scrupulous in making fair housing allocation 'partly
because they wanted to show up their opponents'. Some spoke
as though nationalism was a question of transcending religious divisions and a few spoke as Catholic sectarians in a
language mirroring the rhetoric of unionism. Nationalism as
described by Desmond Fennell embraced both possibilities.[75]

The fundamental difference between the communities
reflected—as it had always done since the conflict became
reciprocal and national—opposed conceptions of the legitimate territory in which 'head counting' was democratic, and
opposed conceptions of the legitimacy of governing institutions. To describe a conflict as national is to say that, in
disputing which community should have the last word, it has
become a conflict about everything because particular 'issues'
become difficult to isolate. They are justifications attached to
one or other pole of the conflict. Since 1920 Nationalists have
confronted a system which can technically claim to be a
democratic expression of a right of self-determination. Even
the Derry Corporation gerrymander was technically defensi-
ble before 1946 according to the principle that property (i.e.
local tax-paying burdens) should be represented as well as
persons. But for nationalists these principles were merely a
framework of rules within which unionist intent to dominate
could be and was expressed.[76] The Irish nationalists' response
to unionist claims for the democratic nature of Northern
Ireland is that Northern Ireland itself is an illegitimate entity,
a massive gerrymander. The island of Ireland is a sacred

territory and it cannot be divided legitimately by anyone. In line with this view that Ireland is indivisible and that the Protestants cannot claim a right to divide it, nationalist attitudes toward Protestants stress their membership of the Irish nation (much as Serbs used to speak of Croats as 'brother Slavs'). It is very rare to find Catholics proclaiming a hostility toward Protestants, though it is not at all uncommon to find them speaking of Protestants as unionists or loyalists, as in fact most are, and declaring absolute opposition to their pro-Britishness. It is their self-proclaimed Britishness (of Orangeism and Loyalism) which is held against them, as it is this that denies the legitimacy of the 'indivisible Island'.

When the few Protestants who have become nationalists— whether through intermarriage to Catholics, revulsion against the proclaimed intent of unionism or for whatever reason—are held up as the standard against which other Protestants are judged, this standard conceals from view the real mechanism that binds Protestants to unionism.

The republican strands of Irish nationalism emphasise the Presbyterian revolt of the United Irishmen in 1798 and the (later) writings of its leader Theobald Wolfe Tone, who is held to be the father of Irish separatism. It is highly debatable whether the United Irishmen were 'separatists'. Wolfe Tone's 1791 *Argument on Behalf of the Catholics of Ireland*[77] spends two-thirds of its text arguing the expediency of Catholic equality to Protestants on the premise that they can give it now or risk Catholic anger later—very much the pre-emptive type of reasoning of the Algerian Popular Front. Furthermore, the areas which rebelled in 1798 in favour of religious equality subsequently provided much opposition to the Whig educational reforms of the 1830s. But the essence of the republican thesis is that if Protestants were republican separatists once, there is no reason why they should not become so again. It can only be the mischievous influence of British Imperialism and the ruling classes that has either coerced, bribed or duped them into becoming unionists. Ireland is seen as one nation and religious sectarianism as an artificial device for dividing it.

This republican interpretation generates two largely opposed strategies. On the one hand are those who argue that

indeed after 1830 Irish nationalism has been heavily impreg-
nated with pan-Catholicism and that unless republicans seek
a class unity with Protestant workers for a non-sectarian
Ireland, no progress is possible. On the other hand, there are
those who argue that the first priority is to drive out the
British presence which means attacking the 'forces of the
crown'. When Britain bows to the armed will of the Irish
nation, then the northern Protestants will come to recognise
that they are Irish. The insuperable difficulty with this view is
that the 'forces of the crown' for the greater part of the history
of Northern Ireland have been drawn from Northern Ireland
Protestants and have enjoyed general Protestant support
against just such challenges. The first variant of republicanism fails to produce the hope for class solidarity; while the
second either belittles or ignores the generality of unionist
opposition to what could in practice only mean their military
defeat. The belief that only *some* unionists need to be defeated
in order that the rest will see their 'Irishness' persists despite
the absence of any evidence to support it.

The mainstream of northern nationalism upholds the aspirations to unify Ireland and can best be distinguished from
republicanism by saying that however provoked it considers
nationalists to be, it regards physical force republican action
as morally wrong, counter-productive for coexistence with the
Protestant society and strategically self-defeating. It seeks a
peaceful reunification of Ireland, hoping that Protestants will
in some way come to see themselves as Irish or that external
pressures will one day encourage them to do so. But this
position is far from straightforward. If, as some nationalists
say, they recognise that a majority in the North must pronounce in favour of reunification they are neither trusted by
many unionists to mean what they say—nor do many other
nationalists consider them to be upholding the right of Ireland
to self-determination. If they uphold the traditional claim to
self-determination, they are charged with giving succour to
the physical force republicans. Because nationalist aspiration
is blocked it generates diverse strands. But it is also the case
that the strands which most sharply mirror unionist egoism
are the ones which most decisively affect unionist perception
of what nationalism is about. This further prejudices the

possibilities of presenting nationalism as a way of transcending 'religious' divisions. Some Catholics go so far as to reject nationalism for these reasons; it is a cul-de-sac that simply hardens the intransigent strands of unionism. These, however, are likely to be held up by unionists as the example that Catholics in general 'ought' to follow—in the same way that Protestants who reject unionism are held up by the republicans in defence of their own claims.[78] The conscious choice of dealignment from the bloc one came from is far more difficult than might be supposed. It is barely recognised as a legitimate choice and is often subject to perverse usage—it is easily drawn into the gambit of seeing the enemies' enemy as one's friend.

In an area of Macedonia once convulsed by Serbian repression and Bulgarian terrorism of IMRO, Rebecca West came across a group of Young Bulgarians whose bitterness against all things Serbian was total. Mentioning that she would visit Veles, one said to her, 'Ah, how I wish I could go with you, for in Veles there lives a lawyer who is a great Bulgarian patriot. We read of him in the Serbian newspapers which attack him shamefully. Later we will go to see him though no doubt the police will persecute us afterwards.' She later found the lawyer who told her, 'Yes, I could weep. For you see I am not a Bulgarian patriot. I am not even a Bulgarian. I can be quite sure about that for when I was a child I saw my father who was a Serbian schoolmaster . . . murdered by Bulgarians because he was not of their blood. But I try to remember that only as a grief and not as a wrong, for I should be a great fool if I did not admit that had he been a Bulgarian schoolmaster, it might easily have happened that he was murdered by the Serbs. But there is another reason why I try to think of my father as having died and not as having been killed. I believe it is time we stopped thinking of such little things as whether we are Serbs or Bulgars. I believe we should rather realise with a new seriousness that we are all human beings and that every human being needs freedom and justice as much as he needs air to breathe and food to eat.'[79] Unlike his youthful admirers, who deduced his identity with their cause from the observation that their enemy seemed to be his also, he had stopped the cycle in his own life.

Civility in social equality—probably even more so than the civility of subordination of the US South—was both a screen blocking empathy and also the anchor of efforts to 'do unto others as you would have them do unto you'. In a world divided, where vigilance and rebellion are latent in the wings, efforts to relate to An Other as just another person like ourselves founder instantly if people feel obliged to discuss the things that mark them apart. The fear of differences, which are rooted in opposed experiences of violence even when they are not erected as righteous causes, cannot be overcome except in the freedom of human friendships. Yet even (or particularly) here, anxiety to preserve friendships acts as a barrier to that freedom. The screen remains and ensures that the relationships of one to the other are mediated by an endless national/ethnic antagonism, itself perpetually repro-duced by the unsymmetrical relations of each bloc to the political power. Students have told me how today at the Union meetings in Queen's University, Belfast, debates about political questions often degenerate into exercises of mutual provocation. By the end they are hard pressed to remember anything except the most virulent and categorical condem-nations of themselves and their communities. They are thus represented toward each other by their own most embittered elements. When it comes to debating issues far away, almost as if by magic, the issue is given a local implication and turned into a proxy for the local antagonism. Long ago in 1873, a Protestant Liberal editor of the *Ballymoney Free Press* noted that the home rule question, then in its early stages, was causing endless recrimination and bitterness. Though he supported the union, he said of some Orange platform speakers that it wouldn't surprise him to hear them proposing the abolition of air and water on the grounds that Cardinal Cullen had need of them. The absence of sacred order and the inability of power to repress endless feuds, all of which are offshots of the larger antagonism, means that in principle no argument has an ending. There is no starting point and no end point; there is nothing that cannot be made relevant. The limited commu-nication of civility was probably the only way this appalling burden could be lived with. But it also regenerated the identities through which it was lived.

Neither supremacist visions of Catholicism as a conspiracy against Ulster Protestants nor the vision of all supporters of the existing order as tools of an evil conspiracy of British Imperialism was anywhere near universal, but all they need to secure political leverage is the space to act out vigilance or rebellion without being criminalised by their own kind. And in achieving this they secure a representative role because they are the risk faced by the 'other'.

The containment of vigilance and rebellion was easiest when it was possible to recognise differences as something that had to be respected. But such mutual recognition was necessarily a reflection of what was possible given the existing balance of powers which was inherently unequal. So long as the metropolitan power upheld or tolerated this balance of powers, people within were trapped in a box. On the dominant side, reasons for accepting the constraints dominance placed upon civility might be legion: self-interest, lack of awareness of what dominance meant for the dominated, acceptance of the traditional, or simply pessimistic fear of the other. Political leadership tended to bridge the gap between restraining and legitimising ritualised vigilance on the one hand and upholding the virtues of civility on the other. As Benjamin Muse, a liberal Republican from Virginia, said, 'Extremists listen more readily to one of their own number who reluctantly takes a moderate course than to leaders who have been moderate all the time.'[80] But such stances either rationalised the existing balance of power, or if they did not they held out only gradualist promises of change.

The US civil rights strategy and the Algerian FLN revolution epitomise two radically opposed efforts of dominated peoples to break out of this system. The first aimed to magnetise the metropolitan government as a Reconstruction force. As the constraints of civility were challenged by non-violent protest, it was possible for sections of the dominant society to sever the links that had bound them to vigilant supremacism. The FLN revolution matched the violence of vigilance with a violence of its own to drive out the whole French presence, excepting only those French Algerians who took the risk of changing sides while the mass of their own kind became increasingly locked into violent antagonism with the rebellion.

On the face of it, it is not at all obvious why Northern Ireland should have become locked into a conflict of comparable severity as either of these. The degree of economic and social subordination imposed upon Catholics is nowhere near as great as in either of these societies with their settlement colonial structures. But this only seems to be a problem if we start from an underlying assumption that antagonism is caused by quantifiable inequalities and its intensity is a function of the scale of these. If this were true then the decolonisation of orthodox exploitation colonies would have generated much more violence than they generally did. In all three societies intent to dominate had institutional expression, and any challenge of the civil rights variety (let alone the revoultionary kind) was certain to trigger off a vigilant response that might sprawl into chaos and unhinge institutional order. The fact that Catholic society was substantially less subordinated than black or Moslem society always meant two things at once. On the one hand relationships of threat and deterrence were more equal and therefore more liable to escalate in reciprocity. On the other hand being more equal, truces of civility meant more genuine possibilities of equal coexistence flowering into mutual co-operation (e.g. in Labour Parties, trade unions, etc). Unionist supremacism spoke not of keeping Catholics in inferiority but of guarding against an enemy. Nationalism blended strands which believed that unifying Ireland would transcend sectarian division (rather than put the boot on the other foot) and strands which tentatively accepted the legitimacy of the union so long as it could be shorn of its discriminatory and dominating intent.

But there were two crucial questions. Firstly, could the metropolitan power be drawn into Northern Ireland as a Reconstructive force in the manner of the US South, rather than locked into a relationship with unionism shaped by defiance actions? Second, could protest against the system be orchestrated in the non-violent manner of the US South, so that moderate unionism could shed its links with vigilant unionism? Or would violent protest set in motion the circle described by Fanon? The next two chapters explore parallels or lack of them with both situations.

Internal Reconstructions and Civil Rights Movements

In neither the US South nor in Northern Ireland, during their civil rights eras, were the USA or the UK acting under the duress of revolution, as was France in Algeria. They were, however, acting under international or foreign pressures abeit at some removes. In the United States segregation in the South was becoming a serious embarrassment to its dealings with non-aligned and decolonising nations. In the UK the Northern Ireland system of unionist rule was the problem area as Britain and the Irish Republic began to reorganise their relations with each other in anticipation of entry into the EEC. Civil rights movements of blacks and Catholics then inserted themselves into readjustment processes, which might otherwise have been cosmetic exercises carried out over their heads, and sought to define them.

In both cases they sought meaningful equality of citizen rights in the hope that this would create a more harmonious relationship with the dominant majorities, white and Protestant. Crucial to the success of both was drawing the metropolitan power into the regional situations and obliging it to act in a reconstructive manner. The past pattern, in which dominant society defiance actions had shaped the totality of relationships, had to be broken.

Necessarily civil rights strategy had to operate on integrationist principles, even if these are only implicit, and build up (while transforming the character of) the authority of the metropolitan state in opposition to the local system of rule of the dominant bloc. But this was a precarious process. The temptation to nationalist alienation consequent on disappointment with the civil rights process was ever present, whether crystallised in an ongoing tradition (as in Northern Ireland) or not (as in the US South). In the US South the civil rights process may have worked whereas in Northern Ireland it has not. But the only ultimate proof that a civil rights strategy had worked with finality would be a situation in which ethnicity itself had ceased to be the axis of political division.

The deeper the ethnic inequalities were at the starting point of civil rights activity, the stronger the chances of generating the cohesive authority required to deal with the more subtle inequalities that continue to be generated within the framework of outward civic equality. This is because civil rights strategy can focus upon overt departures from standards which metropolitan citizens and governments can only see as unacceptable. The process of *de facto* cooperation between civil rights movements and metropolitan power then generates successes as it goes along. At worst technical civil equality is a massive improvement on 1954 Mississippi. It may be much less of an improvement on 1965 Detroit or Belfast.

Blacks were subject to far more drastic inequalities than were Catholics, therefore civil rights made much more difference to blacks than to Catholics. Integration—meaning equal access to public facilities, political participation and equal citizen rights—was a coherent objective for blacks because most of the denials of equality were sustained by segregation.

However, where blacks had no viable method of expressing nationalism when disillusion with the achievements of civil rights set in, Catholics could revert to a nationalism which already shaped much of their previous experience. In the USA federal power—whatever the hypocrisies which make this possible—has acted as an anchor. Ethnic relations may have been reorganised around it on a basis closer to equality, permitting some trans-ethnic coalitions. In Northern Ireland British power has again become the axis around which antagonistic intents revolve.

Many reasons are given for maintaining strict non-violence in civil rights protest. First, to set exemplary standards for future coexistence, to assert equality without letting it become equality in antagonism. Second, not wanting to get people hurt, either in protest itself or in its aftermath. Third, getting whites to listen to the demands of the protest without giving them the means of arguing it away as violence. Fourth, to get the message across to the federal powers and northern opinion which would be needed to get legislation and its enforcement. Fifth, not becoming like the violent opponent. But enforcing agencies and private vigilantes treated black protesters as though they were engaged in violence or provocation nonetheless. White moderates recoiled in fear of knowing what would happen and knowing that the blacks knew what would happen, sometimes repeating in effect the charge of provocation. Any white who broke out of the restraints of the trouble maker veto and indicated sympathy with the protests was likely to be socially isolated by others fearing 'guilt' by association and singled out for intimidation by vigilantes. So the charge that protest was provocation was a bottom line that united determined opponents of desegregation and many who were uneasily aware of the conflict between the customs of the existing order and transcendental precepts. Martin Luther King, after encountering a segregationist Methodist minister, asked himself, 'Why is it that the whites who believe in integration are so often less eloquent, less positive, in their testimony than the segregationists?'[1]

So the refusal to recognise the non-violence of protest was a provocation for blacks. If the whites who could hear would not listen and peaceful protestors were attacked and intimidated what point was there in trying to communicate in a language which white society didn't seem to understand? As one of King's followers put it, 'Aw right, Reverend, if you says so. But Ah still thinks we oughta kill a few of 'em.'[2] The capacity of the southern civil rights leaders to keep such a high degree of non-violent discipline in protest is something I can't pretend to understand. It is not simply a question of having preserved majority support for non-violence, but having made it so near unanimous in the South before 1966 that it prevented a spiral of representative violence from flaring up. To say that this was because blacks knew they would be defeated by sheer weight of numbers doesn't answer the problem. If people are once convinced they are in a war, some at least discard this consideration and their actions implicate everyone else. And anyway a 1963 opinion poll found that half the blacks didn't think they would be defeated in such an eventuality.[3] So the discipline of non-violence seems to have rested on an ever-present awareness of the need to set the example for future coexistence and to avoid becoming like the oppressor; as well as an understanding of how non-violence shaped the process of federal intervention born out by actual results. King once said, when he doubted his own capacity to secure justice for blacks, that he understood why many were tired of non-violence but that he was going to stay non-violent. His own influence was obviously enormous but it seems unlikely that non-violence as a political strategy could have been sustained if it had not been politically effective.

To be politically effective it had somehow to secure changes in the law to bring about civil equality, sufficient precautionary regulation to ensure that such equality would not be bypassed, and a sufficiently high degree of white acceptance and consent that blacks and whites would voluntarily 'fulfil unenforceable obligations towards each other' within that context of civic equality. An authority had to be created from somewhere to secure these results, but from where? Federal government as it then stood could only become that authority on the basis of a hope then kept alight by the role of the Supreme Court—for before 1954 federal power in the South looked rather residual. In a 1963 poll, 45 per cent of blacks reckoned the NAACP (National Association for the Advancement of Coloured People) had done most for black rights. (Martin Luther King 26 per cent, President Kennedy 9 per cent, US Supreme Court 5 per cent, Others 15 per cent.)[4] The background to the development of non-violent protest was the NAACP's gradually successful litigation in the federal courts against segregationist statutes. Non-violent protest subsequently pinpointed these statutes. If protest didn't work directly legal cases could be built upon them. Protest attracted media attention which affected northern congressmen and created international embarrassment by requiring real rather than cosmetic change. And if local authorities failed to observe federal judicial orders, protest could create situations in which the federal executive and eventually congress acted.

Civil rights legislation containing strong enforcement provisions was not passed by Congress until 1964 (the Civil Rights Act) and 1965 (the Voting Rights Act). In the 1964 presidential elections the Democrats won a landslide victory over the Republicans, whose ultra-conservative candidate Barry Goldwater had voted against the Civil Rights Act. While the Republicans slumped everywhere else, they won in the Deep South which had hitherto voted for the Democrats to guard white supremacy. Thus Johnson's victory and the large liberal Democratic majority in Congress overcame long-standing obstacles to civil rights legislation and to welfare and social reform legislation.

At the 1932 election the Democrats had added a huge segment of labour and farm votes to their core of (ethnic and Catholic) urban strength in the north, while retaining their long standing support from southern whites. The relationship between the more conservative southern Democrats and the rest of the party involved a *quid pro quo* in which southerners retained their powerful committee chairmanships earned by seniority while the South cast presidential votes for northern liberal candidates. This enabled them to frustrate any measures which threatened the southern racial *status quo*, although some were supporters of the economic recovery and social legislation of the New Deal era.[5] The Republicans revived with the conservative reaction in 1938 and thereafter until 1964 the southern Democrats and the Republicans often acted as a *de facto* conservative coalition. The first sign of this alliance was their successful opposition to Roosevelt's plan to change the composition of the Supreme Court in order to overcome to resistance to New Deal agencies. But paradoxically his subsequent appointments to the Supreme Court made it the most important of the three arms of the federal government in challenging southern segregationism. In Congress, meanwhile, the conservative coalition blocked the civil rights legislation of President Truman, removed effective enforcing powers from the 1957 and 1960 Civil Rights Acts and frustrated the proposed legislation of Kennedy. As a result of NAACP litigation in the federal courts in the 1940s, the Supreme Court struck down some obstacles to black voting (such as the white Democratic primary which excluded blacks from the only election that mattered in places where they could register at all). It also used the 'separate but equal' principle to prise open institutions of higher education for blacks (on account of the impossibility of providing separate law schools and colleges) and require upgradings of some black schools.[6] Some southern states took the hint and began to improve black schools to pre-empt litigation.[7] Until the 1954 Brown decision that declared school segregation itself to be unconstitutional, there were many whites who believed that the race question would be solved by gradualist changes, so long as segregationists were not stirred up and change was slow enough.[8] The cotton plantation system was decaying. Before the depression the South contributed 30 per cent of US exports, but only 12.5 per cent in the late 1940s. Not only was cotton less important but mechanised cultivation was beginning in the south-west.[9] As blacks moved northwards to the war-expanded industrial centres, they also became a more important voting bloc. In 1948 when Truman took an explicit pro-civil rights position in the presidential election, sections of the southern Democrats broke away to support the Dixiecrat, Strom Thurmond (today Republican senator for South Carolina and chairman of the Senate Judiciary Committee).[10] Although the defection was limited it showed how the Democratic division between northern liberals and southern conservatives would be shaped by civil rights as much as by socioeconomic reform issues.

As the Cold War became the dominant feature of international affairs after 1945, a wave of anti-communism swept through US politics linking together the Soviet threat and all manner of domestic progressive forces. Under Senator Joseph McCarthy it strove to find 'traitors' in the New Deal agencies and the trade unions (particularly inter-racial industrial unions of the CIO.)[11] Had America emerged as the weaker rather than as the much stronger power and really been surrounded by communism it is an open question whether such generalised charges of 'treason' would not have unleashed the same kind of forces as they had done in inter-war Europe. But America's position as leader of the anti-communist or democratic world both required and enabled it to link the standards of anti-communism and democracy. Liberal Democrats, rather than being caught in it, joined in the anti-communist stampede. So it scapegoated a small minority who could be scapegoated and did not success-fully identify social reform or desegregation with communism.

McCarthy was about to fall from favour for extending his witchhunt to the army when the Supreme Court made the Brown decision in 1954. But southern supremacists were quick to link their cause with that of anti-communists infuri-ated by Supreme Court decisions favourable to victims of local and state anti-communist statutes. In 1957-8, with charges of 'communists on the court' being bandied about, Congress came close to passing bills to curb the Supreme Court's powers.[12] Had they been successful and had the southerners successfully linked 'integration' with 'communism', and thereby identified the peculiar institutions of the South with American ways of life, the civil rights movement might have lost one of its crucial levers for making non-violent protest operable.

In the second Brown decision of 1955 the Supreme Court provided that, failing voluntary compliance, desegregation of public schools was to be enforced by filing lawsuits against school boards in the lower federal courts. In most of the Deep South the court's rulings were met with a campaign of 'Massive Resistance'.[13] White citizens' councils set about discouraging blacks from filing cases or registering to vote by economic pressures or blunter methods. State legislatures passed laws to abrogate the right to public education, to facilitate the creation of (white) private schools, to inhibit or ban the NAACP and to undo such black voter registration as had already taken place. Relatively moderate political leaders were either swept aside or changed tack as pre-civil war doctrines of 'interposition' and 'nullification' were refurbished to defy the Supreme Court. In some areas there was little black voter registration before the 1965 Act provided for federal registrars, and little school desegregation before HEW (the federal Department of Health, Education and Welfare) began withholding federal funds from non-compliant districts in 1967. Lacking any means of enforcing its decision, the Supreme Court was often simply ignored.

But while President Eisenhower and the conservative

dominated Congress generally did little about evasion, open defiance created a major problem. In 1957 Governor Faubus of Arkansas announced that he would call out the National Guard (the state militia) to defy a Supreme Court order to desegregate the high schools in Little Rock. Faced with a choice between permitting an open flouting of the US Constitution or upholding a court decision he did not like, Eisenhower sent a thousand troops to Little Rock. After Kennedy was elected in 1960—having secured Martin Luther King's release from a Georgia jail and thus most of the black vote—he used executive enforcing powers less reluctantly. But once again these powers were used most effectively against overt defiance, such as the Mississippi and Alabama governors' attempts to bar black students from state universities, and not against evasion.

It was the most overtly defiant states that provided the major civil rights victories. When in 1955 Rosa Parks was prosecuted under an overtly segregationist statute regarding seating on buses—instead of some outwardly normal law such as failing to obey a police officer—it not only provided the spark for the Montgomery bus boycott but also a test case to take through the federal courts. When the city authorities did try to retreat behind normal laws by prosecuting the organisers of the car-pool for operating a commercial enterprise without a licence, King felt the twelve-month protest was in danger of defeat, but at that moment the Supreme Court ruled the bus segregation unconstitutional. The shout from the back of the courtroom, 'God Almighty has spoken from Washington DC', expressed at least one person's appreciation of the link between King's message of non-violence and political strategy.[14] Protest action did not 'have' federal government support. Rather it made it. The Kennedys were reluctant to use direct federal intervention such as federal marshals for fear of making political opponents, unless the confrontation was against openly outrageous local authority. Thus when King joined the movement to desegregate facilities in Albany, the police chief Laurie Pritchett spiked the effort. There was no visible police brutality, King was given a guard, provision was made to house as many prisoners as might demonstrate ('to fill the jails') and an anonymous bondsman bailed King out of jail, causing him considerable embarrassment. King, knowing the dependence of the movement for success on federal judiciary support, decided to obey a federal court injunction not to march. The attorney-general Robert Kennedy congratulated Prichett for keeping the peace. As the movement lost direction, rioting broke out between police and protestors to which King responded by declaring a Day of Penance.[15] The hold of non-violent restraint was being stretched.

In Alabama the tempo of defiance rose with the election of George Wallace as governor in 1962. The mass protest in Birmingham in 1963 achieved what Albany had not done. The media focused on police using firehoses and dogs against children and made it increasingly difficult to refuse the need for a federal civil rights bill with teeth. The equally highly publicised violence in Selma, the centre of the Alabama plantation district, in 1965 enabled President Johnson to secure the passage of a strong Voting Rights Act.[16]

As the scale of violence, whether killings, intimidation and bombings, escalated in the face of protests in the 1960s—for example, more than sixty blacks were killed during the voter registration drives in Mississippi before 1964 and the end of the Birmingham campaign was marked by a church bombing that killed four young girls—the commitment to non-violence became increasingly a tactical question for some most deeply involved.[17] In the plantation counties of Alabama and Mississippi any semblance of restraint upon white violence crumbled as the cotton harvester reduced the need for much black labour and intimidation reduced the prospective black voting majorities. The voter registration workers of SNCC (Student Non-Violence Co-ordinating Committee) had received some federal government encouragement but found the actual federal protection afforded them very limited. Black power, which grew out of these experiences, expressed disenchantment with non-violence and integration with white America. But whatever its language it never engaged in reprisals or got into direct confrontation with federal power in the South. Ultimately the federal legislation and its enforcement probably made more difference to the Deep South than anywhere else. But the differences made were in the legal and institutional framework affecting the balance of communal powers of blacks and whites. Until the 1970s there was little electoral evidence of whites having accepted the justice of the civil rights changes.[18]

In a 1963 opinion survey 51 per cent of southern whites (and 31 per cent of all US whites) thought blacks were 'inferior to whites', 61 per cent (and 41 per cent) thought they wanted to 'live off handouts', 46 per cent (and 35 per cent) thought they 'bred crime'. Between 47 and 55 per cent (and 20-23 per cent) would have objected to sitting next to a black in a bus, lunch counter or cinema or having their children integrated in schools. From a political perspective there was a striking contrast between the 56 per cent of southern whites who recognised that blacks were discriminated against and the mere 31 per cent who favoured the Kennedy Civil Rights bill; the 88 per cent who agreed that blacks had a right to vote and the 31 per cent who favoured a Voting Rights Act; and the 75 per cent who thoughts blacks should have unrestricted rights to use of trains and buses and the 53 per cent who would object to sitting next to a black. In other words, something in the order of 30 per cent of southern whites actually supported the evolving federal programme that imposed civil rights, being aware of the need for such measures. But beyond them were others who resisted any effort to translate their recognition of black rights into something that could be enforced rather than freely given (or not given) by southern whites.[19]

On the one hand securing white acceptance of black equality was the ultimate objective, but securing the legal and institutional framework in which this could happen was only possible because there were some areas of unrestrained defiance and violence where white moderates had almost no leverage on the situation. It was these places—Selma and Birmingham, for example—that created the shock that brought results. So what happened when white moderates did manage to secure some leverage on the desegregation process?

Both North Carolina and Virginia (24 per cent and 21 per cent black) contained substantial white Republican support at a time when that indicated racial moderation. In the early 1960s black voting registration was at about 40 per cent of white per capita levels. 'Nowhere, except perhaps Virginia,' said V.O. Key of North Carolina, 'have overall relations, year in and year out, been more harmonious.' In neither state were there obvious openings for challenges to the established elites, whether of a socially radical or rabidly racist variety. Dominated by business, banking and industrial rather than by plantation interests, the levels of intimidation and violence were much lower than in Alabama or Mississippi. Their reactions to the Brown decisions were substantially different.[20]

In Virginia the shape of the reaction was affected by the fact that one of its areas of highest black population was the object of an early desegregation order. Prince Edward County School Board took steps to close down public schools if necessary to avoid integration. 'A dynamic and contagious grass roots force joined with a power at the political summit in a combination which moderate elements in Virginia were unable to resist for four turbulent years' (Benjamin Muse). Initially the proposals made at state level (the Gray plan) included a local option clause permitting school boards to integrate or not, through a locally administered pupil assignment based ostensibly on criteria other than race. But it also contained provision for grants for tuition in private schools to escape from public school integration, which (being declared unconstitutional by the Virginia Supreme Court) was put to a constitutional referendum and passed by a 2:1 majority. In North Carolina a similar scheme (the Pearsall plan) became the basis for legislation, but in Virginia after the referendum, the legislature took a stand of massive resistance to the Supreme Court's decision. Senator Byrd's machine amplified Prince Edward County's defiance. State laws were passed requiring a cut out of funds to any public school that integrated, centralising pupil assignment, closing and removing from the public school system any school with mixed race enrollment and hampering the work of the NAACP. The moderate opposition strategy focused on trying to conserve local option. 'Most moderates, while standing firm on crucial issues, sought to conserve their influence by joining in criticism of the Supreme Court and insisting that integration would be held to a minimum.' And where defending the NAACP was concerned all but a handful must have reckoned this a hopeless exercise. 'It is difficult to describe the intensity with which the NAACP was hated by White Virginians. Many who were classed as moderates on the school issue hated the NAACP. Fantastic rumours (about its sources of finance and its alleged links with communism) were given credence.'[21] Three of a hundred delegates voted against all seven anti-NAACP bills. The Republican candidate for governor who had got 45 per cent of the vote in 1953 was reduced to 37 per cent in 1957, standing in favour of local option and open schools. During the contest, the Little Rock intervention was greeted with a shower of bills to facilitate resistance to any similar action in Virginia. Massive resistance seemed popular while its full implications were not exposed.

In September 1958, as a result of court ordered desegregation, some Virginia counties' schools were actually closed under massive resistance laws. This provided the moderates with a strong issue. Now that school closures actually happened, the issue was between massive resistance and open public schools. While in North Carolina token desegregation had been carried out in Greensboro, Winston-Salem and Charlotte in September 1957 amid a fanfare in the national press, Virginia was now plunged into a school crisis. The business community, alarmed at the lack of any new industry established during 1958, while North Carolina's industrial expansion continued, applied quiet pressure to Governor Almond. He had been elected on the wave of massive resistance. But the Virginia Supreme Court came to his rescue, ruling the massive resistance laws contrary to the state constitution, although combining its judgment with an attack on the United States Supreme Court. The state attorney-general described the school closing laws not as a scheme to evade school desegregation 'but a measure of precaution against such violence as had occurred in other states'.[22] Almond, having first lashed school integration as a source of violence and immorality, went ahead and secured the repeal of the school closing laws. Yet right up to the entry of the thirty black children into hitherto all white schools in spring 1959, the expectation of violence remained. The legislature was held in special session to be ready for 'emergency action' and some were obviously disappointed when their prophecies of violence were not fulfilled. The police took action to deter fanatics from making trouble at the integrated schools.

The position Virginia arrived at by mid-1959 was not very different from that of North Carolina. Governor Hodges had pre-empted any massive resistance demands by selling the Pearsall plan as a way of fending off 'extremism'—the NAACP being equated with the Ku Klux Klan. As for the northern praise given to the token integrations of September 1957: 'From the perspective of many Greensboro blacks such phrases described a city on another planet' (Chafe). The preservation of North Carolina's image of progressivism, which kept federal attention off the state until the late 1960s 'consisted primarily of its shrewdness in opposing racial change'.[23]

Whether they used the fear of violent disturbance, magnified it or represented it as they judged it to be, political leaders claimed their actions were precautions against violence and necessary to pre-empt it. That such reasoning could be used even by Governor Wallace does not necessarily prove that it is a fraud in all situations in which it is used.[24] Clearly the risk of being upstaged by white defiance actions, whipped up against an effort by an established leadership to carry through civil rights reforms, would have been very serious indeed if it had materialised. What matters for immediate purposes is that whether moderates felt restrained by the fear of a wrecking backlash or whether moderate schemes were a device to evade the pressures for real changes, they tended to operate along the same lines regardless of motives. Securing white acceptance meant cutting the ground out from beneath any militant segregationists who could whip up a move against civil rights or NAACP 'dictation'. In order to prove that this was not what was happening, every move was accompanied by reassurance that everything was under control. The only acceptable argument from external coercion was the need to obey the law of the land and even that was accompanied by reservations. To maximise the degree of white acceptance the substance of measures had to be limited. Chafe summarises this: 'Justice for blacks would remain contingent upon prior consensus amongst whites'; but he also says in connection with the election in 1960 of the liberal governor Terry Sanford, who sent his own children to desegregated schools, that he 'provided an environment that encouraged racial protest by sanctioning its goals'.[25] Thus it would seem that moderation both tended to deflect federal attention by outward compliance and provided a more hospitable climate for protesting against its own limitations. Greensboro was the birth place of the sit-in movement in 1960 and subsequent mass demonstrations in 1963 were not physically assaulted. They succeeded by mass mobilisations in filling the jails, putting economic pressures on businesses and thus obliging the city and business leaders to secure desegregation of facilities in order to protect its progressive image. Such widespread protest in this context precluded the temptation to resort to repression. In the Deep South, non-violence was perhaps communicating primarily with distant northern audiences, whereas in Greensboro and areas where moderates had some leverage it was communicating directly in the local situation, being reluctantly but none the less recognised as a means of communication.

If this assessment is correct then it would follow that the pace of change in non-defiant areas of the South was indirectly linked to the defiance in the Deep South, which generated federal intervention. Such federal pressures could then be used as arguments for accepting change as inevitable in areas where the prospects of defiance were weaker. And, if so, it suggests several conflicting meanings that might be conveyed by what Key describes as the 'soul-satisfying exclamation' of some southerners, 'Thank God for Mississippi'.[26]

The Civil Rights Acts of 1964 and 1965 illegalised most forms of overt racial discrimination and were supported by about two-thirds of American whites. But the city ghetto riots of 1965, 1966 and 1967, together with northern reaction against civil rights measures which had implications for their own areas (for example the 1966 Housing Bill), weakened federal support for civil rights measures. At the same time the Vietnam War restricted the 'Great Society' programmes— federal aid to education, welfare, community development, housing, health—upon which the hopes of the inner city ghettoes hung. And the war also polarised its supporters against its radical and black opponents. Black nationalism reinterpreted the civil rights experience. Eldridge Cleaver wrote that the domestic conflict over segregation 'became a very pressing problem for US imperialism in its dealings with the black African governments that were cascading onto the international scene . . . Therefore when the federal government "joined" the civil rights movement, the imperialists in control of the government actually strengthened their own position and increased its power . . . Viewed on the international plane, integration represents an attempt by the white mother country to forestall the drive for national liberation by its colonial subjects . . . In fact America's failure is even more obscene and contemptible [than French or British efforts to forestall decolonisation] because, as often happens to exploiters, it has believed its own propaganda, its own lies and it has taken all its perverted deceptions for reality.'[27]

As it is the only place where civil rights strategy has (arguably) worked, Cleaver's vision of integration as a device to stall a decolonisation is a useful starting point. In ethnic frontier zones, the *status quo* between dominant and dominated populations was protected in the last analysis by defiance actions and the creation of confrontations in which metropolitan power was obliged to choose between its own citizens and native nationalism. Having been obliged to choose the former, it got locked into the antagonism with the latter. In the US South it had been spared from getting into this situation because blacks did not in the main support a nationalism. The legend of the Civil War—the North as a liberating force—was given substance by the NAACP federal litigation strategy and by the occasional use of executive power (such as Truman's desegregation of the armed forces). The civil rights strategy depended upon keeping non-violent discipline so that southern violence would be clearly seen to emanate from one source, showing respect for federal law (while in fact securing its change through Supreme Court reinterpretation) and drawing out the contrast between it and local law. Moderate whites for all manner of reasons distanced their approval of change from the black protests that created the pressures and argued instead of the need to accept the pattern of external restraints which federal power built round them. Some were thankful for this, others reluctantly accepted it. Where they couldn't do that and defiance blew up in all its ugliness, it magnified the perceived gap between North and South. If defiance was working according to any plan, wrecking federal intervention by direct means was unlikely to succeed. The only strategy that might have worked was to create racial confrontation which would have permitted the black protests to be treated as an insurrection. Then whatever reforms the federal government legislated would have been undermined because the enforcing process could scarcely have been carried out in cooperation with blacks who were locked into insurrectionary conflict with the same authority. The non-violence of protest checkmated this possibility. Building up rather than undermining federal authority, it obliged it to behave in a way that it very well might not have done. If this possibility is concealed from view and American whites believe 'their own propaganda' about integration it is perhaps because the violence of Selma and Birmingham could not possibly be extenuated as a defence of US territory from a separatist insurrection.

The picture of the race question most forcibly made upon non-southern white people by the civil rights movement was of regional injustice caused by the formal denial of equal rights to blacks. It did not require them to look at the *de facto* inequalities that were generated in their own domains by informal housing segregation, the inferiority of facilities in *de facto* segregated districts, the monopolisation of political power that prevented these issues from securing a remedy and ultimately the degree to which social separation under these conditions allows the relationship between ethnic blocs to be mediated by the law and order system.

In Greensboro after 1963 a council elected by at-large voting contained no black councilmen; the absence of an open housing ordinance kept blacks compacted into a limited residential space; and the school transport system did nothing to compensate for the effects of residential segregation in maintaining *de facto* school segregation. None of this was drastically different from the situation in northern cities. The Taeubers showed how in northern cities other ethnic groups than blacks had been residentially dispersed somewhat *despite* efforts of nationality leaders to secure ethnic consolidation.[28] But *de facto* exclusion of blacks created a situation in which the entry of blacks into an area led to a panic fall in property values and an exodus of whites. And the limited residential space for blacks allowed landlords to gouge an excess rent margin. During the 1960s the black migration from the decaying cotton plantations led to massive population shifts. Detroit—the centre of motor car production—rose from 30 per cent to 40 per cent black in the 1960-67 period with whole districts changing ethnically. As the incomes of the outmi-grants to suburbs exceeded those of incomers by about $1000 per family, the tax-base of the cities contracted while the needs for services rose. Inner-city schools and hospitals became overcrowded and understaffed and some apprentice-ships remained closed to blacks.[29] As black protest focused on more informal and pan-American sources of discrimination in northern cities, the local authorities, the federal government and the northern electorate (which had been the source of the intervening authorities' legitimacy in ending overt segrega-tion) all tended to merge as a huge obstacle. Black power alienation from American society struck roots in northern cities.

The 1967 riots in Detroit, for example, broke out in spite of the fact that the mayor was explicity dependent upon blacks' votes, (though the city council and school board had a negligible black representation); that the black radical con-gressman John Conyers tried to talk them down; and that there was no co-ordinatated plan. Just as in many other cities a key issue was the role of the 95 per cent white police. A survey established that 82 per cent of blacks reckoned there was police brutality before the riots. Fifteen blacks had been shot by whites during the term of office of the incumbent prosecutor. All had been ruled as justifiable shootings 'despite strange sets of circumstances'.[30] Cause and effect rela-tionships here may be very complex, but once a group experiences exclusion and has no effective way of commu-nicating what is happening to it to those who are not affected, the police become a lightning conductor. The worst things done by police, which are neither punished nor for which any kind of restitution is made, come to be seen as representative of the society which tolerates or encourages them. The best elements in the police are compromised by their complicity with the worst. And the most provocative amongst the people they are policing are seen to be acting under provocation themselves—a provocation which is conceived as an intent. If all other avenues of trans-ethnic communication and co-operation are absent, the substance of inter-ethnic relations tends to revolve around the antagonistic axis of law and order.

In an unnamed southern city in 1964 a group composed exclusively of trained war veterans was organised to close the black area to the KKK and to 'restrict the police to their normal functions'. The leader of this group was a convinced advocate of non-violent politics. He insisted upon including within it only people (with families) who had a lot to lose if real trouble started and saw his role as one of deterring. Once the city authorities got round to appointing black policemen they liaised with him. One of the main aims of the Black Panthers was to 'eliminate American police power over black people, i.e. breaking the power of the mother country over the black colony'.[31] The difference between these two positions might have collapsed if the exercise in deterrence had neither worked nor been subsequently replaced by a system of policing responsive to black electoral pressures.

The way in which other issues could degenerate and get caught in this law and order matrix may be indicated by variations in the pattern of full-scale school integration in North Carolina in 1971.[32] Having avoided the spotlight by outward compliance during the high period of civil rights, in 1969 the momentum of civil rights sympathy had largely passed. Nixon was president and Wallace had taken 13 per cent of the national vote winning in five states. Half the Humphrey voters, two-thirds of Nixon voters and 90 per cent of the Wallace voters thought the civil rights leaders had pushed too hard and that the movement had been violent rather than peaceful. In 1971 the Supreme Court upheld the 1969 Swann v Mecklenburg judgment that required North Carolina to produce an integration plan that produced integrated results, which involved extensive home to school travel plans ('bussing').

The decision aroused a lot of white hostility which Nixon's position against bussing echoed. The way it was carried out seems to have varied very much according to the spirit in which it was done locally. In the 1968-9 period black power movements were strong on student campuses. When integration was carried out in acrimonious situations, there were cases of teachers abusing black children, and making them sit at the back of classrooms, school fights in which police took the side of the white pupils in the aftermath, refusals to establish black studies programmes or to recognise the recently assassinated Martin Luther King's birthday as a school holiday. Student protest marches were in danger of confronting authorities which had the last word with police and judicial power. In Vance county the students successfully made their point after the overcrowding of the integrated school was used as a reason for sending some of them back to the old all-black school. In this case the state police pulled rank on local police and used persuasive powers on the school board. In Wilmington a student meeting in a church was besieged by organised white vigilantes and in controversial circumstances the state police were drawn in against the group in the church. The famous case of the Wilmington 10 arose out of their alleged arson of a nearby white store for which they received a total of 282 years' imprisonment. The attentions of the FBI were no longer, as in 1964 in Mississippi, directed primarily against the KKK but against black and anti-Vietnam war radicals and if this most unlikely of alleged insurrections was for real then it served the FBI's purposes. In Greensboro black power had been given a boost by the imposition of a curfew to end demonstrations after King's assassination and by college protests that led to the occupation of black districts by the National Guard in 1969. The pressures generated by black mobilisation brought to the forefront white leadership intent upon reconciliation. Chafe details the story of how the Chamber of Commerce, under the prompting of Hal Sieber, made its own inquiries into the campus protest, vindicated students' complaints about the election of their own leaders, began to organise inter-racial encounter groups that played an important part in the school desegregation process and made representations to the governor that secured the pardon of two radical leaders imprisoned for their part in the campus disturbances. The Greensboro school integration, the preparation of which involved genuine trans-racial cooperation, was described by the NAACP Legal Defence Fund as 'probably superior to that of almost any other city in the south'. Some black power supporters viewed it as a subtle white device to divide blacks on integrationist v separatist lines—to co-opt the black middle class.

Where the civil rights movement had previously asserted the federal government's duty to act, black power asserted the importance of blacks' 'right to define'. Moderate white compliance with federal law had worked with an eye on minimising the scale of white defiance and non-compliance rather than with making any direct overture towards the blacks. The relationship between moderate whites and blacks was essentially mediated and the reconciliatory implications, such as they were, were implicit. Once the federal mediatory relationship disintegrated when race questions were nationalised, this left blacks to face white society with whatever resources they had.

While Cleaver's writings seem to point to an outright national separation, Stokely Carmichael and Charles V. Hamilton explicitly equate Black power with Jewish or Irish power in America, the idea being that Jews and Irish had to develop their own powers in order to secure a place in America. 'Black power simply says: enter coalition only *after* you are able to "stand on your own". Black power seeks to correct the approach to dependency, to remove that dependency, and to establish a viable psychological, political and social base upon which the black community can function to meet its needs.' Their opposition to non-violence is that it is 'an approach black people cannot afford and a luxury white people do not deserve'. They refuse to affirm non-violence merely to satisfy white critics yet their political strategy points towards an eventual coalition in which violence doesn't seem to have much place except as a deterring threat. Had America not already been through the non-violent civil rights stage, it might have been more difficult to develop coalitioning. The rhetoric of violence would have had more political significance than it so far has had.[33]

Today the rather brief civil rights period in Northern Ireland has become history. But as there were at that time signs of hope for new kinds of relationships between Protestants and Catholics, it seems important not to forget it. The difficulties of reconstructing Northern Ireland may be immensely more formidable today than they were then, but the very fact that there ever was such a period is a reason for hoping that 'victory' solutions (which I shall argue in the next chapter are impossible) can be consciously avoided rather than found not to work in practice.

One of the reasons why the traditional nationalist style of opposition was discontinued, to the extent that it was, was because it was in a cul de sac. Until 1948-9 it seemed that constitutional Irish nationalism might still prevail by international pressures. At the ending of the Anglo-Irish trade war in 1938, Britain handed over the southern ports it had retained under the 1921 Treaty. During the war Churchill offered de Valera the unification of Ireland in exchange for the country's entry into the war. But Ireland's neutrality made the North strategically important to the war effort and blunted any Irish international leverage after 1945. The post-war efforts by northern nationalists in the Anti-Partition League to reopen the issue had some effect. A group of Labour MPs, though not the Labour government, showed sympathy. The Irish government under de Valera kept its distance until 1948 when his Fianna Fáil party lost support to the new Clann na Poblachta. There were efforts in the US Congress to make Marshall Aid to the UK conditional upon the reunification of Ireland. When a new coalition government which included Clann na Poblachta ministers declared Ireland a republic in 1948, the Labour government at Westminster responded with the 1949 Ireland Act which had all-party British support and made any future change in the constitutional position of Northern Ireland conditional upon approval of the Stormont parliament. Thus after 1949 the question of Northern Ireland's status seemed to be settled or at least stalemated.[34]

Not only did the 1949 Act blunt Irish nationalist expectations, but the burial of the question was possible because Northern Ireland thereafter had very limited implications for British politics. During the inter-war years Northern Ireland experienced a degree of enforced financial self sufficiency. With its heavy dependence on small-scale agriculture and depression-hit industries, any effort to copy UK policies was pincered between its low tax base and its high expenditure needs, so that public capital expenditure (notably public sector investment in housing) was minimal. After the war the parity principle provided that Britain would make up for any revenue shortfall that arose from Northern Ireland providing similar public sector services while raising similar rates of taxation to those in Great Britain. In this way Northern Ireland was given a strong incentive to copy UK measures and be seen to be copying them. Although unionist MPs voted with the Conservatives at Westminster, the Stormont government gave the appearance of following 'step by step' and removed one of the reasons for metropolitan supervison. This approach was intensified during the 1964-70 Labour government. While the Stormont government of Capt Terence O'Neill needed the approval of London for high levels of public expenditure, the non-intervention of the Labour administration was secured—not only by its own desire to keep its distance—but by the claim that O'Neill was pursuing socially reforming policies with its approval and in consultation with it.[35]

Another reason why Northern Ireland had limited impact in British metropolitan politics was that unionist definitions of British identity cut little ice in Britain itself. There are about six million Catholics in Britain of whom (in the 1960s) about a million were Irish-born and a very much larger number of Irish descent. Speaking English and being (until the 1974 Prevention of Terrorism Act) unrestricted in their movement into Britain, the Irish are not separated by any clear boundary from the British Catholics. Only in south-west Scotland (where they are about a quarter of the population) and in Liverpool was the presence of Irish Catholics associated with explicitly Protestant political opposition. Had educational issues not been effectively removed from the arena of political conflict in Scotland by the abolition of education authority elections in 1929, Gallagher suggests that sectarian confrontation might have retained some vitality,[36] in which case the potential leverage of Northern Irish issues on British politics would have been greater. Irish Catholics were drawn to the

Labour Party before 1918 by the hope that it would be more vigorous in pursuing Irish home rule. After 1920 the party's continuing need for that support may be one reason why the Catholic Church felt satisfied with a largely state-controlled denominational education system in Scotland of the kind the Catholic Church in Northern Ireland feared as a potential source of unionist political control. The Scottish education system was a work of religious elite accommodation. Its control by central government removed it as a serious political issue. Although 'religious' identity continues to manifest itself in football hooliganism, the erosion of sectarian territorial strongholds by post-war housing redevelopment has reduced its implications. The Scottish Unionists changed their name to Conservatives in 1965 and the Labour Party's vague sympathy for Irish unity, allied to its acceptance of the Northern Ireland *status quo*, was probably the line of least resistance. It retained Irish support without repelling any other potential votes. Inter-war Glasgow had had some echoes of Northern Ireland, but by 1966 it was 'much easier to find people prepared to generalise about discrimination than to produce specific examples of it'. The disorder at the Rangers v Celtic football matches was treated as pure hooliganism by the clubs, the clergy, the police and judiciary and had no means of linking itself to any more tangible and substantial issue.[37]

The insulation of Northern Ireland from British politics and the descent of nationalism into a cul de sac in the 1950s was however only partial. Whereas a British government in the immediate post-war years could make light of international pressures, the same was not so in the 1960s. The virtual liquidation of the British empire completed a transition from first- to second-rank power status. From the late 1950s, with the growth of large scale US investment overseas and the formation of the European Common Market, both Britain and Ireland began to readapt themselves to the pressure of European integration; and in the course of so doing to reorganise their relationships with each other. The Republic's abandonment of protectionism and its reorientation toward freer trade went together with efforts to secure mobile international investment. Efforts were made to persuade nationalists to participate in institutions in Northern Ireland. The Anglo-Irish Free Trade Agreement was finalised in 1965 and the (intended) simultaneous EEC entry of Britain and Ireland in 1967 would have occurred but for French veto.[38] What this might mean for northern nationalists would depend upon how Britain influenced the development of Northern Ireland unionism.

The British Labour government elected in 1964 and re-elected in 1966 spoke with two voices about Northern Ireland. Senior ministers spoke of eventual Irish unification as a desirable goal but were generally supportive of the Terence O'Neill government.[39] Some backbench Labour MPs were more critical and echoed the issues raised by the Campaign for Social Justice in Northern Ireland, which focused on the contradiction between the proclaimed social reforming purposes of the O'Neill-Wilson stance and what was actually happening in the nationally disputed areas in the west of the province.

The IRA campaign of 1956-62 had not disturbed Anglo-Irish relations. The Republic's government introduced internment, the Catholic church condemned the IRA, and the campaign was kept away from Belfast. Although Sinn Féin and Saor Éire candidates had electoral successes in the west of the province, in the Belfast areas political developments looked for the first time to be mirroring those of Great Britain. The Northern Ireland Labour Party secured a substantial vote in 1958 and 1962 as a unionist party with a small 'u', opposing the Unionists as a conservative party.

Since the end of the Korean War boom Northern Ireland had suffered a sharp decline in its major industries, ship building, engineering and textiles. The rise of NILP was a response to the unemployment thus generated. As a result of the closer relationships between Britain and the Republic— and Northern Ireland's dependence on British financial support for job creation—any overtly sectarian effort by unionist leaders to combat NILP was precluded. Its programmes of social reform and job creation had 'to be answered on their own terms'. Northern Ireland's limited autonomy required O'Neill to act within the constraints imposed by dependence on a Labour government at Westminster. Although inspecific, these might be summarised by saying that whatever was done had to be done without sensations. For example, in 1968 a *Belfast Telegraph* survey found 50 per cent in favour and 37 per cent against joining the EEC, though the proportions were reversed amongst unionists alone. *NI Progress*, a business journal, said: 'There has been speculation [that] . . . the ultimate consequence would be the disappearance of the border between Northern Ireland and the Republic . . . There will remain a significant residue of feeling, national or regional, which surely rules out the possibility of a realignment of the present border within the foreseeable future. The important thing is to avoid false fears putting a break on increased co-operation between North and South whether inside or outside the EEC framework.'[40]

O'Neill capitalised upon the UK government's regional policy and other capital expenditure commitments while playing his part in talking down the historic issues of Anglo-Irish discord in Northern Ireland. He met with the southern premiers Sean Lemass and Jack Lynch and started cross-border cooperation in tourist, transport and agricultural spheres. Before 1963 Northern Ireland had never built more than 3 per cent of the new UK public sector rented housing; in 1963 financial risks were lifted from the Northern Ireland Housing Trust by a new subsidy system and from that year the proportion has consistently exceeded 3 per cent.[41] The proportion of capital costs to incoming industrial investors was increased (direct and indirect contributions rising to an estimated 73 per cent by the 1970s) and the first manager of the Goodyear plant in Craigavon started in 1966 said: 'We could not have gotten better terms anywhere else in the world.' UK Treasury lending to Northern Ireland rose from £64m in 1964 to £450m in 1974.[42]

But the promotion of new jobs and more particularly houses raised inescapably sectarian questions. Where were they put and who received them? Local governments were largely responsible for housing and local unionist controlled councils in the west of the province rested on sometimes precarious electoral geometry. The reform of local government announced in December 1967 would necessitate redrawing boundaries.[43] Selling it as a necessary administrative rationalisation, the anticipated reform aroused resistance (which would have to be at least largely bought off) from local unionists and premonitions of a renewed gerrymander amongst Catholics. The triangular conciliation of Wilson, Lemass-Lynch and O'Neill, into which the latter was involuntarily caught, was about to be tested for substance by the civil rights movement.

Richard Rose's 1968 survey estimated that there was a 15 per cent difference between the median weekly family incomes of Protestants and Catholics. Catholic families were roughly 16 per cent of the top income bracket and 40 per cent of the bottom bracket. Edmund Aunger found that amongst non-farming males 31 per cent of Catholics and 16 per cent of Protestants were either unskilled or unemployed. The relative positions of the two blocs had not changed substantially since the early twentieth century. More recent figures on relative unemployment rates also show that in any given locality (especially in the high unemployment and more Catholic south and west) Catholic unemployment rates are generally more than double those of Protestants.[44]

The new industry created by external investment was heavily concentrated in the east of the province (although in the end of the 1960s and early 1970s less so). The question of its long-term effect upon relative positions of Catholic and Protestant labour may—since the depression of the post-1979 period—turn out to be academic as much of it has collapsed. It seems likely that in situations where the new investment was neither a question of taking over existing industry, nor of taking up labour from the already defined pool of unemployed skilled labour, it expanded Catholic manufacturing employment.[45]

In the west—where in the late 1970s Murray and Darby found that Protestants tended to learn about jobs from parents and relatives while Catholics depended upon notification of jobs through public agencies—obstacles to apprenticeship in skilled trades left young Catholics to face a hurdle. Free education (since the 1947 Education Act) offered the prospect of professional employment to those who achieved the necessary qualifications. Those who did not faced very high levels of unemployment, irregular employment in unskilled work, low wage work for women in shirt factories, migration or emigration. Derry was largely by-passed in the wave of new industry until the end of the 1960s when the wave was about to end.[46]

In February 1965 the government-appointed Lockwood Commission had proposed the building of the New University of Ulster at Coleraine rather than in Derry.[47] The decision was opposed by the entire political opposition including the Labour party and all the nationalist/republican groupings. It was also opposed by members of the unionist party including many in Derry itself. The motorcade to Stormont to protest was an all-party occasion. If many or most unionists saw this decision as a blow to their city, charges were made (and supported by a unionist councillor) that a group of 'faceless men' had privately expressed opposition to the Derry site which might have upset the delicate electoral geometry of the city. The NI Housing Trust, a public body supplementing the housing position of local authorities, had already had difficulties with the city corporation over refusals of planning permission.

Unlike Britain, Northern Ireland preserved company votes and a householder plus wife franchise for local elections after the Second World War. In 1961 Catholics outnumbered Protestants in Derry/Londonderry by more than 2:1.[48] Eliminating 5,300 Catholic and 2,240 Protestant adults who were not householders and adding 257 Catholic and 902 Protestant company votes left 9,235 Protestant votes and 14,325 Catholic votes, of which 10,130 were concentrated in the near 90 per cent Catholic South Ward with eight councillors. This left two other wards with Protestant majorities, twelve councillors and control of the corporation. By 1965, the corporation had built 2,072 houses and the Housing Trust 1,064. Catholics received 2,212 houses of which only 158 were outside the South Ward. After it had built the Creggan Estate and the Catholic South Ward was full, the corporation built no new houses in 1967, despite the fact that there were families living in Nissen huts. Protestant allocations were overwhelmingly concentrated in the two unionist wards. The council's 177 salaried employees included thirty-two Catholics, not one of whom was among the fifteen departmental heads. However equitable the distribution of houses might be argued to be—although they were distributed by the unionist mayor and not according to any objective criteria—no concept of equity which clashed with the objective of keeping minority political control was to be countenanced. Eamonn McCann wrote: 'The Unionist tactic, we believed, was designed to compel a disproportionate number of Catholics to leave Northern Ireland and thereby to preserve the Protestant majority. It was not the whole story, but it contained a kernel of hard fact which made it rational to believe that Derrymen were sentenced to unemployment for the crime of being Catholics.'[49]

Housing protests had already been organised in the Dungannon area, but the occasion that made international headlines was the police baton attack upon the 5 October 1968 demonstration in Derry which had been banned from marching in the city centre. From McCann's account the radicals who started the protests in Derry early in 1968 were mainly socialists hoping to build trans-communal support and at the same time to break the grip of nationalist politicians on the Catholic community. In a short space of time, however, they obliged traditional leaders to abandon their conciliatory relationship with the unionists (which had not led to a gentleman's agreement on housing distribution as it did, for example, in Armagh) and in the wake of the October march, the Citizens Action Committee was formed, supported by trade unions, businessmen, clergy and led by the future leaders of the SDLP, notably John Hume. Hume had been the organiser of the university motorcade and the chairman of a voluntary housing association which had previously collided with the council over its refusal of planning permission for a large housing project.

McCann says of the CAC sit-down protests that 'no speech from its platforms was complete without a declaration of pacifist intent' and that the average Bogsider who wanted to do something about 5 October 'could go out and march behind Hume, confident that he would not be led into violence, in no way nervous about the political ideas of the men at the front of the procession'. The successful mass breach of a general march ban on 15 November and the holding of a mass meeting in the city centre was followed by

O'Neill's announcement that the corporation would be replaced by an appointed development commission; that housing would be allocated on a points system; that the reorganisation of local government whose preliminary reform had been announced in December 1967 would be speeded up; and that the Special Powers Act would be reviewed. This much was probably a necessary reponse to Westminster pressures after the marches. But the most clear-cut manifestation of change came after another civil rights march in Armagh. Vigilant unionist followers of the Rev. Ian Paisley, armed with blunt objects, took over the centre of the city and prevented the march from passing over the route agreed in advance with the police. Afterwards O'Neill denounced the extreme unionist opponents of change, indicated that pressures of Westminster would be brought to bear if change was thwarted and said to the civil rights protestors: 'Your voice has been heard and heard clearly.' When the Minister of Home Affairs, Bill Craig, criticised the speech, he was sacked.[50]

The CAC and CRA called a marching truce and the 'majority of people in the Bogside and in the Catholic community in Northern Ireland generally believed at this point that the trouble was over.'[51] That indeed is what a lot of moderate unionists may have thought and hoped too. O'Neill's clear opposition to opponents of reform and his legitimation of the protests brought him unprecedented widespread support in both communities. It also began to crystallise a coherent unionist opposition to him both within and outside the Unionist party.

Earlier opposition to O'Neill within the Unionist party had focused upon his meetings with southern premiers, the proposed local government reforms (announced in December 1967) and his refusal to ban republican commemorations in 1966. The fringe opposition of the Rev. Ian Paisley had grown louder since the development of religious ecumenism following the Vatican Council of 1962-5. In 1964, when he was still regarded as the lunatic fringe of unionism, his threat to remove a tricolour from the republican election headquarters in Catholic west Belfast (illegal under the Flags and Emblems Act) embarrassed the government into sending police to remove it and created a riot.[52] When the government, over opposition from its own supporters, refused to ban the proposed 1966 republican parades, Paisley reinaugurated the threat of counter-demonstrations as a means of either securing the banning of both or exploiting government embarrassment at threatened collisions. Hence the significance of O'Neill's strong line against the Paisleyite demonstration in Armagh in November 1968.

Accounts of the history of Northern Ireland between 1968 and the introduction of internment in August 1971 are legion.[53] In what follows I am concerned with the question of how it came to pass that O'Neill's positive and widely supported response to the early civil rights protests should have been eclipsed by the massive disorder of August 1969—and how the British army intervention in that month, which was welcomed by Catholics as a relief from an onslaught upon themselves, was followed two years later by an army internment operation on Catholic areas in support of the unionist government. This locked Britain alongside unionism into a national antagonism with the Catholic community. Certainly what happened in 1971 fitted very much better with historical perceptions of the place of different forces in the north of Ireland, than what happened in 1968-9. And it is indeed true that the balance of probabilities favoured an escalation of representative violence once the fabric of tranquillity had been broken. So the main consideration here is why the hopeful signs of December 1968 were not capitalised upon.

US civil rights successes had little to do initially with whites declaring sympathy with black protests. They had a great deal to do with the protests revealing issues by confronting defiance. Moreover, federal interventions created choices for white moderates between compliance and defiance. It may be that the British government was in no position to do as the US federal government did, but if so that is what needs to be explored.

The first point to make is that the promising start of December 1968 has no US southern parallels. The compliance of North Carolina in 1955 or the efforts of Virginia moderates to secure compliance were both laced with strong antipathies to the organisation preceived to be responsible for the pressures for change in the first place. Before the height of the Northern Ireland Civil Rights demonstrations, Richard Rose found that 75 per cent of Protestants simply did not believe that there was any discrimination. In the light of this, O'Neill's response in 1968 bears favourable comparison with anything in the US South—as does the wave of support he received after it. Thus far, non-violent protest had obviously made a point in a language that large numbers of unionists could recognise without fearful anticipation of the consequences of its having been made. Paisley looked like the source of the trouble rather than the civil rights protests.

More characteristically 'southern' was the response to the demonstrations organised by the student radicals of Peoples Democracy which broke the CAC/CRA marching truce a month later. Michael Farrell, the leader of the march from Belfast to Derry—which was ambushed at Burntollet by loyalist vigilantes (including off duty B Specials) and the arrival of which was followed by rioting and a police attack on the Bogside—explicitly compared it with the Selma-Montgomery march.[54] It was to be an 'acid test' of the Northern Ireland government's intentions, which would 'either protect the march or its impotence to curb unionist extremists would be revealed and Westminster would be forced to intervene'. Just as all black southern demonstrations were provocative to local traditions governing tranquillity so was this one. In this case the troublemaker veto was activated by vigilante attacks and the subsequent behaviour of the police corroded the distinction between the two in the eyes of Catholics. When a week later a threatened counter-demonstration appeared to secure a re-route of a march in Newry, demonstrators rioted against the police, giving substance to the claim that civil rights marches had covertly violent intent. This was the kind of claim that King's Day of Penance in Albany was designed to dispel. The counter-demonstrators had contrived to make the police and themselves appear united—the very impression that O'Neill's response to the Armagh demonstration had tended to unmake. O'Neill's reaction to the Burntollet ambush was to deplore the violence against the march but to suggest that it was a foolhardy and irresponsible exercise.[55] This almost certainly expressed overwhelming unionist feeling about the march. For the rest of his period in office he set about attempting to get unionist support for the main demand of the Burntollet march, 'one man one vote' (or universal adult franchise in local government elections) while distancing himself as far as possible from the sources from which the demand came.[56] Here his actions seemingly resembled those of North Carolina and Virginia moderates devising schemes that would permit integration while distancing themselves from the NAACP. In both cases the main preoccupation was to remain in control of the situation and argue the necessity for change from any other argument except the duress being applied by militants. When O'Neill appointed the Cameron Commission to inquire into the disturbances (with the expectation that it would report in favour of universal adult franchise in local government) the unionist revolt focused on the charge of bending to dictation. But the election that he called to strengthen his hand was far from showing either unionist mass rejection of reform or Catholic disenchantment with moderate civil rights leaders. It could only be judged a disaster from the standpoint of anyone expecting these two elements to merge or opponents to wither away (it seems that O'Neill himself may have had some such expectations). Pro- and anti-O'Neill groups contested for unionist nominations. At least five non-Orangemen secured these and in the general election the official candidates were opposed by either independent O'Neill supporters or Paisleyites depending on the position of the official candidate. In such contests the Pro/Anti votes were Belfast: 42,000 to 32,000 (plus 14,500 for the Labour party); Antrim 45,000 to 28,000; Down 21,000 to 20,000; and the four western counties 27,000 to 40,000. In nationalist majority seats, CRC/CRA leaders beat sitting Nationalist MPs, though PD candidates despite substantial votes did not.[57] In the aftermath O'Neill just secured a majority in favour of one man one vote from the Official Unionist MPs. About this time a series of explosions occurred in the province. These were widely believed to be the work of the IRA and O'Neill resigned shortly afterwards. It later transpired that the explosions were the work of a Protestant paramilitary organisation. Fearing the consequences of renewed collisions the government secured a Public Order Bill designed to curb civil rights demonstrations and ban counter-demonstrations. From a moderate unionist viewpoint this seemed like a sensible way to proceed. But from a civil rights standpoint the measure throttled the only way of demanding reforms and left events to depend on the internal developments within the Unionist party. Seeming to put down counter-demonstrations, its effect was to do their work for them. Governmental fears of counter-demonstrations led to a fatal preoccupation with eliminating the situations (civil rights demonstrations) that gave rise to them, and magnified the dangers of police-civil rights confrontations. What looked to unionists like an even-handed treatment of 'extremists' of both kinds looked to many Catholics like Paisleyites telling the government what to do.

If from the point of view of many Catholics the unionist response seemed to be dictated by Paisley, even if at several removes, that is not very different from the way blacks perceived the pace of white reform in the US South—except in one very crucial respect. The pressure of black protest was indirectly shaping the force of federal intervention and could expose failure to comply with federal requirements. In the North of Ireland there was no working equivalent of the federal 'outposts'—the judiciary—with which to short-circuit the local political system. This was demonstrated by a test case brought against a Republican Club banned under the Special Powers Act by Craig in 1967.[58] The police gave evidence that the Club had no seditious pursuit and the magistrate dismissed the case. But in the Northern Ireland Court of Appeals the ban was upheld, as it was on a final appeal to the House of Lords in June 1969. The highest British court had effectively upheld the legality of the most obnoxious piece of Northern Ireland legislation. Admittedly there was no long established build-up of litigation (as there had been for years, often with limited success, by the NAACP) but once direct action protests started there was no way in which they could be plugged into an ongoing litigation procedure (as they were, for example, in the 1955 Montgomery bus boycott).

But there was possibly a more fundamental difficulty with the litigation procedure. The Special Powers Act could be justified by reference to actual insurrectionary history, quite unlike segregationist statutes. And even if the law might have cut into gerrymandering (as the Supreme Court in the USA got into in 1962-4) it would have been unlikely to focus on the *de facto* inequalities of Northern Ireland with the same ease that overt legal enforcement of status differences in the US South could be cut down. What seems likely is that because many of the malpractices of Northern Ireland clung to security pretexts/reasons, any judicial sweeping away of these things would have been far more probable if those pretexts could be seen to be fictions. That would depend critically upon the successful discipline of non-violent civil rights protest. Thus the closer approximation to equal citizenship in Northern Ireland than in the US South—however deficient in the spirit of equal citizenship—made it much more difficult for moderate civil rights leaders to develop a total march and litigation strategy for short-circuiting the Stormont system and creating links with British political power, even after allowance is made for the less interventionist approach of British rather than American courts. A more sweeping institutional imposition would have been needed to achieve anything quickly—and what happened in the US South was very far from being quick—hence Michael Farrell's expectation that the Burntollet march would lead to a Westminster intervention. Once that march had led to polarisation, it was indeed true that only a Westminster intervention could have arrested the downward spiral that followed.

In theory direct legislative intervention in Northern Ireland by the Westminster government would have been easier than any comparable intervention in the US southern states, because the constitution of Northern Ireland was an act of the Westminster parliament that could be repealed by it. The US states, by contrast, are a federation enjoying constitutionally entrenched powers of their own. But the Labour government indicated that it had no intention of using such powers unless O'Neill or 'his ideas' were overthrown by extremists.[59] Whatever public indications it made in favour of particular changes, they were followed up by statements of confidence in the unionist ministers to manage their own situation. Rather than threaten intervention it gave private warnings about the possible constitutional implications of lending military support, which were calculated to deter the unionist ministers from making any such request. In other words, they showed a strong determination to make the unionist governments responsible for managing their own affairs.

If that was the case, then what pressures did they bring to bear? The Anglo-Irish *rapprochement* in its triangular phase had depended upon evidence of conciliatory intent while respecting O'Neill's need not to rock his boat more than he judged he could. The civil rights protests inserted themselves into this framework and attempted to define it. Britain of 1969 was no longer the premier power of 1949 and it would have been far more embarrassing to have a fellow European Irish government raise civil rights questions about Northern Ireland than it was to have a small wartime neutral raise territorial demands. Even without the pro-Irish unity and pro-civil rights sentiments inside the Labour party, the option of letting Stormont ignore the civil rights protests was precluded. Why not then, in the light of the general lack of sympathy for unionism in the Labour party, intervene?

First O'Neill was compliant and—given the absence of machinery for finding non-compliance, such as judicial intervention—would remain so, as would his successor Chichester Clark. The unionists were left to define compliance themselves. In May, for example, Chichester Clark told Wilson that sections of the Special Powers Act potentially conflicting with the European Convention on Human Rights would have been revoked already but for certain recent outrages.[60] Second, so long as compliance was evident, it no doubt seemed sensible to let the unionist government proceed with local government, housing and anti-discrimination measures rather than risk creating a defiant opposition that would wreck the chances of Catholics and Protestants fulfilling non-enforcible obligations toward each other within a framework eventually reformed. The defiance that obliged the reluctant Eisenhower to act in Little Rock was missing, nor did the machinery exist to define it in this situation.

This comes round then to the big difficulty. To have

responded to the historically unprecedented Catholic call for British rights for British citizens (as it was occasionally put by those most distanced from Irish nationalism) would have meant an intervention at a time when unionist extremists would have resisted it. Wilson's verbal Irish unity sentiments were the strongest strategic arguments any unionist could give to convince doubtful supporters that defiance of Westminster would provoke disaster. Had an actual intervention been carried out, the unionist defiance would have been magnified. Had Wilson intervened before August 1969—when, in fact, intervention could no longer be avoided—he would have had to override devolved government and integrate Northern Ireland fully into the United Kingdom. Only by thus securing the constitutional position of the unionists could he have possibly stifled their protests at his concessions to nationalists. This would have raised difficulties with both the pro-Irish unity element in the Labour party and with the Republic because it would have hardened the British sovereignty claim to Northern Ireland. It would have made Britain's responsibility for and involvement with Northern Ireland greater, whether it worked or failed. These risks and difficulties obviously had no southern US parallel. But to have pursued the civil rights scenario of the US South, *some* external authority would have had to impose a framework which could draw moderate unionists and civil rights-oriented Catholics into compliance under its authority. The Anglo-Irish accommodation which rested on a less than total British claim to sovereignty in Northern Ireland made this a perilous adventure to embark on voluntarily. Leaving the unionists to determine and define the pace of change meant that when the whole system blew up, London's intervention looked like a 'peace keeping' exercise in a distant and rather un-British place rather than a conscious reconstruction. The preservation of that distance between Britain and Northern Ireland is the one single consistent strand in British policy throughout the whole troubles. The civil rights period was the only period in which a reconstructive integration of Northern Ireland into Britain might have been attempted (it is another question whether it would have worked) and during which British power might have acted as a centripetal force as federal power did in the US South. It might, however, have been derailed in which case the strengthened claim to sovereignty implied in it could subsequently have turned Northern Ireland into a potential Fiume or an Algeria—a focal point for an outburst of metropolitan national egoism.

The indirect nature of Westminster pressures therefore left the pace of developments to depend upon majority consent within unionism. This was a very different situation from the US South. It would have been like expecting a southern governor to secure a majority within his Democratic legislative caucus, under a vague threat of a cut-off of funds if he himself couldn't convince federal powers that he was doing all he could to pass measures for which civil rights protests—which the police were curbing—were being attempted.

The capacity of moderate Catholic leaders such as John Hume, now MP for Foyle, to secure any kind of restraint upon police-Catholic collisions was sorely stretched. After a confrontation in the city centre in Derry, the police pursued demonstrators into the Bogside and beat a man in his home so badly that he subsequently died. While Hume called the inhabitants to a meeting away from the massed police, Robert Porter, the Minister of Home Affairs, had the police withdrawn before the meeting ended. This was one example, notable for their declining frequency, of instances in which leadership accommodation defused an explosive possibility.[61]

The approach of the traditional June-August marching season in 1969 tended to corrode all forms of restraint. The police protection of Orange marches contrasted with their role over the previous six months in preventing civil rights marches. PD leaders who favoured keeping up the pressure of civil disobedience had always advocated, but were decreasingly able to sustain, non-retaliation. In Dungiven they took part in an effort to make a non-violent gesture emphasising the contrast between the legality of Orange parades and illegality of civil rights parades. Initially successful, this broke down into clashes and attacks on the Orange Hall in this overwhelmingly Catholic village. In Belfast, when intending aggressors attached themselves to an Orange march past the mixed residential Unity flats at the bottom of the Protestant Shankill Road, residents saw no impartiality in police actions which implicitly equated residents and attackers. During and after the main July parades menacing sectarian incidents multiplied, so that Porter was confronted with a dilemma over the Derry march in August. If he banned it and (as Scarman puts it) 'if the Protestant extremists should get out of control . . . the police were not certain of their ability to deal unaided with the ensuing situation; but on past experience they believed they could deal with Catholic rioting'.[62]

The pitched battle between the police and the Bogside after the march, the public and private requests to the British and Irish governments to intervene, the Irish premier Jack Lynch's speech about the Republic 'not standing by', and the calls from Derry to supporters elsewhere to make 'diversionary actions' to take police pressure off the Bogside swept everything in their wake. Lynch explicitly opposed the use of British troops, called for a UN Force, and for British-Irish negotiations on the Northern Ireland constitutional position. CRC/CRA/PD leaders had in different ways sought British intervention in the past. There was no way to talk down this quasi-insurrection that seemed likely to bring it or an intervention from the Republic. But if some unionists would have welcomed an intervention at an earlier stage for fear of the forces within their own society, it was made clear to Porter that before the British government would provide military support, the unionist government must first exhaust its own resources.[63] That meant calling the B Specials out in force with all its escalatory implications. The conditions applied by Westminster were in effect that the disorders had to be treated as full-scale insurrection—which is what such B Special mobilisation implied—before the army would appear. Lynch's speech, meanwhile, convinced many unionists who did not need much persuasion in the first place that a full-scale republican insurrection had begun. So when the British army did arrive it came in circumstances where it could only look like a peace-keeping force, obliging the police, the B Specials and loyalist paramilitants to withdraw from Catholic areas. Between direct attacks on Catholic areas and intimidation of Catholics from others, about 5 per cent of Belfast Catholic households were forced to move. Many moved into Catholic West Belfast, from which about half of one per cent of Belfast's Protestant households were also displaced.[64]

While traditional republican objectives played little part and traditional republican actions even less, even a token insurrection of this kind depended for its success on the presence of the Irish Republic and its relationship with Britain. It was not a republican objective to get the British army to intervene. As a prelude to a general reconstruction of Northern Ireland, it might very well have been a civil rights objective. But reconstruction on a basis of equal citizenship presupposes that both communities will in King's words 'fulfil unforcible obligations towards each other'. The traumas of August 1969 had begun to dissolve any basis of possible coexistence in some areas. Strictly distributive questions of housing and employment discrimination, the reorganisation of local government, would all tend to become secondary to the question which had become uppermost in August 1969. The trigger had been the way that state force had been deployed to secure the passage of Orange marches where it had previously been used to curb civil rights marches. The right to march had become a visible expression of the more intangible question of proprietorship over law and order. The legitimacy of the army's presence for Catholics depended on the exclusion of the police and unionist processions. Paisley's attacks on the unionist government now focused on the existence of these 'no-go' areas, where the army liaised with neighbourhood committees.

The decision to leave the Stormont system in operation and to pressure it to put through reform measures such as the centralisation of housing under the Housing Executive (NIHE) and the reorganisation of local government, meant that the British government had to respond to the unionists on the issues which both they and Catholics—in an opposite sense—now felt most strongly about. When Wilson forced Stormont to disband the B Specials, the army became involved in its first firearms encounter on the Protestant Shankill Road. Anti-reform unionist successes (such as Paisley's election to Stormont in April 1970) made a compelling argument for allowing Orange parades. Otherwise the local administration which Britain depended upon to execute its reform programme was unlikely to survive. Around this question Britain's role in the all-important law and order question was to be subsequently defined, despite efforts to reform the police.

Dublin, thanks to Mr Lynch's speech, had managed to convince the RUC and loyalist auxiliaries that they faced a genuine insurrection. The reality was somewhat different. The attempt to raise the question of partition at the UN was rebuffed on the grounds that Northern Ireland was an internal question for Britain. Early plans to provide arms for Catholic self-defence groups in the North evolved in a twilight zone of approval until the dismissal of two cabinet ministers, Neil Blaney and Charlie Haughey, and their prosecution in the September/October 1970 Dublin Arms Trial signalled that these efforts were to be regarded as the unsanctioned activity of individual ministers.[65]

The role of the south in northern politics has subsequently operated on three levels. The coming together of the independent civil rights leaders and Labour MPs from nationalist areas into the Social Democratic and Labour party (SDLP) in 1970 provided a broad umbrella for constitutional Catholic politics.

The three main southern parties, Fianna Fáil, Fine Gael and Labour, and the southern governments (both Fianna Fáil and Fine Gael-Labour coalitions) looked upon the SDLP as the legitimate voice of northern Catholics, and echo its message in diplomatic and international arenas. At the second level the presence of the Republic has provided a relatively safer haven for republican paramilitary groups, which are not considered legitimate by any of the three southern parties. The IRA reformed after the August 1969 chaos and split into two wings. The official wing was Marxist and the Provisional wing a more direct successor to traditional republicanism. The absence of an Irish military strength on the southern side of the border comparable to the British military strength across the border, the lack of extradition facilities until recently, and the capacity of republican paramilitary groups to rely on some local sympathy in border areas made the south a source of strength to paramilitarism. At the third level the Republic's claim to the territory of the whole of Ireland, whether it is taken in the most restrictive sense as an assertion of guarantor status on behalf of northern Catholics or in its most unrestricted sense as a licence to armed warfare against the 'British occupation', makes the Republic co-responsible in the eyes of many or most unionists for the IRA. In the more conspiratorial vision it is seen to be part of a conspiracy orchestrated against the Protestants of Ulster.

Although the Conservatives supported the reform programme they had some sympathy with the unionists. Until 1968 the relation between unionism and conservatism had been one of formal alliance. The military escort given to Orange parades in July 1970, shortly after the return of the Conservatives to power in Britain, had direct implications for the development of wider policy. Gun battles arising from Orange processions through two Catholic areas were followed by the imposition of a curfew and arms searches on the Falls Road. Unionist ministers were taken round by the army in an obvious effort to demonstrate that the government was maintaining order and to reassure its own doubtful supporters. But the effect on Catholics was to demonstrate that the British government was now intent upon propping up Stormont and reasserting its control over areas from which it had been excluded after August 1969. The deterioration of relations between the army and Catholic areas proceeded rapidly with Catholic leadership unable either to orchestrate effective restraint in their areas or to shape the evolution of policy. From early 1971 the Provisional IRA began to engage in shooting confrontations where previously the heaviest weapons used by rioters had been petrol bombs. In the first half of 1971 six civilians were killed by IRA bomb explosions as well as fifteen soldiers and policemen and the British government became more responsive to the appeals of the new Stormont Prime Minister, Brian Faulkner, to introduce internment without trial. This move, in August 1971, effectively declared war on many Catholic areas, aligned British power with unionism and massively increased support for the IRA. The renewed housing flight, propelled by the heightening of the dangers, made territorialism a fact of life. For many it was almost the main fact of life.

Fred Boal's work has shown just how little residential

mixing there was in 1972 in Belfast: 99 per cent of Protestants
and 75 per cent of Catholics lived in streets where they were in
their own majority; 78 per cent of Protestants and 70 per cent
of Catholics lived in streets where they were part of a 90 per
cent plus majority. In 1969 the respective figures were 69 per
cent for Protestants and 56 per cent for Catholics. In public
sector estates nearly all mixed streets had Protestant majorities. In lower valued private sector housing, mixed streets
with Catholic majorities tended to be in transition to larger
Catholic majorities. The Protestant households were older
and had been there longer. 'The limited amount of ethnic
residential mixing present in Belfast in 1972 cannot be
assumed to have much significance as an indicator of ethnic
assimilation, first because of its limited extent and secondly
because, at least in the circumstances of the early 1970s, much
of it is of a transitional nature.'[66] In the massive movements of
1969 and 1971 people fled either because they were directly
intimidated or felt uncomfortably sure they might be if they
stayed or because their houses were bombed or set on fire or
occupied. To start expulsions in an area requires an initiative
of a small group. To prevent such an initiative from getting
under way requires the bulk of people of an area to feel able to
pre-empt it—and the minorities in danger of expulsion to feel
their neighbours have pre-empted it. That is a much taller
order than it sounds to someone who has never been anywhere
near such a situation.

Michael Poole, who has investigated the degrees of segregation in different towns in Northern Ireland, finds that the
strongest correlation with 1971 segregation indeces are the
segregation indeces for 1911. It seems probable that some
towns having avoided ructions in the past may have managed
to preserve the kind of intercommunal relations that prevent
trouble 'elsewhere' from causing panic to spread to them. To
preserve residential mixing is a long-term achievement, easiest if it is not even seen as a problem, but to break it up an
incident has to happen only once. Many estates and areas in
1969 and 1971 gave birth to community groups and peace
groups consciously motivated to prevent the rot from spreading. A concerted and large-scale effort was made in the Upper
Springfield area of Belfast, to the west of the main zone of

contestation in 1969—an area predominantly Catholic but having substantial Protestant districts. But two confrontations arising from Orange parades in Easter and July 1970 were followed by Protestant evacuation of the New Barnsley estate, strongly encouraged by certain Unionist leaders. The Rathcoole estate, described by Boal in 1972 as 'one of the very rare examples in the urban area of an ethnically mixed public housing estate' was steadied by a peace committee in 1969 but efforts to do it again at the time of internment were less successful. Intimidatory pressures against Catholics built up from early 1971 when the provisional IRA began to engage in shooting exchanges with the army, even though no such things were happening in or near Rathcoole. The shipyard peace meeting organised by trades unionists in 1969 managed for a while to prevent the spread of the troubles to east Belfast.[67] In both 1969 and 1971 the police and (in 1971) the army were engaged in conflict with Catholic areas. The space for intimidatory actions against Catholics in Protestant areas increased so that efforts to prevent this, where they were made, had to be made by people of the estates without much recourse to enforcing powers. In Catholic areas in 1971 the main preoccupation of republican groups was with those suspected of sympathy with the army or police—a category that would include most Protestants. The worst possibilities in each case are the ones that fugitives take precaution against—being suspected of being an IRA sympathiser (which for some Protestant paramilitaries is a very wide category indeed and puts any Catholic at risk) or finding oneself in an area of conflict, mass internment sweeps and house searches, threatened by or uncomfortable with the climate of hostility to the army/police.

These developments have drastically belittled the significance of any administrative reform measures—by 1971 all the original demands of the CRA had been legislated (though implementation is a wholly other matter) except the abolition of the Special Powers Act. The massive pressure of Catholic demand for housing in west Belfast has created a problem of overcrowding which is not, for example, experienced in the Protestant areas adjacent to it. There the decay of the older housing creates a different problem. The NIHE, formed to deal with what was called the worst housing problem in Europe and to enforce fairness in distribution by a points system, has from the beginning had to face the fact that there are two separate housing demands according to where people can safely live. Squatting, the sheer weight of demand, the difficulties—and inefficiencies—of the repairs systems, the poor quality of much of the stock taken over, and the pervasive influence of territorial questions (affecting whether to build the Poleglass estate to meet demand for houses that could not be met in Catholic west Belfast) are examples of issues facing it.[68] The territorial and political fragmentation has also inhibited the growth of any cohesive tenant organisation, something that became increasingly serious once UK-wide cut backs reduced allocations to NIHE.

Within these territorial enclaves all manner of other differences are sharpened. For example, in 1978 the patterns of travel to work from working-class west to east Belfast (the main industrial area of the shipyard) were an inverted image of the differential unemployment rates. Protestant west Belfast with 18 per cent unemployment had 25 per cent of its employment in east Belfast. Catholic west Belfast with 40 per cent (in inner zone) and 25 per cent (in outer zone) unemployment had 5 per cent of its employment in east Belfast.[69] This reflects the pre-1969 situation but the weight of sheer physical risks is now an unquantifiable element that would affect any efforts to deal with the chronic economic debilitation of Catholic west Belfast.

Until 1975, when the beginning of the effects of the world-wide recession combined with knock-on effect of government expenditure cuts, a general consensus prevailed in British politics on Northern Ireland that the inequalities between Protestants and Catholics would be dealt with by raising the incomes and living standards of the whole province. The level of personal disposable income as a percentage of the UK per head was 76.6 per cent in 1971 and 78.1 per cent in 1974 (for comparison the next lowest UK region, the north of England, it was 88.9 per cent in 1971 and in 1974 in Wales at 89.7 per cent) But whereas social security benefits were 9.5 per cent of UK household incomes, they were 16.4 per cent of Northern Ireland household incomes.

The oil price hike from 1973 onwards hit Northern Ireland industries severely in at least three areas. In the 1960s a conscious choice was made in favour of the oil-based production of electricity. Harland and Wolff had been adapted to building very large oil tankers (VLCCs) for which demand collapsed after the 1973 oil crisis. And the man-made fibre plants, dependent on oil for both naphtha feedstock and energy, were placed in competitive disadvantage with the US where oil prices remained lower. The drying up of new industrial projects after the onset of the troubles had a delayed action effect, while those in the pipeline continued to come on stream.[70] But the general picture has been contraction rather than opening opportunities. The distancing of Northern Ireland from the UK is nowhere more unwittingly displayed than in arguments that the chronic economic debilitation of Catholic society should somehow be remedied at the expense of Protestants rather than Britain.

The post-1971 period was only in one sense a 'return' to the inevitable. There must be many nationalists and republicans of the early adult generation of 1969 who were being accused by Paisley of 'republicanism' long before they became whatever they subsequently did become. The forces pulling and pushing in this direction are clear enough in the stance of John Hume and Ivan Cooper. In October 1969 Hume, welcoming the proposed reform programme, called on civil rights supporters to play their full part in the life of the community because it would require a great deal of effort to make the reforms work and to produce 'the change of heart and mind that is absolutely necessary to make the equality that the law proposes a reality.' Fifteen months later, after relations between the army and the Bogside had deteriorated (with relatively random arrests of rioters who were then liable to a mandatory six-month sentence), his efforts to curb conflict were becoming fruitless. Hume and Cooper were 'being told by fifteen year olds to fuck off' (McCann).

McCann says people were 'almost relieved gradually to discover that the *guiltily discarded tradition* on which the community was founded was, after all, meaningful and immediately relevant' [my emphasis]. And conversely back in August 1969 Max Hastings listened to a police gunner harangue a group of his colleagues on the Falls Road where they were using machine guns against what they took to be a revolution. 'You know, of course, Dr Paisley has been telling us this would happen these nine months but *none of us had the sense to listen . . .*' [my emphasis][71]

Eric Gallagher and Stanley Worrall speak of a phenomenon endlessly repeating itself in their story of Christians in Ulster (1968-80): 'Christian leaders making constant appeals for moderation and reconciliation, but forced always to look over their shoulders to see how far they were isolating themselves from their own flocks.' Of the accusation of double-talk levelled at Northern Ireland clergy, Eric Gallagher comments: 'It must be said . . . that the impression of double-talk sometimes arose from the sense that clergy had of the need to say something against the other side in order to gain a hearing for the restraining advice they sought to give their own people.'[72] The costs of showing open solidarity or trust of the 'other' are real, not only when they lead to charges of treachery, but when the hopes for reconciliation, without which trust is difficult to vindicate, disintegrate. Obviously the Protestant liberal clergy and liberal unionist political leaders would have found their message much more persuasive if they hadn't encountered everywhere the essence of the policeman's argument.

The introduction of internment destroyed the British government's remaining chance of a purely internal reconstruction. So long as the army insulated Catholic areas from direct Stormont control, the possible implications of police/law and order/justice reforms remained uncertain. But as the British government became more responsive to the unionist government's possible electoral vulnerability and itself receptive to demands to put down the IRA, the SDLP were trapped in an increasingly impossible position. Withdrawing from Stormont after the refusal of a public inquiry into two deaths in shooting incidents, the imposition of internment a week later necessarily blew any chance of persuading their followers of the importance of the reform programme. The bulk of the Catholic community were united in opposition to internment and the Stormont government that imposed it. Though the SDLP continued to denounce the violence of the IRA, they were now obliged to take up a modified nationalist stance. With Britain and the unionist government locked into alliance against the Catholic community, any future settlement would have to involve the Irish government at least to the point of ensuring that such an alignment was broken and could not reappear again. This minimum went together with a revived aspiration to reunification of Ireland, and increased the SDLP's dependence on support from the Republic's major parties. Any unionist who had always believed that civil rights was a Trojan horse for Irish unity could now point to what appeared to be proof of the fact. Many, forgetting their earlier thoughts about 'extremists on both sides', could regard Paisley as a prophet—and Catholics regarding this could equally logically declare that moderate unionism must have been a shallow facade.

To conclude, the US southern and Northern Ireland situations suggest what is necessary if a system of communal deterrence is to be broken up and replaced by something more closely resembling normal metropolitan order. All communal deterrence relationships were held together in the last analysis by defiance actions. Defiance actions or the threat of them constrain white/unionist moderates, deter any metropolitan interventions, and convince blacks/Catholics that the system will always operate against them. If the blacks/Catholics become convinced that defiance action has worked, then white/unionist society and federal/British power look like a huge united obstacle. The only way to cut through this arrangement was for federal/British power to confront agencies of defiance to prise open a clear-cut division between vigilant and moderate whites/unionists. But for the effect to be lasting, this had to be done while potentially compliant and uncertain blacks/Catholics were able to orchestrate a positive response to it. The more cohesive the non-violent leadership of blacks/Catholics, the more time was given to the metropolitan power and the greater became the likelihood that the whole process would be successful. The growth of black/Catholic violent alienation from the process tended to dissolve the distinction between moderate and vigilant whites/unionists.

The metropolitan power would never have considered taking the risk of confronting such defiance—it would have continued to tolerate 'regional peculiarities'—unless pressures of external and international opinion had made it necessary. But where these pressure were exceedingly indirect as in the USA, federal power could prevaricate for much longer than could British power in Northern Ireland. Here the immediacy of the Republic enabled alienated Catholics to give up non-violent protest much more quickly. Black power, however provoked, could not circumvent King's non-violence with the same ease that the Bogside insurrectionists of August 1969 could circumvent Hume's non-violence.

However, when all is said and done, the failure of Britain to override the devolution system before August 1969—and its failure to impose integration before August 1971—meant that the kind of confrontation with agencies of defiance necessary to make a reconstruction work never happened. The question of blame is not important. It might be possible to 'blame' the British Labour government; or the Dublin government for any anticipated objection to a strengthening of the British sovereignty claim; or Northern unionists and nationalists for objecting to such British intervention. Richard Rose's 1968 survey found that Protestants divided into two equal parts. 'Ultras' approved of 'any measures' to keep Northern Ireland Protestant, while the compliant segment did not. Catholics divided into three equal parts. Some supported the constitution, some were 'don't knows', and some opposed it, though only one eighth approved 'any measures' to end partiton.[73] Though Rose was exceedingly pessimistic (and realistic) about the possibility of forming a consensually based regional government, the failure to attempt a reconstructive intervention allowed these limited assets to burn up. Today it is often observed that unionists are 'not really' British because Britain doesn't want them or because their loyalty is to themselves and not to Britain. And the similarities between the language and behaviour of the sharper edges of unionism and that of settlement colonial defenders (e.g. in Algeria) is used to argue that they are really 'settlers' (who happen to have a local majority but one which for that reason is denied any democratic validity at all). To put these kinds of charges into perspective it is now clear that the US southerners were lucky that the civil rights reforms were imposed upon them and that George Wallace's 1968 vote was of no avail against them. In the end it allowed a new generation of southern moderates to appear whose links to supremacists were visibly severed. The unionist misfortune, for which the British policy of safety-first is at least partly responsible, is that they did not have such an imposition placed upon them at a time when a majority of them would probably have disliked it. Had that happened it is possible that the difference between moderate and vigilant unionists would have become much clearer than it actually is, and enabled the former to grow at the expense of the latter.

However that is not the end of the story. To assume baldly that US civil rights problem was solved in the 1960s would be a self-affirmative white judgment. Vincent Harding illustrates this point by saying that in white history the civil rights movement begins with the judgment of nine white men (the US Supreme Court) whereas in black history the simultaneity of the Bandung conference of colonised people and the Montgomery bus boycott is no accident.[74] Even if the apparatus of federal intervention continued to be a positive asset to blacks in the most defiant states of the South, once the momentum of civil rights ran out and the federal arm could not be used as a lever against local obstacles, black self-organisation had to launch out on its own. Taking up where I left off earlier, Black power had several alternative destinations. It might be simply a means of building up black society so that it could engage in the usual US coalition style politics on an equal basis with other groups, or it might be a separatist nationalism. To say that the civil rights era 'worked' in the USA is to forget about these developments and the ongoing question they pose for US society. In so far as this question also relates to Northern Ireland, could the subsequent revival of Irish nationalism have followed the first Black power path rather than the second one?

Before attempting to answer this, it is necessary to notice how Black power has (if anything) been stronger in the northern cities than in the South where the main weight of the Second Reconstruction fell. By contrast British cities with large Irish populations experienced no obvious ripple of Irish organisation spreading from the Northern Ireland crisis.

Perhaps, although I don't know the answer, the strength of the Catholic and Irish middle class and equal participation of Irish within the labour and trade union movement in Britain may be one reason why this didn't happen. But there seems to be much more symmetry between black experience in northern cities and Catholic experience in Northern Ireland itself. Despite the battery of civil rights legislation and affirmative action programmes (which have only weak counterparts in Northern Ireland) blacks remain massively disadvantaged economically and unrepresented politically in public offices.[75] There may be limits to what civil rights legislation can achieve against *de facto* inequalities as distinct from formally entrenched mechanisms of discrimination. These can be simply struck down by law.

Since the 1967 riot Detroit, once known for the strength of the UAW (United Automobile Workers) in politics, has become sharply race-polarised and residentially segregated. Widick said of Detroit in 1972 that it 'seldom has a moment or respite from racial incidents'. With one handgun per eight inhabitants (80 per cent of which are unregistered) serious incidents between blacks and police were not infrequent. He pointed to black inroads into unionised work and possible development of a strong middle class. The formation of a black caucus in the Michigan Democratic Party was a challenge to form a coalition of equals. 'Otherwise the current rise of separatism may turn out to be more than the detour we hope it is on the road toward an integrated society.'[76] For this hope to be realised it would be necessary that polarised relationships between whites and blacks became channelled through the political process and not mediated by the system of law and order operating as a white shield against black protest. Otherwise, all issues of economic inequality and discrimination would become bound up with black alienation from the law and order system. Hence the long-term importance of 'pockets of black power [becoming] illustrations of what legitimate government really is'.[77] The election of black mayors and judges and the appointment of black police chiefs all tend to reduce the possibility that policing can be conducted without regard for the rights of those being policed. Only in these circumstances is there any chance that economic and distributive questions can be dealt with by normal political bargaining. And only when blacks experience the institutional order in a way similar to the experience of other population groups, can that order be taken for granted *or* made the object of general grievance.

None the less even the election of black office holders reveals a new layer of problems. Black mayors elected in increasing numbers in the 1970s preside over some of the poorest jurisdictions. There is 'an increasing concentration of have nots in a small minority of state and local jurisdiction of steadily weakening political influence' (E.K. Hamilton), 'threatening to limit the impact of newly attained political representation for black constituents' with a possible result of 'some polarisation on racial lines between state governments and city governments on revenue allocation and taxation matters' (Elliot Zashin).[78]

It is not clear that the black coalitioning within the Democratic Party will produce satisfactory advances on the socio-economic front. But as the Democrats cannot win elections without black votes that at least makes the coalitioning arrangement compelling. Furthermore, until black office holding is more widespread, law and order/justice questions will retain dangerous possibilities.

In Greensboro, Chafe concluded his study about the time when Hal Sieber, one of the driving forces on the white side of the reconciling process, resigned from the chamber of commerce after failing to get it interested in investigating police brutality—'one of the sorest points in Greensboro's black community'. In fact the Supreme Court chose the issue of complaints against police forces to adopt 'the most extreme position it has yet taken on federal judicial impotence' (Louise Weinberg). In 1976 Rizzo-v-Goode, the Supreme Court overturned a federal judge ruling that Philadelphia establish a citizen complaint procedure in its police department on the grounds that the ruling 'offended principles of federalism'. One of the triggers of the 1980 Miami riot was an all-white jury acquittal of a policeman charged with murder.[79]

The possibility that Black power in the USA will become like Jewish or Irish power is a real one, but it depends heavily upon the ability of blacks to secure positions of power and responsibility at least in the areas where they are heavily numerically preponderant. The existence of these possibilities depends upon the capacity of the US political system to sustain a very high degree of local self-government. Like my earlier comments on US judicial system, this is not intended as a euology of American ways. The system only works because no internal groups with a high level of local power can be seen as a threat, a sort of agency for external intervention. And that is so only because the US is one of the strongest powers in the world. It is that strength which enables the generality of its people, if they wish, to disregard the view that particular kinds of ethnic power concentrates are a 'danger'. If some black separatists see US power as an obstacle, there must be others for whom that strength is at least a partial blessing. It reduces the chance that black self-organisation will be stigmatised as a threat and treated like one; and in doing so it may reduce the institutional provocation to respond in a separatist manner, with all that that entails. If this helps to account for the existence of white moderates or liberals with whom blacks coalesce in the Democratic Party, then the role of black non-violence in the US South in the first half of the 1960s is crucial, if quite unquantifiable.

History and politics tend to focus on clashes of antagonistic intents, whereas non-violence was a 'no' to mimetic temptation. Martin Luther King's notion of non-violent protest might have had much reduced 'significance' in political or historical terms if it had been largely overtaken by confrontationism. The power of its Christian foundation was a barrier to internal mediation with white supremacism. John K. Ansbro says of King that he 'uncovered a paradox in the black power movement. While its members continued to insist on not imitating the values of white society, by advocating violence, they were imitating the worst and most brutal values of American life.' None the less after 1965 King, to use Cleaver's words, became a 'stubborn and persistent stumbling block . . . The contradiction in which he was caught cast him in the role of one who was hated and held in contempt, both by whites in America who did not want to free black people and by black people *who recognised the attitude of white America* and who wanted to be rid of the self-deceiving doctrine of non-violence' [my emphasis]. In death his legacy may be part of the sacred order that restrains both of the forces Cleaver describes as hating and holding him in contempt while he lived.[80]

If this interpretation of the possibly integrative consequences of Black power is correct, then its implications for Northern Ireland are clear. Nationalist dependence upon some kind of unspecified support from the Republic will remain and, even if it does not, it will always be suspected or guarded against by unionism and by Britain, so long as Britain's relationship to the Republic and the relationship of both Britain and the Republic to Northern Ireland remain either ambiguous or antagonistic. In order to place Northern nationalism in a position where it could develop in a manner similar to the integrative strand of Black power, it would be necessary for it to relate to the state structure in the same way that unionism does. Logically this points in the direction of joint sovereignty. But joint sovereignty is only a concept, for which there are no very good precedents and any such arrangement is loaded with risks for both British and Irish governments. These are the subjects of the two remaining chapters.

8

Solutions and the Insoluble

Since the disintegration of the civil rights process in Northern Ireland in 1971, some people have identified the IRA campaign to secure British withdrawal with the FLN campaign to secure French withdrawal from Algeria. Although these comparisons are usually only made *en passant*, Ken Livingstone, the former Labour leader of the Greater London Council, has drawn rather more direct parallels and argued that a withdrawal should be carried out speedily to prevent the growth of a loyalist reaction similar to that of the OAS in Algeria.

It is true that these situations are (were) the most difficult areas for France or Britain to withdraw from. If the 'neat' solution of the US civil rights process, tighter integration of the southern states into the USA, is no longer possible in Northern Ireland, one of the other 'neat' solutions is an independent United Ireland. There are enough instances of situations where neat solutions have come to pass even though many who knew most about them would have doubted they could happen. Algeria may be a case in point.

Even if the sovereignty of many third world countries today may be rather fictional, the 'norm' of national independence has the attraction that national citizens, recognising the state's monopoly of the use of force, are freed of force fields running through the society. People are then neither tempted, forced, nor able to appeal to external forces to strengthen themselves against internal opponents. The best test of this condition being arrived at is universal agreement as to what forces are 'external' and what are not. Clearly Algerian decolonisation, whatever else it involved, produced a 'neat' solution.

The French minority in Algeria (10 per cent) were an economically privileged element. But it was their limited numbers rather than their 'privilege' which made decolonisation a possibility. When the rebellion broke out in 1954 their dependence upon metropolitan French military backing was enormous. When that support was removed they had no possibility, except in some limited enclaves (of which more later), but to accept Moslem majority rule or to leave. That is why decolonisation worked.

Republicans in Northern Ireland believe that if Britain announced its intent to withdraw most unionists would recognise that they were Irish. Only 'diehards' would behave as the 'diehard' colons behaved in Algeria (where in fact only 5 per cent stayed after 1962). So there is a problem with the analogy. It depends on a very substantial number of unionists behaving in an altogether different manner than did the mass of colons. Even if we look at Ireland as a whole with a 20-25 per cent British minority, that is substantially more than the 10 per cent French in Algeria and would produce much larger zones of British physical predominance.

Perhaps the most striking weakness of this 'analogy' is that the reason the Algerian colons acquired so much political leverage over France was the build-up of nearly half a million French soldiers committed to the objective of keeping Algeria French. Without these troops and the heavy military commitment to keeping Algeria—which has no parallel in Northern Ireland—the obstacles to withdrawal would have been very much reduced. The French presence that caused de Gaulle so much difficulty was the military rather than the civilian presence.The relationship between Britain, Ireland and Northern Ireland is more like that of a disputed nationality zone with dependency upon two powers.

If we stick to the 'analogy' as it relates to the whole of Ireland, the most striking difference is the priority that the British and Irish governments (representing about 85 per cent plus of the Irish nationalist population) have placed upon preserving good relations with each other and preventing Northern Ireland from antagonising their relationships towards each other. They have avoided sharpening their conflicting sovereignty claims in a way that some elements

internal to Northern Ireland would wish and thereby provided anchors for those internal elements who are glad that
they have not done so.

Wherever representative violence is a significant possibility,
the behaviour of the quite small numbers necessary to activate
it—as well as the capacity of those seeking to restrain
it—depend in some measure upon the stances of external
forces that might be magnetised into the situation. Once
epidemics of representative violence have occurred, the definition of internal groups is sharpened (because most people
experience representative violence as a threat or injury to
themselves rather than inflict it). The volatility of situations
can increase, weakening the powers of restraint against new
outbreaks. The dependence of each group upon external
forces and the threat each pose to the other increases.

It may be that the proliferation of nations and claimants to
nation status in the Balkans and the Middle East—when
contrasted with the relative stability of, say, multilingual
Belgium or Switzerland—owes more to external dependency
syndrome than it does to differing degrees of 'cultural diversity' in the west and east of Europe. The nineteenth-century
great 'Christian' powers made it their business to protect
Christian and other minority elements in the Ottoman
Empire, whether in order to break it up, secure clients for
themselves or to render its rule dependent on their support.
Perhaps groups which might have behaved differently in a
Belgium or Switzerland now relate to each other not as
religion or language groups but as nations. 'The principal
lesson,' says Raymond Pearson, 'to be drawn from continental
experience, steadily reinforced as the century progressed, was
that nationalist successes depended less on who you were than
where you were'.[1] Switzerland's recognised eternal neutrality
and Belgium's sovereignty guaranteed by Great Power Treaty
in 1830 may have made it much easier to avoid getting caught
up in the external dependency syndrome, which once created
generates endless reasons for itself. Once groups are locked
into antagonisms with neighbour-enemies who have recourse
to external backing, they also need it. Each would be more
secure if the other's external backers could be removed or
cancelled. Their own (of course) are a necessary protection

and as often as not cease to be seen as 'external'. The objective basis for the distinction between 'internal' and 'external' disappears.

We must now consider the wider consequences of two nation states related to each other by a mixed nationality zone where the internal antagonism threatens to shape their relations with each other. If armed elements in a mixed zone were operating in a situation where the relationship between the two wider nations were already hostile, it might be possible for them to magnetise these nations into a conflict in which the contested zone became something of a cockpit. The more the two states were committed to back up 'their' nationals in the conflict zone, the greater would be the contribution of armed elements to shaping of the course of events. On the other hand, if the two states in question are committed in the first place to a direct working relationship with each other, they are less likely to be distracted by the claims of their competing nationals in the mixed zone. There will, however, always be a tendency for national states to support the representative violence of their own sides if they cannot find ways of resolving or accommodating conflicting sovereignty claims to be disputed territories.

Conflicting sovereignty claims to disputed nationality zones are inherently unresolvable. They cannot be renounced without risk of enthusiastic national movements taking up the cry of national 'treason', using the 'renounced' people of the frontier as a flag. There is no 'rational' way of avoiding this. National conflicts, after all, uproot the only principles upon which political rationality can be based. Frontier antagonisms simply expose the fact that nations enjoy no sacred worldly authority above themselves. Nations are bodies of people owing mutual obligations to their members. Their relationships are potentially lawless.

The closest any two nations could get to resolving conflicting sovereignty claims to disputed national zones would be to accept the joint sovereignty of both within them. This would be the only way in which both internal comunities could relate to the state power in symmetrical ways. And in so doing the state might cease to be the axis of antagonism between them and become instead a focal point for co-operation. This is, however, only a theoretical possibility. It would only be likely to be attempted because relationships between the two communities had already been acutely antagonised under another arrangement. The relationship between the two states would have to be strong enough to ensure that it could not be disrupted by defiance of their own nationals in the disputed zone. While a joint sovereignty might increase both states' powers of acting together to curb internal antagonism it could also increase the capacity of forces of chaos to expose the limits of both states' power in a conclusive manner.

Until 1985 the British and Irish governments attempted to moderate antagonism within Northern Ireland but Britain took much refuge behind the need for positive electoral support for anything proposed, thus avoiding these kinds of joint responsibilities. The 1985 Anglo-Irish Agreement is a quantum leap in the direction of interlocking and increasing them. It is both a potential opportunity for the people within and a risk to both states themselves. If the two states can co-operate to create something closer to equal citizenship and to ensure that Northern Ireland cannot any longer be ruled by securing conditional legitimacy from unionists and by controlling nationalists, it might become a stronger anchor for internal recognition of the equality of communities. It is impossible to predict what the two governments would do if both loyalists and republicans treated the Anglo-Irish Agreement as an obstacle to 'real' solutions and generated a mutually reinforcing chaos. But what they are likely to do is to manoeuvre themselves out of any position of responsibility for clearing up the chaos. Many names might be given to whatever they agreed to thereafter but all would have the same tendency to allow them to reduce their involvement under varying pretexts until people discovered that in this particular situation peace would not come through chaos. Chaos would produce some new form of separation under a new political label. There would be intense antagonism revolving round the choice of the label, but the substantial issues at stake would tend to disappear, leaving only the antagonism behind.

In the sections of this chapter, I shall deal first with the way in which France became locked into the commitment to

French Algeria and the background differences this demonstrates from Northern Ireland. Second, I will look at the way in which the conflict in Northern Ireland developed between 1972 and 1985 within the framework of a British-Irish posture of hoping for voluntary internal agreement, followed eventually by the more interventionist approach of the Anglo-Irish Agreement. Third, I shall use the Algerian analogy from 1959-62 to demonstrate why decolonisation was possible and produced a neat solution there but would be very unlikely to do the same in Northern Ireland. In chapter nine I will look at Cyprus and Lebanon to show how external dependency syndromes can generate crises which are about everything and nothing. I will draw out the redeeming features which make it unnecessary (but not impossible) for Northern Ireland to go the way of either. The capacity for co-operation between Britain and the Irish Republic, contrasted with the relative incapacity of Greece and Turkey in Cyprus and the total incapacity of Syria and Israel in Lebanon, is the main source of difference. So long as this co-operative capacity is treated as an asset and not as an obstacle, Northern Ireland will not become like Cyprus or Lebanon.

Since 1972 Britain has never made the defence of the union between Britain and Northern Ireland a touchstone of national strength in the way, for example, that it elevated the Falkland-Malvinas in 1982. Whatever the levels of metropolitan anger against the IRA, no major tendency in British politics has ever seriously contested the legitimate interest of the Irish Republic in the affairs of Northern Ireland. Whatever the inconsistencies and misunderstandings or conflicts of interest, in the last analysis Britain has behaved toward the Irish Republic as another member of the EEC to which it must accord a recognition of the kind it expects itself. Britain of the 1980s is in no position to treat Ireland as France of the 1950s was to treat North Africa. British parties have not tried to score points off each other over their continuing failures to prevent violence in Northern Ireland. And most of the British people have come to accept the idea that the problem in

Northern Ireland is about 'religion'. Even if they were quite wrong about this, their understanding is important for what it does *not* say. The issue in Northern Ireland has not so far been seen as a question of keeping the British flag flying. Quite the reverse of this situation developed in Algeria between 1954 and 1959. While France was moving toward decolonisation of most of its territories, it stuck hard to the claim that Algeria was not a colony but part of France, a position for which it could claim some external recognition (for example in the NATO Treaty of 1949).[2] In France (and otherwise only in Italy) the Communist party had played a crucial role in the resistance to the Nazis and a bedrock of 20-25 per cent of the French electorate stood by it when it was frozen out of office in 1947 after the escalation of the Cold War decimated communist support in most of Western Europe. Generally supporting decolonisation, its exclusion from governments left the other parties favourable to decolonisation in a weak position in coalition governments and ensured that such moves were only taken when they seemed unavoidable.[3]

Two of the middle ground parties, the Socialists and Christian Democrats, were firmly committed to upholding parliamentary democracy and supported the US sponsored and funded moves toward European integration. But the party of General de Gaulle, the titular head of the resistance, was stridently anti-communist, opposed to the subordination of French imperial interests to the Euro-integrationism sponsored by the USA and intended to force the parliament to accept a constitution that would provide for presidential rule. Securing 20 per cent plus of the vote in 1950 it remained another source of total opposition (besides the communists) until 1952 when some of its members defected to join a government, whereupon de Gaulle disbanded it and 'retired' from political life. French governments in the 1950s were a permanently shifting coalition arrangement.

In 1954 the French army experienced actual military defeat at the battle of Dien Bien Phu in Indo-China where they had been fighting since 1946. Pierre Mendes-France was elected premier with a promise to disengage from Indo-China. He also began the process leading to the independence of Tunisia and Morocco, the two North African countries with large

French populations, bordering Algeria to east and west. But when the FLN rising broke out in November 1954 he reaffirmed the view that Algeria was part of France and appointed Jacques Soustelle, a Gaullist, governor-general.[4] Soustelle's goal was to make the formal integration of Algeria into France a reality, breaking down European opposition to equal rights for Moslems and making them full French citizens. Integration, which in the 1930s had been a progressive concept for breaking down colonial statutes, was about to become a formula for resisting any kind of Algerian autonomy and for increasing French self-assertion in Algeria.

In 1944 de Gaulle's resistance government had belatedly done by decree what the European mayors' strike of 1937 had prevented—extended French citizenship to around 80,000 Moslems. But in 1945 pro-independence manifestations during a VE day parade were followed by violence in which some hundred Europeans were killed. This was followed by a massive repression running into thousands of Moslem deaths. Instead of extending citizenship as de Gaulle had done, a second electoral college was set up for Moslems (both Europeans and the nine times more numerous Moslems elected fifteen deputies each to the French parliament) and the elections to the Algerian assembly in 1948 (on the same bicommunal system) were rigged by the army and administration. So when the rising of 1954 broke out many Moslem leaders who had previously called for integration faced an entirely altered situation.

For the French army, fresh from the defeat at Dien Bien Phu, Algeria was an outpost everyone in France seemed keen to keep and until August 1955 they contained the rebellion fairly easily. In a rising in the eastern Constantine department that month thinly dispersed Europeans were massacred, and a military reprisal massacre on the principle of collective responsibility was carried out. Moslem elected leaders from this area (without the support of their counterparts in the more heavily Europeanised Oran department in the west) were caught between the violence of the FLN and the French authorities and took a stand against integration. In France the non-communist left, now led by Mendes-France, called for Algerian autonomy in opposition to Soustelle's integrationism.

In the 1956 French election the non-communist parties divided between a left bloc in favour of autonomy for Algeria and a right bloc in favour of integration on the *status quo*. But the increase in communist seats and the appearance of the Poujadists with 12.5 per cent of the vote (protesting both about measures unpopular with small shopkeepers and peasants and in favour of the *status quo* in Algeria) deprived either of the main blocs of a clear majority.

The left bloc's proposals were not particularly clear anyhow. Autonomy was to be preceded by the setting up of institutions elected under a single electoral college (Moslems and Europeans voting together) nothwithstanding that in 1956 it had been impossible to conduct elections at all. Social and economic reforms were to be carried out. But first a military reverse was to be secured against the FLN. The prime minister, Guy Mollet, appeared to respond favourably to an angry Algiers European crowd—suspecting he intended to negotiate with the FLN—by introducing conscription and giving the army an increasingly free hand. So the differences that had been so apparently sharp in the 1956 election became rather muddy. Military autonomy in Algeria grew inexorably. Right up until 1958 the French parliament was bogged down in efforts to pass a bill that included a single electoral college. It was finally passed in January 1958 only to be overtaken by events of greater magnitude.

France's determination to keep Algeria was gradually isolating her internationally. The FLN secured international recognition at the Bandung conference of non-aligned nations in April 1955. The independence of Morocco and Tunisia was to give the FLN neighbouring sanctuaries. And the extent of Franco-British decline in the world was revealed when, in league with the Israelis, they attempted to deal a blow to President Nasser of Egypt, the rising leader of Arab nationalism. The US ultimatum that obliged them to call off the Suez adventure focused smouldering imperial discontent against the USA. In Algeria itself the army was given full powers in 1957 to put an end to an outbreak of assassinations and bombings, using torture on a massive scale (and with the consequent disappearance of some 3,000 people in Algiers in 1957). In the eastern zone, near the Tunisian border,

Europeans were fleeing rural areas which were held by military power alone. The 1957 decision to undertake pursuit against FLN incursions from Tunisia led in February 1958 to the bombing of the Tunisian village of Sakiet. And although the government stood over the military action, the international outrage was such that it felt obliged to accept an American-British mediation between itself and Tunisia. The government that accepted the mediator's report as a basis for Franco-Tunisian negotiations was defeated and eventually after a prolonged governmental crisis, on 13 May Pierre Pflimlin attempted to form a government excluding all well-known supporters of French Algeria, with a promise of further military action against the FLN as a prelude to ceasefire negotiations with the possible help of Tunisian or Moroccan intermediaries. The military in Algeria and the governor-general warned President Coty against any 'abandonment' or 'diplomatic Dien Bien Phu'. But Pflimlin wasn't likely to secure a favourable vote with the communists and the right against him.

In February 1957 the army had 340,000 men in Algeria. The military commanders were impatient with European efforts to block integrationist measures of equal citizenship. The policy of integration had become a fixed purpose and to secure any kind of Moslem support against the risks of FLN attacks, they knew they had to be a permanent presence. On the day Pflimlin was seeking investiture, a crowd of European activists took over the government buildings and when the army commanders arrived on the scene General Massu agreed to join a 'committee of public safety', hoping to keep control of it and to convince the parliamentarians to change course. The actual effect was that the Communists abstained on the vote and Pflimlin was elected by a substantial majority. The defiance action in Algiers to stop a government of 'scuttle' had actually ensured its election, and in the process massively increased its implications for metropolitan France.[5]

The army had connived at this revolt to secure a parliamentary reshuffle so that their mission would not be compromised. But sundry extreme rightists and Poujadists in Algeria and France saw the possibility of a general rising with the military pushed to its head. The Communists, to the partial embarrassment of the government, switched to out-right support of it and thereby increased its dependence upon them. Pflimlin, hoping that the army were really only controlling and not leading the revolt, confirmed General Salan's powers in Algiers. The military initiatives were to organise massive Moslem attendance at the perpetual demonstrations and to insist upon the inclusion of both Moslems and military personnel on the committees of public safety, to dilute the influence of the European activists, keeping metropolitan fascists from arriving and raising the temperature, and linking up with the quite limited local following of General de Gaulle. The more serious the crisis became the more unambiguous became their calls to de Gaulle to declare his position. Their attitude toward the main Gaullist spokesman for French Algeria, Jacques Soustelle, was governed by a fear that his arrival would be too provocative to the French government (and would discourage its resignation) and the fact that the locally recruited European territorial units arrived at the airport and prevented them from sending him away. The volatile influence of the territorials was reflected in their takeover of the most European city in Algeria, Oran.

On the other side of the Mediterranean the government initially contemplated resistance but discovered that they had no control over the state apparatus. De Gaulle, responding to a speech by Salan which had concluded 'Et vive de Gaulle', made it plain that he understood why the army had acted as it had, that he was available, but it was up to the Republic to elect him premier legally. Until the Algiers-based invasion of Corsica, the government contemplated holding out. But after they failed to prevent this, they faced a choice between acquiescing in the election of de Gaulle or attempting citizen resistance (which would have magnified their dependence on Communist backing) to parachutists invading Paris. De Gaulle was elected by the assembly against the opposition of the Communists, half the socialists and the remnants of the Poujadists. Algeria had been made a focal point of a number of larger questions. The army saw the acceptance of Anglo-American mediation as acceptance of an external constraint upon the policy in Algeria to which they were committed. The European activists were not in themselves of enormous importance. The Poujadists in France had already fallen back from their 12.5 percent in 1956. But they created a question mark for the army, which did not want to put down their initiative, because they too disliked the Pflimlin government. That the issue could so easily trigger a major reaction in metropolitan France in its favour must have depended partly on Pflimlin's dependence on the Communists—the very development of such an arrangement raised a host of other issues with far more direct metropolitan implications—and partly upon the existence of the de Gaulle option. The de Gaulle alternative enabled the military to build up the pressure without risk of starting a coup or a civil war, and gave the parliamentarians a way of giving in to a legal alternative rather than face a *coup* or civil war. If Algeria had become so important to France it was because it had been elevated to the status of a test of French power; the only possible responses to Sakiet were either to accept the constraints of international pressures in a manner that exposed the government to charges of national weakness or to raise the standard of national self-assertion even higher.

The events of May 1958 brought de Gaulle to power in circumstances which virtually tied him to keeping Algeria French. Pierre Laffont, editor of *L'Echo d'Oran*, describes how he had been receiving favourable responses to an editorial he wrote in favour of reform in a power-sharing direction. The revolt of May 1958 killed off this development because it brought a hope or expectation of total victory.[6] A French captain described how he led about 15,000 Moslems from the Casbah to the Forum to demonstrate for de Gaulle. This was the area that the parachutists had saturated militarily and in which torture had been used systematically to break up the FLN. 'Who would have thought this possible a year ago . . . there were barely fifteen of us in all [French soldiers] and none of us even carried side arms. It was a truly spontaneous movement . . . Whatever may be said this was a splendid recompense for us. The rest will follow automatically.'[7] When Algeria voted as a single electoral college for the first time in November 1958 nearly all the 71 deputies elected to Paris were integrationists. And at that stage the FLN did indeed seem to be on the defensive. The European-Moslem fraternisation during the May 1958 demonstrations became the focus of a myth. It would be impossible to sort out how far these manifestations were voluntary and how far they were created by coercion. But what is clear is that neither their scale, nor the confusion about how voluntary they were would have been possible without the massive French military presence and its commitment to stay in Algeria in perpetuity.

In August 1958 52 per cent of metropolitan French people thought integration a good idea (though only 40 per cent thought it possible) compared to 21 per cent who thought it a bad idea (and 26 per cent who thought it was impossible).[8] The French army outside the cities was engaged in warfare with openly organised FLN guerilla bands spread across a massive area, whereas in Northern Ireland the concentrated and urban space makes any such IRA activity largely impossible. None the less the contrast between the 400,000 French soldiers in Algeria and the peak of about 20,000 British soldiers in Northern Ireland is a difference of an order of magnitude. Likewise, the casualty rates are of different magnitudes. Whereas in Northern Ireland in sixteen years to date around 2,500 people were killed, in the first two and a half years until April 1957, 40,000 were killed in Algeria (30,000 FLN, 5,600 Moslem civilians, 900 European civilians and 3,400 French soldiers): roughly thirteen times higher per capita per year.[9] Where civil administration has remained in Northern Ireland, the military took over from the civil administration during the Battle of Algiers and much of their activity in the countryside was directly administrative. The military commitment of France to Algeria was much greater than the corresponding commitment of Britain to Northern Ireland.

It is often said that the French army in Algeria was more politicised than is the British army in Northern Ireland. Without going into the argument at length there is an obvious sense in which this must be true.[10] The investment of an enormously much larger French military presence involved a far more ambitious prospect, with correspondingly greater requirements of constant political support from metropolitan France and French governments. One of the things that made the eventual withdrawal from Algeria so difficult was that in order to pursue the project of military integration, the army had had to reassure not only Moslem military personnel but also civilians that it was there to stay. Thus the revolt of the generals in April 1961 was joined by many French soldiers because they saw the negotiations with the FLN as betraying their previous assurances.[11] The politicisation of the French military therefore had a lot to do with the fact that they had been launched into a project that could only be carried out with a massive and permanent commitment, and the events of May 1958 escalated the political development in what amounted to a military veto on government policy, creating a host of force-based illusions about the feasibility of integration. It is therefore probably true that the lower level of British military involvement in Northern Ireland also means a lesser temptation to the military to attempt to dictate policy.

Temptations to the military to intervene directly in political questions probably depend upon how proposed political decisions affect the cohesion and discipline of the army itself and upon how likely the intervention would be to succeed without making it obvious that a military intervention was being made in the first place. Short of outright military revolt and *coup d'état* there might be a continuum of possible types of intervention running down through refusal to carry out an order on grounds of conscience, honour etc; demand for greater resources to carry out what they are told to do which in the circumstances amounts to a veto; to a request for clarification of an order designed to draw out implications that are either concealed in or not spelt out in the order itself. Clearly the more a project has come to shape the military itself, the more any sharp change of priorities is likely to affect military cohesion. And a mutiny by a politicised element is more likely to be put down if the government is one the rest of the army feel confident in obeying. In the May 1958 situation the Pflimlin government was vulnerable both because it seemed to threaten an entrenched military commitment and because opposing it seemed likely to prise open metropolitan political divisions in a way that was very likely to produce a change of government.

The likelihood of anything like this happening in the context of Northern Ireland can probably be narrowed. First, the British political system doesn't contain (at the moment) the kinds of division that would make it easy to change a government by a May 1958 type shock. It might be a different matter if in the future the SDP-Liberal Alliance became an indispensable part of government in a parliament without a majority. But secondly, so long as Northern Ireland is not made a 'test' of British national self-assertion and is not linked up with or does not come to be proxy for major issues in British politics, the temptations to overt military defiance are probably low. For the same reason the capacity of unionists in Northern Ireland to trigger a defiance action with the expectation of military support are low.

The other side to this question is that the relatively low level of the British military presence means that it would be likely to object to proposals that required it to take on enlarged obstacles. Their reluctance to take strong action against the UWC strike of May 1974 may be a case in point.[12] While there is no strong evidence at the moment that the British army would resist its withdrawal from Northern Ireland, these kind of considerations might be of paramount concern in determining what the result of such withdrawal would be. 'Troops out' would be likely in practice to mean exactly what it said.

If British and the Irish Republic had become locked into antagonism over their conflicting sovereignty claims to Northern Ireland in 1971, they would not only have reduced the prospects of any internal agreement but would have allowed the antagonisms generated within Northern Ireland to shape their relations with each other more than they have actually done already. From 1972 there has been a zone of agreement between them to the effect that a solution requires some kind of bi-communal administration in the North with developing links with the Republic. For the Republic these links are the starting point of some form of Irish unification; for Britain they are a way of settling its relations with the island of Ireland as a whole. But whereas Britain has until 1985 accepted that an adverse unionist majority can block this process, the Republic's leaders' response to this blockage has

been periodically to call for either a British statement of intent
to withdraw or to revoke the unionist 'veto'

Since 1920 Northern Ireland has never been 'threatened' in
a way that might have made it a focal point of British national
egoism. Anglo-Irish understanding has made it unlikely that
it will ever be so. It has, however, been a perpetual preoccupation of the Irish Republic for which it is a 'lost' territory.
Opinion polls show in the 1970s that people of the Republic
are more strongly in favour of keeping the constitutional claim
to the whole island and more keen on the British declaring
intent to withdraw from Northern Ireland than are the
northern Catholics themselves.[13] The lost territory tends to
delegitimise the Irish Republic as the severance of the 'Polish
Corridor' did to the Weimar Republic, Yugoslav possession of
Macedonia did to Bulgaria, or the uncertainty over Fiume did
to pre-Mussolini Italy. The Irish case is only one of the most
spectacular such irredenta that has survived the upheavals of
the Second World War. But the Republic's claim to the North
is—in the absence of an entrenched guarantor role in relation
to Northern Catholics—the only way of upholding its guarantor role in an internationally recognisable form. The tacit
British recognition of this has been implied in the less than
total claim to sovereignty over the North (only so long as a
majority wishes it). This convergence helped to create the
constraints within which O'Neill had to operate, the space
into which the civil rights movement inserted itself and also
the reluctance of the British government to take decisive
interventionist steps in response to the civil rights movement.
(Harold Wilson's memoirs make it appear that Bernadette
Devlin's opposition to a strong intervention before August
1969 confirmed such reluctance.)[14] But once the British state
was trapped into its 'normal' national alignment with unionism after the introduction of internment in August 1971, the
inter-governmental understanding shaped the route taken
when the army shot 13 unarmed civilians at an anti-
internment protest in Derry in January 1972 (Bloody
Sunday).

The abolition of Stormont and the search by the Secretary
of State William Whitelaw for a bi-communal solution began
to draw the line as to how far Britain would go to assert the

kind of solution that could only be upheld by perpetual recourse to physical force. To make Northern Ireland as 'British' as Scotland would have generated military commitments and corresponding force-based political illusions that could only be sustained by everlasting military commitment. Given that where conflicting sovereignty claims are concerned, clarity can only mean antagonism, the effort to work for an internal solution with institutional links between the North and the Republic, necessarily generates a degree of uncertainty about sovereignty issues. At one level this uncertainty has helped to keep alive hopes for a reconciling rather than a repressive outcome. But at another it has made plain and may have magnified the lack of control of the two states (most importantly that of the ostensible sovereign Britain) over the internal situation.

In the whole period from 1969 to 1983, the year 1972 had most deaths, accounting for 21 per cent of the total. To mid-1983 2,304 people were killed by the violence of the 'troubles': 34 per cent of these were Catholic civilians; 22 per cent Protestant civilians; 7.5 per cent RUC and 6 per cent UDR; 16.5 per cent British Army; 9.5 per cent Republican paramilitants and 2.5 per cent Loyalist paramilitants. To November 1983 57.5 per cent of deaths have been caused by Republican and 26.5 by Loyalist paramilitaries. 11.5 per cent have been caused by the security forces; within this last figure civilian deaths caused by the security forces were 6.5 per cent of the total. A civilian was defined for this purpose as one 'without manifest connections with paramilitaries, security forces, prison service or police.'[15]

The pain caused by these violent deaths is not like that of losing someone close in an accident or by disease. The knowledge that it was intended by someone intensifies the loss and becomes haunting. Maura Kiely founded the Cross Group, a fellowship of families who had been bereaved by all the forms of violence of the troubles (both kinds of paramilitary and security forces violence.) Bitterness threatens to infect all moments of silence and reflection. 'Being bitter,' says Maura, 'gives them two for the price of one.' Representative violence—killing people because of what groups of people they represent— is a cancer that could know no limitations, dragging all its live victims into a cauldron of revenge against the people whom the killers purport to represent. To an outsider this might seem to be the most striking difference from his/her own society. But far more remarkable is the counteracting tendency. Despite having good reasons to be bitter and to see all-pervading malignant intent in the 'other', legions of people who have suffered appallingly do not do that. These people are not just being 'sensible' or 'rational' (these kinds of words can only be applied to people who are not actually at risk). They are showing faith in something that keeps them at one with others, refusing to see malignancy of motive wherever it might conceivably be, and in little or large ways taking risks to express that faith. If it wasn't for this, Northern Ireland would have torn itself to pieces long ago, there would be no possibility of co-existence under any conceivable political order and the avenging of every death as a martyrdom for a national cause would have produced two monsters intent upon inflicting absolute defeats upon each other.

However, representative violence doesn't need to trap everyone to have a coercive political effect. It is only necessary people who share the experiences of provocation that lead others to commit acts of violence, to feel that it is somehow provoked, to become convinced that only the removal of the source of provocation (the violence of the 'other') will enable their own condemnation or disapproval of the violence within their own environment to take effect. Politics is therefore largely concerned with the violence of the 'other'. The diametric opposition of political blocs reflects the different quarters from which violence is anticipated. Opposed political stances are not in most cases supports for opposed violences and so long as this remained generally true it was possible and frequent for some politicians of both sides to unite in condemning violence. It is often said by the politically apathetic that Northern Ireland would be fine if it wasn't for the politicians. Apart from the fact that they are elected by people's votes, this sentiment—benign in so far as it is a way of indicating that the speakers wish for peace—is one of the many ways in which the persuasiveness of violence remains unappreciated. People may live and endure all manner of risks and provocations, but political leaders cannot preach that they ought to endure without seeking remedies for them. When one group's risk is another's precaution, it is only by exercise of some restraint and acceptance of each other's good faith that politicians avoid accusing one another of intending violence against each other's constituents.

The SDLP, for example, never justifies IRA violence but it treats contentious cases of security forces violence as essentially similar, knowing very well that such violence provokes IRA terrorism. It is sharply critical whenever there is *prima facie* suspicion in the eyes of its constituents. It must be because there will be no respect for the law unless it is seen to be radically different from terrorism. Yet when these criticisms are linked up with statements to the effect that Northern Ireland's system of justice is wholly unreformable, such statements can be latched upon as 'proof' that the SDLP is really engaged in undermining the security forces in a more subtle way than the IRA. Likewise unionist support for internment or for the security forces in contentious situations may be motivated by a fear of undermining their morale and capacity to respond to the IRA. But the occasional outbursts about removing the restraints upon the security forces so that they can 'root out terrorists' can be latched upon to 'prove' that what unionists want is unbridled repression of Catholic areas. There is a general tendency in Northern Ireland—which is quite rational when the 'other' might be a source of real threat—to remember the statements from the 'other's' political leaders which seem to magnify that threat, and a tendency to infer that silence or a more cautious expression differs from these more hyperbolic utterances only in being more hypocritical. Verbal hints of violence are like violence itself: a magnet of attention.

Since 1971 the Provisional IRA campaign to secure a British withdrawal from Northern Ireland has been ongoing. It is the primary axis of confrontation because it is a direct challenge to state power, is incompatible with any internal agreement and has the capacity to exacerbate the underlying differences between the stances of the British and Irish governments. Despite the overwhelming self-description of Protestants as British (67 per cent) or Ulster (20 per cent),[16] the IRA and Sinn Féin believe that most would recognise they were Irish if Britain decided to withdraw. Such restraint as its campaign shows depends upon its belief that it is fighting an occupying force rather than an enemy population. Its violence is directed primarily at the security forces including the police (RUC) and locally recruited army regiment that replaced the B Specials, the Ulster Defence Regiment (UDR). But its claim not to be opposed to ordinary Protestants doesn't give much comfort to most unionists and Protestants who regard these British forces as not only their protection but part of themselves.

Loyalist paramilitarism was active during the August 1969 and August 1971 waves of intimidation. In 1972, shortly before the introduction of direct rule, Bill Craig launched the Ulster Vanguard movement, which included the Ulster Defence Association (UDA).[17] At a series of mass rallies, he threatened to set up a provisional government to oppose Westminster moves to change the constitutional *status quo* and spoke of 'liquidating the enemy'. The UDA and UVF (Ulster Volunteer Force), acting on the supposed lesson of the IRA that Catholics got what they wanted by violence, set out to do the same. If Catholic 'no-go' areas existed, they would create Protestant 'no-go' areas unless the British army put down the former. If the IRA bombed their territory, they would bomb Catholic territory. But whereas the IRA's primary enemy was the security forces and its bombing campaign was primarily against government and economic targets, the loyalists' enemy was the IRA which it couldn't identify. The random killings of Catholics escalated in 1972. Once the IRA was a real presence, vigilante beliefs in a general Catholic conspiracy against Ulster revealed gruesome implications. Restraining forces within unionism were severely stretched and 'to some who had criticised the [Orange] Order in the past it now seemed a source of stability and restraint compared with Protestant paramilitary bodies that had grown up.'[18] Protestant paramilitarism has tended to increase at times when expectations of a British 'sell-out' are high and to decrease at other times. It has also, since the UWC strike of 1974, attempted to find a political direction. In 1972, however, the rise of Bill Craig revealed something of the degree to which British distance from Northern Ireland was self-reinforcing. Ian Paisley, in a sharp change of stance influenced by Desmond Boal, the lawyer MP for the Shankill,[19] had opposed internment shortly before it was introduced. They both opposed the Payment for Debt Act passed to secure payment from anti-internment rent and rate strikes. And Paisley also supported the army over Bloody Sunday and did not oppose direct rule. If these stances were an effort both to secure possible alignment with the SDLP and to argue that intensifying the connection between Northern Ireland and Britain was part of a solution, the partial eclipse of Paisley by Craig in 1972 suggests that the distance between Britain and the loyalists was already a reciprocal and self-reinforcing tendency.

When Whitelaw set about putting together the power-sharing Executive, there was in the background a very high level of violence of all kinds. Only the recently formed Alliance Party had substantial bi-communal support with 9 per cent of the total vote, so the SDLP with 22 per cent (almost entirely Catholic) was indispensable to any bi-communal system. It has always contained two tendencies that cannot be clearly distinguished. The nationalist persuasion, despite opposition to the IRA, believes that with sufficient diplomatic clout and eventual British determination, the unionists could be required or persuaded to accept the 'justice', 'inevitability', geographically 'natural' qualities, etc. of Irish unification. On the other hand, there is a tendency to see the role of the Republic as a guarantor for a reconstructed system within the North in which Protestants and Catholics will relate to each other as equal citizens. Such a unity of hearts might lead to unforeseen developments in political identities. This is an effort to transpose the logic of the civil rights movement onto the escalated question of opposed national identities and break the ongoing antagonism between Catholics and the northern state. The unionists participating in the power-sharing system were that part of the Official Unionist party which remained with Brian Faulkner, the ex-Prime Minister, and secured 26 per cent of the vote in 1973 for the partnership concept. Unlike the Alliance party, which was built explicitly around the commitment to power-sharing within the

Northern Ireland context, the Faulkner Unionists had to draw supporters towards the idea of partnership and fend off the charge of slipping down the slope toward Irish unification. The various opponents of power-sharing and any Irish dimension (Craig's Vanguard Unionists, Paisley's Democratic Unionists and Harry West's section of the Official Unionist Party) collected 34 per cent of the vote split evenly between them.[20]

The power-sharing system could work so long as neither the Faulkner Unionists nor the SDLP used their ultimate resignation weapon to settle disagreements with each other or protest at the decisions taken by the Secretary of State over areas which remained his responsibility (notably security). In this case the Executive would lack support from both communities and the system would revert to direct rule.

It has been argued that it is extremely difficult to demonstrate that political decisions are objective and free of sectarian intent. It has also been argued that given the pervasiveness of territorialism, all distributive questions are intrinsically sectarian. O'Dowd et al argue that O'Neill's reforms merely substituted regional geographical sectarianism for the more blatant institutionalised sectarianism of the old local authorities.[21] My argument has been that it is never possible to remove the suspicion of sectarian intent or indeed possible to prove its absence so long as power is monopolised by one bloc. Power-sharing between representatives of the blocs was the obvious way in which precedents could be worked out for making fair distributive arrangements to unavoidably sectarian constituencies and allowing the different parties publicly to give each other credit for good faith. And so long as Westminster was prepared to foot the bill this had real possibilities. Overt clashes of sectarian interests could be avoided by ingenuity when resources seemed unlimited. In the longer term (after the onset of the 1975 recession and expenditure cuts) this would have become an ever more taxing problem for the executive had it survived.

The more fundamental difficulties focused on the possible use of resignation threats to protest over security policy and the development of the substance of the 'Irish dimension'.[22] From the Faulkner Unionist angle, the two things that the

Irish dimension might bring were greater co-operation in combating the IRA and southern recognition of the North as a legitimate entity. The SDLP—which had originally boycotted talks with Whitelaw in protest against internment and published its own proposal for British-Irish joint sovereignty as a transitional stage toward Irish unification—viewed Irish dimensions as steps towards unification. Where the ending of internment was for the SDLP essential to reduce the recruiting base for the IRA, the Faulkner Unionists might have accepted it only as a response to declining IRA violence. In fact, however, this was the period of peak loyalist violence and the introduction of internment for loyalists blunted the otherwise sharp edge of this question.

The Council of Ireland agreed between the British and Irish governments and the parties to the Executive at the Sunningdale conference was to prove the lightning conductor of loyalist discontent. Containing equal representation from the Executive and the Republic's government, it was to evolve its powers only by mutual (and unanimous) agreement. From John Hume's vantage point, some kind of reconstruction of the policing system was essential and only through the council would it be possible to find a way of breaking the antagonism between the Catholics and the police. But any effort to make the formation of the council a way of according a stronger recognition of the legitimacy of the North was blunted by the defence of the Sunningdale agreement argued against Kevin Boland's case in the Republic's courts.[23] The court ruled that the Sunningdale agreement did not contravene the constitutional claim to sovereignty over the whole island and provided fuel for loyalist charges that it was a half-way house to united Ireland.

The scale of loyalist opposition to the agreement became clear in the Westminster elections of February 1974 when all the pro-power-sharing Unionists were defeated by loyalist candidates. So the Ulster Workers Council (UWC) strike in May 1974, backed by loyalist politicians and paramilitaries, began against a background of proven support for its objectives. The argument that a more determined military obstruction of the early phases of the UWC strike might have allowed the Executive to survive ignores the essential vulnerability of an arrangement that was wholly dependent upon positive electoral support, as distinct from mere compliance. While it is true that the military did not obstruct loyalist road blocks in the way it would have republican road blocks, it did not want to create an overtly two-front confrontation (with both loyalist paramilitaries and the IRA) without a good reason for doing so. To have confronted the strike in this way, it would have been necessary to have a cast-iron commitment from the Faulkner Unionists to back up all the measures it took. In other words, it required a commitment from the Faulkner supporters not to resign and let the Executive fall, regardless of the scale of loyalist opposition that might have materialised in such a confrontation.[24] Had they appeared to sanction the use of heavy military force against the loyalist action, the fiction that Faulkner was engaged in a conspiratorial deal with the Republic, the SDLP and the British government would have gained ground rapidly and strengthened the loyalist counteraction. What the Faulkner Unionists might then have done, had the Executive survived through its dependence upon the military and in spite of (by then) exacerbated loyalist opposition would have been an open question. The UWC strike therefore put the Faulkner Unionists in the impossible position of having to give open-ended approval of measures necessary to thwart the strike and to secure enough electoral support afterwards to allow power-sharing to continue. It is certainly true that the strike was helped by intimidatory pressures, but given the level of popular support it enjoyed, the risks people took in opposing it would not have disappeared after it was over. Anyone with a family and nowhere else to go would have had to think not of the next week, but the next month or year. No military action could have removed that kind of risk. Finally the popularity of the strike was not without important positive aspects.[25] Some of the hitherto unknown leaders thrown up by it called for an end to internment (rather than just an end to internment for Protestants), attempted to articulate a concept of 'voluntary' as distinct from 'enforced' power-sharing, and broke democratising ground already broken in Catholic communities by the experience of the anti-internment strikes and self-organisation of community groups. Political initiative from paramilitaries began to grow in its aftermath, only to encounter obstacles from established loyalist politicians.

While some argue that the power-sharing system failed because Britain didn't take a strong enough line against loyalist opposition, another line of argument is that the SDLP and the Republic's government pushed for too much and the Council of Ireland prejudiced the future of power-sharing. Thus the suspension of the Council announced in the middle of the strike came too late to save power-sharing. The difficulty with this argument is that the SDLP, mindful of the problems of undoing the alienation generated by internment and Bloody Sunday, could hardly have entered a coalition government with the unionists without the explicit support of the southern government and the expectation that it would in some way anchor their position in the decision-making process in the North. They needed to appear anchored in some way and the Council was conceived as a means of doing this. To think ahead of the future development of the Council, no government in the Republic could ever abrogate the constitutional claim to the North (with all the difficulties of a referendum) until it could convince itself, the southern electorate and northern Catholics that either its own guarantor role in the North or that of northern minority representatives was entrenched and secure against a reversion to unionist majority rule.

After the fall of the Executive, the Convention elections of 1975 produced an absolute loyalist majority of 55 per cent and the Faulkner Unionists fell from 26 per cent to 8 per cent of the vote.[26] Not only did this bury the Sunningdale system but the efforts of some of Bill Craig's party to orchestrate an alternative system of 'voluntary coalition' never secured more than limited support. Thus the problems involved in securing Catholic influence in devolved administration were never seriously reopened. It is not likely that the SDLP would have been able to accept such a precarious arrangement, but the Convention majority report (which merely offered the SDLP chairmanships of some legislative committees) repudiated power-sharing in favour of majority rule. Since 1975 loyalist opposition to power-sharing (meaning anything the SDLP could call power-sharing) on the one hand and the SDLP's requirement of an Irish dimension (meaning a guarantee of permanent rather than transitional SDLP influence) remained fixed symbolic expressions of an unbridgeable difference.

The British government's rejection of the Convention report and the restoration of direct rule allowed the loyalist parties and SDLP to veto each other's mutually opposed desires for devolution without tending to reduce the distance of either bloc from Britain or to make direct rule a permanent arrangement. Only Enoch Powell and a section of the Official Unionist party wanted to strengthen direct rule and transform it into an effective integration of Northern Ireland into the UK on the same basis as the parts of Great Britain. But the very manner in which this integrationist position is argued indicates that it shares the sense of Northern Ireland's distance from Britain common to all other political tendencies. Integration is seen as a way of enforcing upon Westminster resistance to Dublin's 'interference' and obliging Britain to uphold Northern Ireland's membership of the UK in a way it does not at the moment. For almost identical reasons Ian Paisley wants the restoration of something like Stormont as a guarantee against the duplicity of British politicians. For the SDLP, devolution is a necessary part of expressing the Irish dimension which Powell and Paisley want to resist. For the Alliance party and the small Workers' party, important local decision-making bodies are necessary forums in which trans-sectarian politics can be practised.

The only thing all of these positions share in common is the sense that Britain, as it is at the moment, lacks the power and authority to bring internal cohesion and tranquillity. Direct rule was apparently the least divisive formula of government in the late 1970s, because it seems to have balanced all the conflicting alternatives in a mutually vetoing powerlessness. About two-thirds of both communities in 1978 believed Britain didn't really care what happened as long as there was not too much civil unrest. Around 60 per cent of both thought that but for the British government things would be worse than they were.[27]

The implications of this balancing rather than resolving of differences were brought out in various ways by the peace people, the hunger strikes, the electoral rise of the Paisleyites, and the appearance of Sinn Féin. The peace people were formed after a car driven by paramilitants crashed into and killed the Maguire children when its driver had been shot by a soldier.[28] Their aunt, Mairead Corrigan, and Betty Williams launched a series of marches for peace which were enthusiastically supported by massive numbers throughout the province. Many saw it as a women's initiative to put an end to a largely male-orchestrated chaos. What it showed was how much more widespread was the desire for peace than was the extent of agreement about what peace meant and how to achieve it. Once necessarily political questions emerged, so did their differences. But even if the scale of support for the peace people shrank after the period of marching failed to end the violence, the bonds it created amongst the shrinking numbers went far past the oratory about there being no differences between people. People with different experiences of where the violence came from communicated with each other and understood why they differed politically and what respecting each other's differences might mean. It is very unlikely that this period is the failure it is now represented as being by those who judge things entirely by 'decisive results'. What can never be quantified is what evils may have been prevented.

If the peace people showed how widespread was the desire for peace, the hunger strikes of 1980-81, during which ten republican prisoners died, revealed the roots of diffences very sharply. After 1975, when phasing out internment, the British government decided also to phase out the special category status of sentenced paramilitary prisoners. These, like internees, had been held in compounds which allowed them to largely organise their own routine. Secured by a hunger strike in 1972, this status left them in a twilight state between prisoners of war and ordinary criminals. People sentenced for crimes committed after March 1976 were to be housed in cells (H-Blocks) under tighter supervision. Courts are presided over by judges without juries ('Diplock Courts'). Frequently prisoners are held on remand for long periods (years) and then released without the charges being pressed, a form of backdoor internment. And large numbers of cases are tried in which the evidence consists of uncorroborated confessions extracted during interrogation.[29] More recently mass trials have been based upon the evidence of supposed accomplices who have turned prosecution witnesses ('Supergrasses'). And although mass house searches are not as common as they were in the early 1970s, patrols in republican areas frequently stop and search or ask the same people for identification week after week. Although some of this was experienced by loyalist areas, for the greater part it was a republican experience.

The restoration of direct rule after the fall of the Executive was regarded as a partial satisfaction by many loyalists who opposed its initial introduction in 1972, as the growing dependence of the security forces upon the RUC and the UDR rather than the British army made the direct rule administration more obviously aligned with unionism. Protestant paramilitarism declined sharply between 1976 and 1977. A second UWC strike (organised with Paisley's support but not that of the Official Unionists) to secure a restoration of devolved government and local control over security policy failed—and the police were active in resisting it. Whereas in the late 1970s 80 per cent of Protestants and 90 per cent of Catholics supported the view that Britain should take a tougher line on Protestant paramilitary groups, 55 per cent of Catholics and 95 per cent of Protestants took the same attitude toward the IRA.[30] When Bernadette Devlin stood in the EEC election of 1979 campaigning around the prison question she got 34,000 votes (6 per cent), at a time when H-Block prisoners were engaged in the 'dirty' and 'blanket' protests.

The hunger strikes of 1980-1 to demand what amounted to the restoration of special category status became a virtual referendum—not on support for or opposition to the IRA—but on whether the prisoners were 'ordinary criminals', as the government insisted, or not. A more certain way to polarise people round their own experiences of violence would have been hard to devise.

If most unionists had little sympathy with the loyalist paramilitary prisoners, they experience the IRA as murderers of their friends and relatives, whether RUC, UDR or prison warders. The circumstances of their deaths do not resemble military combat in declared wars, and most felt that any concession on this question would be a straightforward victory for IRA terrorism. But many Catholics who did not support the IRA, yet who came from areas of the internment sweeps of 1971, who knew people wrongly arrested or were themselves exposed to stop and search procedures, might all have felt as the one who said: 'I detest paramilitarism and deplore all violence. But no one is going to tell me that the paramilitary violence isn't provoked and that it's like self-gain criminality. It's twisted idealism but idealism all the same.' The Moxon-Browne survey in 1978 showed that Alliance party Protestants generally agreed with other Protestants in their rating of the three wings of the security forces. Alliance party Catholics were closer to Protestants than to other Catholics on the rating of the army, roughly half-way in between on the RUC and rather closer to Catholics in general on the UDR. But on the specific issue of RUC treatment of suspects in custody 'opinion polarises sharply between Catholics and Protestants within the Alliance party as well as outside it.'[31] Despite the efforts of clerical and peace groups, the Commission on Social Justice and the SDLP to represent the prison issue as a humanitarian question and to take account of the emergency procedures under which prisoners were convicted, all efforts to break the polarity failed. And when ten died they made a point about not being 'ordinary' criminals in a language which was unmistakable.

Although there has been a strong republican voting tradition in Fermanagh/South Tyrone, the election of the hunger-striker Bobby Sands as its MP and after his death the election of Sinn Féin candidate Owen Carron heralded the entry of Sinn Féin into electoral politics. To many Protestants it looked like a vote for murder. To many Catholics it seemed the only way to deny the British government's claim that the prison issue was a conflict between civil society and terrorism.

From 1981-2, when the Paisley DUP expanded electorally and Sinn Féin emerged, both have tended to absorb the socio-economic protest generated by the recession. Unlike the various small leftist parties or *ad hoc* protest groups, both of these parties have the attraction that any issue they take up gains clout as a result. The British government does not need to respond to protests about job losses, increases in public sector rents, social security cutbacks or school rundowns, because Northern Ireland's votes are no direct benefit to them and its concerns have no effect on British political alignments. The sense of Britain's distance is a two-way self-reinforcing process. The way to frighten British administration into taking notice is for the parties which are least inhibited about respecting institutional and bureaucratic procedures to take issues up. If the strategy works it convinces people whose primary concerns are material questions that this militancy pays. If it does not, it proves that Britain doesn't care. Both ways it undermines the legitimacy of institutional processes. Hence Paisley's opposition to monetarism and the presence within his party of people whose language on housing, welfare and employment questions would put them in the Labour party in Britain. Sinn Féin's socialist republicanism absorbs such tendencies without any of the hint of contradiction that characterises the Democratic Unionists. And the obvious consequence is to reinforce the tendency for all distributive questions to be seen in sectarian-territorial terms, and not to consolidate any class unity.

The polarisation generated by the hunger strikes, the rise of Sinn Féin and the Conservative government's plans to make an attempt to devolve powers to a local assembly raised difficulties for both the Alliance party and the SDLP. Although the Alliance party, which is committed to power sharing within Northern Ireland, has been able to raise about 30 per cent of the vote in the Belfast suburbs and the middle-class residential areas of the city, it has never been able to exceed 15 per cent province-wide. The 1982 Assembly elections faced it with a challenge to make power-sharing work in some form despite its compressed support. But the SDLP now faced a challenge from Sinn Féin which charged it with collaborating in the restoration of Stormont. At this stage it decided to boycott the assembly and to seek the support of the southern parties to oblige Britain to take seriously the need for something more than restored devolution. The very presence of Sinn Féin threatened to undermine the SDLP whose efforts to secure power-sharing had been thus far in vain and to make it more difficult for the SDLP or the southern government to guarantee any settlement. The New

Ireland Forum brought the SDLP and the three major southern parties together in an effort to work out the agreed position of constitutional Irish nationalism in relation to Northern Ireland. Meanwhile, the Alliance party and the two Unionist parties met at the Assembly.

The Forum report of 1984 spoke of three options: a United Ireland under a unitary state, a federal Ireland and a joint authority between Britain and the Republic over the North. It expressed its preference for the unitary state. It recognised that the unionists in the north wanted to preserve their Protestantism, their British identity and the economic advantages of the link with Britain. And it declared that unity could only be by consent. The subsequent interpretation of both the concept of consent and the preference for the unitary state delivered by Mr Haughey, the Fianna Fáil leader, seemed to boil down to the view that the unionists would have to accept the unitary context—the other two options would not deliver peace, he said—and could then consent or not to the details of the new constitution. The implications of the Report drawn by John Hume, Dr FitzGerald and Mr Spring, the Labour party leader, were very different and all saw it more as a statement of position for a conference agenda. But whatever way it was looked at, the unionist parties were not going to consent freely to any of the Forum proposals, since 59 per cent of all northern respondents and 83 per cent of Protestants rejected all three proposals. Thus, the application of strong pressures by the British government was presupposed in any of the various conceptions of the Forum.[32]

To get the difficulties created by and faced by the Forum into perspective, it is best to start from the Alliance party's criticisms. Oliver Napier stated that the Nationalists 'should not be tempted to confuse [their] aspirations with reality.' For example a joint sovereignty proposal would be seen by unionists as a halfway house to a united Ireland which would 'be resisted totally and absolutely'. The Forum had spoken of the need for a British response and its warning that failure to respond would lead to the collapse of constitutional nationalism sounds, said Napier, 'uncomfortably like blackmail'. But he also observed that the unionists by refusing to share power with constitutional nationalists 'had an enormous responsibility for the rise of Sinn Féin, whose victory at the polls was a justification for murder'. Unionists, he said, had to realise that power-sharing was not a demand by the minority but the 'minimum acceptable concession for support for the Northern Ireland state. No leader of the minority could now or at any other time deliver his support for anything less.' Since the Report was published with its preference for a unitary state and 'nothing about how you would build an administration in which both communities could participate', he said 'it was not practical politics.'[33]

As subsequent events have shown and the possibility was clearly visible at the time, the Alliance party are certainly right about the scale of loyalist disorder that would face any move tending to involve the Republic. They are also entirely sincere in making the warning without in any way summoning up the threat they speak of. But on the assumption that the unionist parties will retain an electoral majority they can also thwart any power-sharing scheme. The Official Unionists in their proposals, 'The Way Forward', sought what amounted to an integrationist mechanism for by-passing the power-sharing question. Despite having sizeable support amongst their followers for power-sharing they were, no doubt, wary of competition from the DUP. [34] A devolved institution would be like a local authority with administrative powers rather than the legislative powers of a parliament, and hence without the need of cabinet government 'with its concomitant requirement of a dependable constant majority'. They proposed a Bill of Rights passed by and amendable only by the Westminster parliament to deal with the fears of discrimination and accepted a case for state funding of Irish cultural activities.

The Alliance party saw the polarising potential of any initiative based on the Forum report and believed that only persevering in the context of Northern Ireland would ever deliver peace. The SDLP was aware that if they and the Republic's leaders did not exert themselves to find some way of entrenching nationalist influence in the North, there was a real danger of being outflanked by Sinn Féin—at which point no negotiated solutions to anything within Northern Ireland would any longer be possible.

Whether out of conviction that the Forum would lead to

Irish unification or sensing the need to take the wind out of the sails of Sinn Féin, the aftermath of the Forum was followed by a big drive to secure sympathy and support for the Forum's options from all elements, American, European and British, that could impress upon the British government the need for a positive response. Sinn Féin's attitude toward any such diplomatic and negotiating process is clear enough. Danny Morrison of Sinn Féin: 'In our opinion the British government is not ready to negotiate. She has not been tired out. Their will to stay has not been broken . . .' and Martin Mc Guinness of Sinn Féin: 'Loyalism is fascist—it is the major component in Britain's oppressive system—its leaders and its paramilitary forces must be confronted at every level . . . until loyalism as a political philosophy is destroyed, there can be no hope of justice, peace or freedom in Ireland.'[35]

Margaret Thatcher's early rejection of the three Forum proposals lifted unionist hopes and deepened nationalist dismay. But the Anglo-Irish Agreement of November 1985 has probably changed the situation irrevocably. The Agreement creates an inter-governmental conference at which proposals made by the Republic's government will be discussed and 'determined efforts' made to resolve any differences. But at the same time if any devolved administration is created, which both governments want to see happen, any matters becoming the responsibility of the devolved administration are no longer the concern of the inter-governmental conference. Britain remains the sovereign power but will facilitate a Northern Ireland majority wishing to unite the province with the Republic. The Republic recognises that the present status (i.e. British sovereignty) cannot be changed without the consent of the majority.[36]

The main changes from the previous situation are the commitment of the British government to make a 'determined effort' to resolve differences with the Irish government, and the latter's acceptance that majority consent is required for any change of status of Northern Ireland. Sinn Féin see this acceptance by the Republic as a derogation from the claims of Irish self-determination. The loyalist parties see the commitment to the conference as a form of Dublin control. The Alliance party, after initial hesitation, has decided to support it, the more so since physical loyalist opposition has materialised. Some sections of the SDLP see it as a way of securing communal equality of Catholics in the North; others see it as a step on the road to a united Ireland. The ingenuity of the agreement was to give expression to a joint governmental resolve in such a way that it also created strong incentives to unionists to start negotiations with the SDLP on power-sharing in order to reduce the impact of the conference. But with a few exceptions unionist leaders have taken the view that the agreement strengthens the SDLP's bargaining hand too much to make such discussions worthwhile. Hence the 'Ulster Says No' campaign, in progress at the time of writing.

Although any number of arguments might be presented to show why the efforts at voluntarily agreed solutions from within Northern Ireland failed before 1985, it was intrinsically unlikely that they would succeed. The British and Irish governments' stances certainly tended to reduce the capacity of internal forces to convulse the situation or to draw them into deeper conflict with each other. To some extent they allowed the antagonism at the base of the society to be expressed in relatively civilised differences of opinion about the form devolution might take. But they did not create a clear and coherent goal that different elements could be brought around together. That, of course, is because the easiest way to clarify opposed sovereignty claims is to magnify their non-negotiability. The safest way to avoid doing that is to preserve ambiguity. But ambiguity is not a very good anchor for anything, least of all when it requires positive electoral legitimation, as Sunningdale did but the much less ambiguous US civil rights process, which only required compliance, did not. The Anglo-Irish Agreement has attempted to clarify opposed sovereignty claims *without* making them the source of non-negotiable differences.

The onset of mass loyalist defiance of the Anglo-Irish agreement may seem similar to the Algerian colons' reaction to General de Gaulle's self-determination offer of September 1959. But as we shall see, the relationship is by no means simple and the outcomes are unlikely to be the same. Reading de Gaulle's task backwards over the years 1958-62, he had somehow to disengage France and its army from a commitment which was not only costly but created enormous difficulties for France's relationships with the rest of the world. This commitment was a perpetual source of possible disturbances which might feed back into France itself as they had done when he came to power. 'Needless to say I approached it with no strictly pre-determined plan,' he wrote. 'Only gradually, using each crisis as a springboard for further advance, could I hope to create a current of consent powerful enough to carry all before it. Were I to announce my intentions point blank, there was no doubt that the sea of ignorant fear, of shocked surprise, of concerted malevolence through which I was navigating would cause such a tidal wave of alarms and passions in every walk of life that the ship would capsize.' Of the military installations and contingencies he found in Algeria: 'On this vast apparatus, effective in preventing the situation from worsening but incapable of solving the insoluble, a wealth of ingenuity, conscientiousnes and patience was expended.'[37]

It is sure that he did not in 1958 or '59 envisage the kind of independence that eventually appeared. To use his own metaphors, the 'springboards' were to enable him to deal with each of the various questions separately which, had they been taken together, would have 'capsized the ship'.

At least four relevant questions can be separated. He had first to replace his dependence upon the military and civilian population in Algeria by mass support in metropolitan France; second, to expose the difference between the various notions of 'integration' so as to divide those who saw it as a possible choice for Algerian Moslems from those who saw it as a French imposition; third, to get the metropolitan French and the army to see that having accepted the principle of Moslem autonomy there was no one else to negotiate it with except the FLN; fourth, to secure some kind of workable safeguards from the FLN for the European population, holding up the possibility of partition of Algeria as a last resort if such safeguards were not forthcoming.

To deal with the last point first. It is doubtful whether he ever meant to partition Algeria at all, though he says that he found himself 'seriously considering it'. Ageron makes it clear that he never thought it practicable, despite the large number of advocates it had in 1960-61.[38] But even if he had done so at one stage, the possibility of retaining, say, Oran and Algiers must have become increasingly unattractive, first because they would have had to have been defended by the army which revolted against him in April 1961 and even more seriously because such French enclaves, which would then be part of French national territory, fell under the control of the OAS during the last year 1961-62. To have regularised relationships between France and these enclaves would have required direct co-operation with the OAS on an ongoing basis, with all the dangers that entailed. If no other reason had already made him decide to ditch partition, that certainly would have done.

Having reorganised the electoral system and the constitution in late 1958, de Gaulle was armed with emergency powers, the use of the referendum, and a system of government which was impregnable to all assault except that of an absolute majority of deputies voting against it. The electoral system boosted the size of his own UNR and virtually removed the Communists from the assembly. Before September 1959 the UNR and conservative supporters of French Algeria had a majority; after September 1959 the UNR and the left and centre parties would block any challenge to his self-determination proposals and any risk of a repeat of May 1958.[39]

In May 1959 and 1960 local and cantonal elections in Algeria produced an overwhelming majority of Moslem office holders, so that Europeans in Algeria had a very limited power to use local machinery to frustrate French policy changes by such actions as mayors' strikes. Their powers of disruption depended upon support they could gather from either the army or from metropolitan France. Otherwise they were limited to zones where they were predominant. The police, although often sympathetic to Europeans' political positions, had, since 1955, been reorganised within the metropolitan police system. A large part of the army was composed of conscripts whose enthusiasm for French Algeria was limited. The relatively independent Moslems elected in 1959 and 1960 could fudge their political position by calling themselves followers of de Gaulle (to distinguish themselves from nationalists or integrationists). Few were prepared to present themselves as a 'third force' and as de Gaulle's acceptance of the inevitability of independence increased, so did the advice he received from elected Moslems to the effect that he should negotiate with the FLN (GPRA).

The self-determination proposal of September 1959 was exceedingly nebulous. It offered three choices to the Algerian electorate—integration, total separation (which included partition to regroup Europeans), or association between an independent Algeria and France—but not until several years after a ceasefire. The crucial point about it was that the Moslem majority would have the last word and it was this that alarmed many of the colons and sections of the army who saw that it indicated a reduction in French commitment to the perpetual use of force. The revolt of the barricades in Algiers was a defiance action—the occupation of several public buildings by colon organisations—intended to force de Gaulle to retract the self-determination offer. In fact, it drew a crucial distinction between upholding integration as the only way to keep Algeria French and integration as a choice Moslems might be encouraged to make by such actions as de Gaulle had already taken—the single electoral college, the Constantine economic plan, the reservation of 10 per cent of French administrative posts for Moslems. Although some of the parachute regiments with substantial local membership tacitly supported the revolt, most sections of the army saw self-determination as quite distinct from power to the FLN (which at this stage it was) and did not support the barricades. When the insurgents shot and killed members of the gendarmerie, metropolitan French sympathy for the revolt evaporated. All de Gaulle had to do was to make sure that the revolt was unable to connect itself up with any metropolitan sympathisers. Hence, for example, when Amiens farmers demonstrating about farm prices took up the cry ' Vive Massu' (referring to General Massu whose criticism of self-determination and subsequent sacking by de Gaulle triggered the revolt), their immediate grievances were promptly bought off.[40] By simply refusing to reconsider self-determination, de Gaulle forced the revolt to buckle and in its aftermath compliant units of the French army dispersed insurrection sympathisers and closed down the locally recruited territorial regiments. The revolt of the barricades had buried the integration option by revealing what its keenest supporters meant by it. To reassure the military and to force the FLN into a negotiating stance, de Gaulle intensified the war in 1960 and secured a virtual military pacification inside Algerian territory.

The military success in 1960 was of limited significance given the 35,000 ALN forces in Morocco and Tunisia and growing international support for the FLN (notably from Russia and China). Having failed in the first negotiations with the FLN to secure a ceasefire, no other Moslem leadership materialised to negotiate about self-determination. In fact even the Moslem deputies elected in 1958 favoured negotiations with the FLN, a course toward which de Gaulle was necessarily obliged to move. When he spoke in October 1960 of a 'future Algerian republic', the gap between self-determination and an FLN government seemed to shrink, and his last visit to Algeria in December 1960 was marked by FLN demonstrations of urban Moslems and several European plans to assassinate him. When he put the self-determination proposal to referendum in January 1961 it was passed overwhelmingly in both metropolitan France and in Algeria, though the highest 'no' votes were registered in Oran and Algiers where Moslems observed an FLN boycott and Europeans voted against.

Shortly after renewed negotiations with the FLN were announced—but still within the context of negotiating with 'all tendencies'—came the generals' revolt of April 1961. For many of the military participants, such as its leader General Challe, the revolt was a question of honour. Having accepted that self-determination did not mean FLN power, they had refused support to the barricades revolt and intensified the military action in 1960. They now hoped that by taking power in Algeria they could step up the campaign and somehow present France with an effectively secured Algeria that de Gaulle could not refuse to accept as such. Clearly this scenario was a non-starter. But for other military elements and for the European OAS the revolt was aimed at toppling de Gaulle himself and extending military rule to France to ensure full backing for the campaign in Algeria. Colonel Argoud, for example, considered that France had won a military victory in 1960 but it was corrupted by the consumer society. Europeans were outnumbered and that was the major problem but they lacked determination ('preferring their casseroles to machine guns').[41] With Rhodesia and South Africa in mind he dreamed of mobilising France to making Algeria really French, which if it was to mean anything in practice would have implied a renewed thrust of settlement colonisation backed up by an imperially orientated France. De Gaulle appealed over the radio and TV to the conscripts and loyal sections of the army to immobilise the insurgents and the last military obstacles to his policy were removed. It was to spare France from this kind of adventure that just about the whole French political spectrum supported de Gaulle. He had diagnosed the military enthusiasm for French Algeria as 'a sort of crusade in which values attendant on risk and action are developed and affirmed', and once the 1961 revolt made it clear what keeping French Algeria involved, comfortable bourgeois as much as the left recoiled from French Algeria. Presented with a straightforward choice between de Gaulle's order and Argoud's crusade, there was no choice.

The military campaign in Algeria had uprooted whole areas and about 1.5 million people in a so-called regroupment strategy to destroy 'terrorist bases' and facilitate control over them. The worst of these were virtual prison camps. This same strategy also, together with rising Moslem rural under-employment, led to an enormous growth of Moslem population in the main urban areas which had once been much more European.[42] Once the generals' revolt collapsed and the negotiations with the FLN were no longer part of a supposedly larger negotiation with 'all tendencies' but about the future organisation of Algeria, the French state control in European zones of Algeria shrank dramatically.

In Algiers and Oran the OAS spread rapidly . In July, during a breakdown of negotiations, de Gaulle threatened to partition Algeria and rioting broke out in Algiers and Oran as rival elements attempted to assert territorial control. The ex-military element in the OAS leadership opposed partition and the efforts of indigenous European elements to treat this proposal seriously were crushed between French refusal to discuss the question with armed elements and the OAS murder of 'partitionists'. The deterioration in Oran which had been relatively tranquil in mid-1960 was total as the OAS tightened its grip.[43]

The French administrative centre was moved out of the cities to fortified encampments and its largely fictional control in the cities depended on the 25,000 (metropolitan) gendarmes and CRS. The OAS strategy, insofar as there was one, was to prevent the negotiations between the French government and the FLN from reaching agreement, by stirring up such strife that the FLN and French army, of which there were still about l00,000 soldiers in Algeria, would be forced into collision. In the last six months of the war in the Algiers zone, the OAS killed three times as many people as the FLN had killed since 1956.[44] There were about 2,000 to 3,000 OAS members in Algiers (about 1 per cent of the European population). The OAS is probably one of the clearest exmaple of violence generating reasons for itself, finally proving that violence that has corroded all restraint is nothing except violence. The ultimate objective of breaking French control and forcing France back into a confrontation with the FLN was intended to leave de Gaulle with no choice but to negotiate with the OAS and re-establish French rule through it. It continued to talk of restoring the fraternisation of Europeans and Moslems of May 1958, claiming to know the difference between pro- and anti-French Moslems. Parts of it made efforts to prevent straightforwardly racist attacks, but it had only one asset—its control over its own areas—and one weapon of communication with those outside its strongholds: violence. At one moment it would describe its actions as intended to reassure pro-French Moslems that they were not alone, and at others to wipe out Moslem professionals to force Moslem society to depend on European professions. At one moment it would 'condemn the lie' that it had told Europeans to dismiss Moslem employees, and at another it would exclude them from European areas for fear of espionage. At one moment it would punish Europeans to prevent them from leaving and at another, attack Europeans who intended to stay (when the Evian agreements were signed).[45] But its main effect was to ensure that so great was the danger of Moslem reprisals in the event of victory that the vast majority of Europeans, whether innocent or guilty of the OAS atrocities, felt unable to stay if ever it should be defeated. At the end of 1961 it looked as though it might be succeeding and the FLN feared to make a ceasefire with the French lest the OAS establish control in the cities. But by then it was spreading through metropolitan France with attacks on communists and liberals—and French anger against it mounted. To both the French government and the FLN, OAS seemed, at that point, a greater threat than either was to the other. In reaching agreement on a transitional Provisional Executive, the French and the FLN agreed to leave the control of Oran and Algiers in the hands of French administration. The FLN did this in order to avoid getting caught in conflict with the OAS and jeopardising the ceasefire; the French did it in order to provide some ostensible protection for Europeans. At this point, the OAS declared war on the army (as well as the police) leading to the battle of Bab-el-Oued. 'How have we been able to arrive at this confusion, at this defiance, at this collective suicide: to declare war on the French army? We have fallen in to a derangement without hope and we are stuck there. Since nothing can be saved, everything might as well be destroyed,'[46] said Gabriel Conessa, a young man from Bab-el-Oued, shortly after the Evian Agreement. In fact the OAS attempted to do precisely that—'to leave Algeria as they found it in 1830'—before it collapsed, plunging the million people who feared reprisals for its actions into the exodus of 1962. Algeria endured enough territorial conflict in Oran and Algiers to reveal the possible implications of such violence had the opportunities for it been more widespread. The OAS hold over the European population within its territory rose in proportion to the danger of reprisals for its actions. It had outside odds of success which depended on forcing the French state and army into renewed combat with the FLN; but the odds were sufficiently low that they eventually led to the self-defeating attacks on the French army and police to force them into alignment with itself. The OAS could not have withstood the FLN alone. Once on a losing trajectory without a clear strategy and reduced to gambling, violence was used for a legion of self-contradictory purposes. When success became more and more elusive anything might be attempted because no single approach would work. So long as people clung to what were in fact impossible objectives—and it was difficult not to, when to question them was treason or contemplation of the ultimate horror of defeat—virtually any suicidally and often self-contradictory reasons for violence remained 'rational'. That is a reasonable definition of irrationality. Those who had either persuaded or imposed upon the working-class colons the view that French Algeria could be held had trapped them into a fireball, in which reasons for violence sprawled in all directions.

By contrast the FLN capacity for violence became by the end more and more latent. There were 35,000 FLN forces in Morocco and Tunisia, able to enter Algeria after independence compared to about 6,000 within Algeria. The OAS violence to force the FLN and the army back into conflict with each other had had the opposite effect of making them more anxious to reach agreement. But if the Oran/Algiers situations had covered a wider part of Algerian territory, it is doubtful if the FLN would have taken the risk of agreeing to leave them under French control after the ceasefire or of so resolutely attempting to prevent reprisals for OAS violence. The weakness of OAS numbers therefore led first, to the self-defeating OAS attacks on the French state apparatus rather than simply trying to hold its ground; second, to the preparedness of the FLN to risk leaving Oran/Algiers under French control; and third, to the certainty of the exodus when it was over. In the end the violence of the defeated plunged into irrationality, while that of the victor became more restrained, instrumental and approximate to that of a rule-governed state, which it was about to become.

The central point about any analogy between de Gaulle's treatment of Algeria and the likely behaviour of British governments in relation to Northern Ireland is almost certainly not a similarity of outcome. It is rather that de Gaulle's priority was always to be seen to be in control of events—even when his control was nearly fictional—and never to allow Algeria to visibly dislocate French state power again as it did when he himself was brought to office. Britain, given the limits of its capacity to control events in Northern Ireland, probably has no more of a fixed 'plan' or interest in a particular outcome. It certainly does have an interest in avoiding impossible obligations, as the failure to fulfil them would dramatically expose its powerlessness. Republicans believe that Britain could organise an orderly withdrawal leading to Irish unification. Loyalists believe that Britain could repudiate all efforts by the Republic to shape what is going on in the north and at the same time crush the IRA militarily. If these beliefs are not fictions, they are certainly obligations of a kind that Britain is unlikely to adopt. If the pressures of violence and disorder wreck the Anglo-Irish Agreement, an altogether more probable outcome would be to conclude that there was no way of preventing both blocs colliding directly and finding the way to minimise British responsibilities for regulating the outcome. In that respect they might copy de Gaulle but with quite different results.

If, after the Forum Report, something like the Anglo-Irish Agreement had not been made, the Republic's only way to vindicate its proclaimed guarantor role would have been to raise Northern Ireland related questions in international forums. This would have drawn the British government closer to unionism both because the repudiation of the Forum would have been total and because it would have had to defend itself in essentially unionist terms against international criticism. There have been many border incursions,[47] but the chances of one being transformed into a Sakiet would have risen (even without the incident having anything like the same military characteristics). That Britain has chosen not to confront the Republic's claim, but rather to find a way of recognising it and institutionalising it, reflects a refusal to turn Northern Ireland into a test of British national self-assertion. In the long run it may turn out to have reduced the risks of polarising British opinion on Northern Ireland in ways that would have been far more dangerous for people in Northern Ireland itself.

Like the revolt of the barricades against Algerian self-determination, the loyalist protest against the Anglo-Irish Agreement has probably magnified the distance between the metropolitan British and Northern Ireland unionists. As during the barricades, attacks on the police by people who had been supposed to be their supporters had negative effects on the metropolis. But that is where the necessary similarities stop. The self-determination proposal could not have worked without a Moslem 'third force' appearing or without an FLN ceasefire and participation in the process. Neither of these things was likely to happen and the revolt of the barricades probably reduced any chance of the first. Thus whereas self-determination was, as Colonel Argoud put it, a 'question mark' or, as de Gaulle might have called it, a 'springboard', the Anglo-Irish Agreement creates an institutional procedure between the British and the Irish governments without any 'question marks' about negotiating with the IRA. It does not *need* to become a 'springboard', though it might become one if sufficiently disrupted.

The hopes of both the Republican and Loyalist opponents of the AIA hang upon making it valueless or unworkable by disruption and heightening of tension. Significantly for both, not only their own but also their opponents' violence and disruption are an argument in favour of their own positions. Escalation of IRA activity could thwart the improvement in security which has been one of the main arguments offered in its favour. It could be a pretext for Britain not to respond to the Republic's proposals dealing with reforms in the administration of justice, an added obstacle to any efforts to improve relations between the security forces and Catholic areas. The escalation of loyalist violence is already creating a second front deterioration in relations between the police and loyalist areas, generating threats to Catholics which the police are hard-pressed to deal with. Fear of loyalist reaction also might frighten the British government away from Irish government proposals. The whole process might convince both the British and Irish metropolitan parties that the exercise has been futile. In this case there would be no other position for Irish parties to fall back upon except the view that Northern Ireland was 'unreformable', to demand that Britain 'withdraw' and themselves to shed as much responsibility for anything that happened there as possible. If the agreement collapsed it would be hailed as a victory by extreme loyalists and leave Britain ruling an area on terms that appeared to have been dictated to it by demagogues who had threatened 'civil war'. That could not be seen by British politicians as other than a demonstration of weakness, unless there were some British politicians who chose to make Northern Ireland a test of national self-assertion.

A move by British politics in this direction would depend on an outburst of popular national egoism sufficient to sweep away concerns about Anglo-Irish co-operation or relations with the EEC. Conceivably a default by a major debtor country might set off a worldwide economic crisis, creating a domino effect of bank collapses and sharp international credit squeeze. The disruption of trade and economic activity generally might create impossible conflicts of interest within the EEC and force it into collapse in national recriminations. If these exacerbated Anglo-Irish relationships, and the economic radicalisation that the crisis gave rise to became linked up with heightened national egoism, it is not inconceivable that both countries might generate large political currents identifying more closely than any do at present with opposed national antagonists in Northern Ireland. But this possibility takes us backwards into hopefully improbable analogies with chapter five. It suffices to say then that the prospect of a British government making or finding the collapse of the AIA a proof of strength rather than weakness (and backing it up with heavy military force to affirm that Crossmaglen is as British as Finchley) is highly unlikely. It is far more probable that the collapse of the AIA would be treated as an indication of a fundamental loss of control. It is these possibilities that I shall follow up now.

In what follows I shall suppose that there are no strong metropolitan British interests in favour of keeping Northern Ireland for reasons of their own (there may be, but their existence won't substantially complicate the argument). What Britain does not need at the moment is a flood of refugees from Northern Ireland. When the colons went to France in 1962 it was during an economic up-swing with near full employment. So far, having not made Northern Ireland a test of national self-assertion and having preserved the semi-fiction that the conflict is a 'religious' conflict, Britain has had only limited difficulty in repudiating the unionists' claims that Northern Ireland should be governed according to their guidelines. But if the AIA were wrecked, expelling British citizens from the UK would be an altogether different proposition. Northern Ireland unionists, unlike Algerian colons, can make a strong case (that it is contested is not the point) on principles of democratic right of national self-determination. For a British government to accept openly a 32-county self-determination right as superior to that of the six counties would be quite different from saying either that it itself had no interest in keeping the six counties any longer than their inhabitants wished or that so long as unionists are part of the UK, they must accept the will of the UK parliament. Even de Gaulle hedged this kind of question as far as French public opinion was concerned by talking of partition to create French enclaves in order to make people in France believe that all conceivable solutions were being studied for protecting French nationals. [48] He only abandoned these notions publically when the OAS activity escalated. Then he concentrated the risk of a French backlash against overt abandonment of the Algerian French minority into the last year when the 1961 military revolt had been put down, when self-determination (in the abstract) had won an overwhelming referendum majority and when OAS violence had become an overt threat to order in metropolitan France. Furthermore by this stage France had already gone through and seen the consequences of such self-assertion in relation to Algeria. A British government deciding to accept the 32-county Irish self-determination claim would run the risk of taking the Northern Ireland question into an area it has hitherto not taken and a headlong collision with all the latent forces of British metropolitan egoism.[49] It is scarcely realistic to suppose that any British government would move into these waters without very compelling reasons indeed. If loyalists began to behave as the OAS had done, that might be such a reason, but even if it was, the faults in the 'analogy' would rapidly surface. Whereas it was only necessary to pull out the military supports from underneath French Algeria to let it collapse, to achieve the same effect in Northern Ireland—given relative weights and strengths of sectarian numbers—would require positive action against loyalists of a prolonged nature. The prospects of a concurrent ceasefire arrangement between the

British army and the IRA while this was going on are not only more remote in principle but far less likely to be sustainable; yet this was a background condition during the brief period when the French military exerted itself against the OAS. By far the safest way for a British government, concerned to shed responsibility for Northern Ireland after having had the AIA collapsed by internal pressures, would be to let unionism expel itself from the UK, to remove metropolitan troops and reduce the level of financial support to a successor regime so as to enfeeble it and ensure that it had to develop some co-operation with the Republic; yet at the same time not to run the risk of driving it into complete collapse and starting an exodus. Above all else, once Britain had placed sufficient distance between itself and a successor regime, it could wash its hands of direct responsibility and place the burden of 'wooing' unionists entirely in the Republic's hands.

For de Gaulle, the preservation of co-operative arrangements with independent Algeria became the key to his worldwide neutralist policy and his massive influence in the third world. The Oran/Algiers enclaves would have required large-scale metropolitan military protection, would have destroyed friendship with Algeria (and conceivably complicated the Sahara oil question). It was much simpler to let them simply fold up. There would be no comparable advantage to Britain in attempting to coerce northern unionists into a united Ireland. None the less it may be argued that there are British parties that support Irish unity 'by consent' and there is widespread support for 'troops out' of Northern Ireland. A Labour government (or a coalition including the SDP/Liberal Alliance) might come to power elected on a programme of 'united Ireland by consent' and 'troops out'. It might call an All-Ireland conference which no unionist leaders attended because they knew they could not deliver support for the outcome. Meanwhile loyalist paramilitants built up readiness to create citadels. If the British military were ordered to squash this development, they would demand a very large troop increase to do it, because under these circumstances they would be unlikely to get any kind of local security force help (even if they didn't find themselves in direct collision with them). Immediately the contradiction between 'united

Ireland by consent' and 'troops out' would become glaringly obvious. In Algeria the OAS offensives against French police and military were designed to force the French state back into alignment with them, because without that happening they were defeated, so the military response only needed to be episodal. In Northern Ireland action against loyalist citadels would have to be prolonged because they could resurrect themselves and survive after the disengagement of metropolitan British troops. As the full implications of this unfolded, the risks of a successful defiance action might rise rather than fall. For loyalist purposes the mere departure of metropolitan troops would suffice and it is easy to see how confrontation would be avoided. It is absurd to suppose that loyalist politicians would not agitate for immediate mobilisation to strengthen their 'bargaining' hand. If they could get up such a strong agitation against the AIA, the reaction to impending Irish unification is not in any doubt at all. The idea that most ordinary unionists would have the space to resign themselves peacefully to the prospect of Irish unification, if they were anywhere near the possible (and numerous) focal points of defiance actions is simply foolish. A policy based on the pretence that this would happen would either get shipwrecked or it would be either intentionally or half intentionally a disguise for a quite different policy. The belief that eventually a British de Gaulle will be 'strong' enough to create a 'clean' solution to Northern Ireland is a chimera, because it fails to grasp that de Gaulle's magic was to give his very limited power over events in Algeria the appearance of strength. There is all the difference in the world between eventually giving the OAS a bloody nose when it was already gyrating into the irrationality of total defeat, and preparing a major effort to induce Northern Ireland loyalists to 'consent' to Irish unification. Insofar as Algerian colons consented to anything it was the impending ALN troop arrival, not French power, which did it. A British government might make carefully limited gestures to do this for the record but actually set up a process in which loyalist self-expulsion from the UK was a tolerated alternative outcome.

Whatever pretences surrounded a British withdrawal process the precautions likely to be taken would include:

avoidance of commitments to dismantle loyalist defiance that would become ongoing, as distinct from episodal; avoidance of situations in which there were risks of clashes between British metropolitan and Northern Ireland security forces; dismantling of any obligations for physical re-engagement under any short-term pretext; provision of sufficient economic resources to whatever 'interim' successor institutions that were left behind to prevent a massive dislocation; the occasional use of cuts in those resources as levers to oblige successor institutions to negotiate with the Republic, though to what end might remain carefully ill-defined. But these kinds of sanctions would scarcely be precision instruments and the one consistent guiding thread in the whole procedure would be to minimise British responsibility for things which it judged it could no longer control. It would leave itself as much latitutde in defining acceptable outcomes as it reckoned would cover all likely or possible developments that the use of economic leverage alone couldn't prevent.

9

Beginning of the End or
End of the Beginning

This last chapter has an internal and an external focus. Internally it is addressed to the people of all politics and none who despite their political differences know that chaos will bring more chaos and that peace requires its prevention. Externally it is directed towards anyone who, after reading this far, is feeling uneasy with the way in which I have suggested that simple political solutions are exhausted. Where does such a conclusion stand in a comparative perspective?

The complexities of the conflict are a warning that the ways of developing any coherent authority may be nearly broken. Without overt and institutionalised co-operation of the British and Irish governments, sustained by a substantial degree of internal compromise, we are back in chapter eight. Both points can be illustrated in the recent histories of Cyprus and Lebanon. Endless, very complicated arguments might rage about which internal group or groups broke up either country. But it was a sufficient condition for their break-up that the external powers drawn into each had little interest in building an authority embodying any joint responsibilities (as distinct from their powers). There is no certainty that the British and Irish governments have such a determination either, but at least the chances are much better than with Greece and Turkey in Cyprus, or Syria and Israel in Lebanon.

The major subject of discussion in this area is the Anglo-Irish Agreement of November 1985. It is held to be undemocratic both by unionists because it lacks majority support in Northern Ireland and by republicans because it accepts the partition of the island of Ireland, which they consider is the legitimate unit. The only way to create an authority equally desirable and equally objectionable to both communities is to impose the framework. Internal forces must then develop the detailed rules which permit the framework to be overturned only by an agreed alternative produced by both communities. Headcounting in an ethnic frontier arena is only democratic when its favourable and unfavourable aspects seem to be evenly distributed. If such authority is not imposed *then* the claims often made that Northern Ireland is a zero-sum conflict might very likely come true.

Secondly, to get to any kind of symmetrical situation in the Northern Ireland context it is clear that it must begin with a shift in the balance of power toward nationalists. In chapter seven we considered what the future of Northern Ireland might have been if Britain had imposed integration before August 1969 when few unionists favoured such a move. One can only speculate as to what would have happened, but the result could scarcely have been as bad as what has actually happened. Today total integration is becoming more popular among unionists, but the spur to organise in favour of it is clearly the hope of neutralising the Anglo-Irish Agreement. Likewise many unionists now believe that power-sharing is the solution, though in 1975 many who may have agreed with it in the abstract voted against it in practice in order to oppose the particular version that had recently been overthrown. Dominant societies are always constrained. Moderates fear to act lest their initiatives be jeopardised by the militants in their own community, who effectively have a veto over their actions. In such a society, it is impossible to wait until internal agreement can be found before making moves toward communal equality. The Anglo-Irish Agreement has the virtue that it has imposed something which in the first instance requires no more than compliance.

Consider how the US South might look had George Wallace's 1968 vote there been translated into a veto upon the 1964 and 1965 Civil Rights Acts. White southern moderates who cautiously argued that these were actions of the federal government which must be complied with would have been set back. By contrast, what has actually happened is that as compliance has become routine, it is now much easier to call these acts foundations of a more just new order. Although there can be no way of proving the point, it is probable that the exercise of authority that once secured only compliance eventually generated legitimacy.

In Northern Ireland, external imposition would indeed be undemocratic if there were signs that both blocs had a common understanding of the undeniable evils of British mediation. Yet the pattern of past development has never created the space for such an understanding or compact. Britain has remained a feeble pivot of antagonism, allowing it to regenerate itself but also restraining its worst possibilities.

After the re-imposition of direct rule in 1972, unionism was largely compliant, and British power was locked into something like an occupation of some republican areas. To nationalists the alleged 'shoot to kill' policy looked like a licence to err on the side of incaution, knowing that killings in contested circumstances will be condoned (even where actual intent is not imputed, as it often is). To unionists, meanwhile, any effective means of stopping IRA murders often seemed welcome. People who experience the security forces as a threat and people who experience them as their defence against terrorism cannot possibly view them in the same light, even when both condemn violence and use such influence as they have to prevent it from emanating from their own community.

Only one kind of authority has a chance of becoming legitimate and of being seen to be restrained within the law. It is an authority that would undermine *itself* were it to rely on one community to maintain tranquillity by policing the other. Thus, unless both the British and Irish governments have both powers and responsibilities as guarantors of the respective communities, no legitimate authority is *ever* likely to emerge. How this works out in practice cannot be foreordained: it is a process. What was certain was that the first steps in this direction would be greeted with cries of betrayal (of unionism by Britain and of republicanism by the Irish government). If betrayal means the abrogation of undivided claims to sovereignty it is hard to see how it could be otherwise. But lest any metropolitan think otherwise, people on the ethnic frontier who utter cries of betrayal are not just being 'unreasonable' in a metropolitan way. All nationalisms conceal possibilities for force and the apparently normal condition of tranquil nation states sets up temptations to violence amongst those who don't enjoy such 'normal' conditions.

The rest of the world seems to teach us a lesson: violence works. The parts of the world most of us know anything about are often scenes of violence. The world is full of respected political leaders who were once 'terrorists'. Most of us perhaps owe more to violence done on our behalf than we know. Major Denoix de Saint-Marc's question about whether he would have survived the experience of Nazi concentration camps had it not been for the 'terrorist bombing raids' of Dresden and other German cities pinpoints a much more universal question relevant to people who live in the shade of metropolitan order.[1] Violence does often bring a much deeper peace than whatever went before. The Algerian example is an obvious case in point. A clue as to why this might be so is that at the end, when FLN factions were fighting each other over the inheritance, peasants threw themselves between them crying 'Enough, leaders.'[2] In other words, only when the original pretext for violence had disappeared was it possible for the mass to restrain those for whom it had become a way of life. An example better related to the resolution of national conflicts and leading to a higher form of co-existence would be that of the Yugoslav communist Partisans. In a country chronically traumatised before the war by Serb/Croat conflict, the Italians and Nazis set up a puppet Croat dictatorship over much of Croatia and Bosnia-Herzegovina. (Bosnia Herzegovina was roughly one-third Croat, one-third Serb and one-third Moslem.) Had the Partisans, as the Allied powers insisted they do, allied themselves with Serbian Chetniks, the liberation from the Croat Ustashi would at least in some areas have been a Serbian vengeance for Croatian extermination, and the victory would not have been a multinational achievement. Two things may have helped to avoid this: first, the Croatian partisan involvement in the liberation of Italian annexed (rather than Ustashi controlled) areas of Croatia; second, the strength of the Partisans when Italy capitulated and the backing eventually accorded to them by the Allied powers. Thus, the Partisans were able to assemble a fully multinational army *before* the victory, excluding no national bloc from participation in the defeat of Nazism, Fascism, Croatian Ustashism or Serbian Chetniks. The long-run solution to ethnic antagonisms in Bosnia-Herzegovina may have been the Moslem birth-rate (now over 50 per cent of the population) and their recognition as a separate nationality.[3] But in this case, as in Algeria, if the outcome had delivered peace, it is because the victory was simply overwhelming— and the enemy in each case totally discredited. The OAS violence and its weakness cemented the FLN-French agreement. The Ustashi went down with the Third Reich in total war, the communist Partisans having full Allied backing. These successful violences work, not because they are intrinsically just but because they create a category of expelled devils. In other words, the cohesive values of the new order are religious. And in that way they resemble the nationalisms of longer established nation states. It is not that nationalisms are necessarily wrong about the evils of those expelled. In the final phase of conflict, when everything is antagonised, they are right by definition, because everything is judged from the standpoint of those who are still there afterwards. No nationalism would be cohesive if it *didn't* make these claims. But along the way the less spectacular or 'effective' ways in which opponents upheld values of co-existence get forgotten. Every colon who did not give the OAS encouragement—and there must have been many who were trapped in a position where they were forced to live in its shade—or who left without burning their furniture or wrecking their apartments to prevent Moslems using them, not to mention the firemen who dismantled the tanker bomb the OAS planned to launch into the Casbah, did more for peace in Algeria than those in Paris who voted the way de Gaulle called upon them to do and who may have been tempted to compare their civilisation with the chaos of the colons.

Violence 'works' when it draws a very sharp line between the liberating violence of yesterday and the order of today; when internal distrupters of the peace can be criminalised and relations with foreigners monopolized by the state. Internal force fields between citizens are abolished. And this 'lesson' is in one way or another taught to everyone everywhere who lives in the middle of a force field. What is not necessarily taught—indeed it cannot be because the example is set by victorious violence—is how much purely capricious violence, how much trauma is buried, how much sheer hatred is dressed up as virtue. Just about any atrocity committed by victorious violence can be shown to have 'shortened' a war and gambling with violence can be safely portrayed as a celluloid 'adventure', so long as the victory is a secure fact. Victorious violence converts half-truths and some lies into what pass for truths.

So what is it that is so attractive about this secure national order? Is it that the nation can celebrate the expulsion of 'evil' as that which unites them together; celebrate the triumph of arms that led to it; and compare its own virtues with the lesser qualities of other nations (particularly the ones it has developed in antagonism with)? Or is it that once sacred order actually exists and non-state justifications for violence have been abolished, people can live in peace? If it is the second thing, then it is also recognised that if this condition is good for us, it is also good for other peoples. Other nation states are like our own and ours is no more righteous than anyone else's. What matters is that all who are under the prevailing authority are alike in being under the same authority which relates to all alike. In the first 'nationalist' vision, the nation state is a citadel of national virtue. In the second 'internationalist' vision, the nation state is a sanctuary which gives us the best approximation we are likely to get to being under one common authority. Nation states at birth are obviously still much closer to the 'national' than the 'international' vision. In fact the second is only likely to prevail beside the first where the expelled 'evil' can with a good conscience and relative objectivity be labelled 'fascist' or 'colonist'. But nation states in general are a context in which the two visions are not clearly separable. The debt owed by the 'international' vision to national violence in the past is an unknown quantity. All that can be known is that it is a mercy that a line is drawn between violence in the past and the internal tranquillity of the present. If national state histories seem to teach that what is most valued is secured by decisive acts of violence, it is because the people who were left behind were all united by common opposition to the expelled 'enemy'. Hopes for peace through decisive acts of violence in Northern Ireland are hopeless and productive of chaos but they are not 'unreasonable'. Temptations to violence generate their own reasons.

Where the temptations to violence are pervasive, they also uproot any possible rational economic strategy. Fanon, for example, in speaking of decolonisation observed that only after decolonisation (which, it must be remembered, meant the expulsion of the colonial presence and therefore the end of the political ethic that what is good for 'us' is what is bad for them) was the 'true economic state' unveiled. Leaving aside the opportunity created by the colons' departure for economic redistribution and the contribution of the anti-colon violence to weakening the grip of any new native elite, the violent reciprocity served as a distraction from the deeper laid realities of colonial economic relations. These could not be overcome by the violence of decolonisation. The young independent nation 'sees itself obliged to use the economic channels [of the export trade] created by the colonial regime', lest disaster threaten. When he points to the existence of 'a sort of detached complicity between capitalism and the violent forces which blaze up in colonial territory', he conveys the strong suggestion that the real stimulus to violence had much less to do with economic exploitation than with the explosion of the force relationships between settler and native. And so long as this reciprocity was unabated the 'true economic state' was veiled.[4]

The role of antagonism in concealing the 'true economic state' in Ireland is all the more drastic for the absence of any supposed 'solution' of expulsionism. The relatively high (i.e. not Third World) levels of income in both parts of Ireland are the benign face of the malignancy of mass emigration, without which mass underemployment and qualitatively lower wage levels would be a norm. In the Republic this issue is an objective problem, a fact which can be approached with rational policy choices and whose scale can be clearly grasped. In Northern Ireland it is not. Unionist dislike of emigration pressures has been tempered by an awareness that the differentially high rates of Catholic emigration offset the corrosion of the unionist majority by differential birth rates.

Evidence of this disposition provides nationalists with a culprit, a hostile intent, more oppressive than the objective economic forces themselves. The only authority that has any real power to check the emigratory decay of Northern Ireland is the British government, but the violence provides magnificent pretexts or reasons why it need not treat such an obligation as a serious one. While internal elements attack 'fifth columnists' and 'collaborators' the insecurity multiplies the pressures to emigrate and British governments can use projected static or falling populations to 'rationalise' the provision of schools, houses and hospitals, offering at the same time very generous-looking investment grants safe in the knowledge that few will find them attractive. On Britain's part, little effort is required: certainly nothing as well planned as a conspiracy. The struggle for the territory goes on while it becomes a desert. Freedom is for many secretly redefined as an escape from the territory which many proclaim their anxiety to free. The decay lifts the level of dependence on UK public expenditure by destroying the income-earning tax base and increasing the numbers dependent on a welfare state structure that is none the less being chiselled away. Some believe and hope that the scale of the UK subvention will eventually lead Britain to 'withdraw'. Others believe that in some independent Ulster, Britain could be obligated virtually to continue the subventions. These opposed hopes are both examples of the concealment of the 'true economic state'. Britain 'withdrawing' and providing only enough economic support to prevent total collapse (and an exodus to Britain of flood proportions) will in the words of Tone 'play upon the fears of the Protestant and the hopes of the Catholic . . . plunder and laugh at both'. The real economic situation will remain a dim shadow, so long as there is no common authority in relation to which both communities see themselves as symmetrically placed. Until that happens they will lack the power to oblige whatever authority that is to treat the decay as a malignancy for which it is responsible.

Returning to the Anglo-Irish Agreement, it is probably pointless to search out the motives that led its authors to produce it. It is reasonably certain that they didn't know exactly what results would follow. Judged from the standpoint of whether it promises a future peace in Ireland, it is clearly deficient. It is not a permanent arrangement (so that it can be represented by unionists as a stepping stone to Irish unification) and it is not a full joint sovereignty (so that it can be represented to nationalists as a subtle British ploy to deflect international criticism while changing nothing). But neither government could have taken the risk of proclaiming such a permanent joint responsibility without leaving themselves with escape routes if the whole exercise backfires. If it is to develop into a promise of peace it will require internal forces to shift it in that direction. The Irish Republic cannot accept joint responsibility for the North without being given some joint power over it, which anchors nationalist leverage on the decision-making process. Nor can unionists be expected to see Britain as 'their' guarantor in such an arrangement if the increased nationalist leverage isn't matched by evidence that nationalists and more particularly southern governments accept the arrangement as permanent rather than transitional to some eventual unification. Any steps toward political reconciliation are going to be vertiginous. Neither compliant unionists nor nationalists who articulate the need to replace the demand for Irish political unification by the fact of entrenched nationalist power in the North will have an easy time. Whether it is possible for either to win out will depend in the last analysis on how the two external powers develop their relations with each other. The situation in which the Anglo-Irish Agreement has placed people in Northern Ireland is not unlike that created in Bohemia by the ad hoc measures of Austrian power to placate the Czechs. Out of the confusion emerged transnational class-based party alliances of a kind which had only an ephemeral presence in Prussian Poland or the North of Ireland. The shift of state power can be seen as a threat or an opportunity.

Many who have looked at the political situation in Northern Ireland have suggested that it is hopeless. It is easy, for example, looking at Lijphart's conditions for consociational democracy (a system in which power is more or less permanently shared) to come to the conclusion that consociationalism only works when it isn't very necessary (or indeed when it isn't strictly necessary at all). But as Lijphart says, most models of political co-operation 'are not alternatives to consociation but are subsumed to a large extent under the consociational model'.[5] To look at its relevance to Northern Ireland it is best to concentrate on cases where the consociational system was so necessary that when it broke down there was chaos. Leaders of different blocs in a consociational system are often more 'extreme' than the mass of people they represent. But this is not necessarily a purely self-interested disposition. If their followers are spread over a spectrum, the leader's most serious problem is to prevent his own 'extremists' from imperilling his own leadership, starting physical force confrontations which the other side react to and in the process turning everyone into an 'extremist' A strictly necessary consociational system would be one in which leaders of blocs were aware of this danger, kept displays of mutual deterrence within carefully conscribed rules that applied to all segments and knew that however much extreme language they spouted they had a solid secret understanding that matters must always be settled by accommodation between themselves. The more successful they are, the less provocation keeps extreme tendencies alive, the more conciliatory their own language becomes; and the greater the prospect that one day consociation can give way to simple majority rule. By contrast the closer the threats of violence to the surface of political life, the more the preservation of tranquillity looks like accepting a balance of communal deterring powers, knowing violence may rapidly escalate beyond the point at which it can be criminalised.

Dangers of this kind are greatest when there is a possibility that an internal element will appeal for support of an external ally, act as though such a support can be taken for granted, or be encouraged by such an external ally. Such risks are capable of multiplying themselves as the people threatened by it react perhaps in a similar manner. It may be that the most successful and properly called consociations are ones which keep these prospects so buried that no one except a few maniacs hope for such external support to cancel the power of their internal opponents—or ones which are lucky enough never to have external 'allies' to dangle tempting offers before them. An example of the first might be the way the language question in Belgium has never been made a pretext for Dutch or French assistance to Flemish or Walloon blocs. An example of the second might be Hitler's lack of interest in incorporating Switzerland into the Reich. An example of a danger which was limited by the distance of France from Canada might be the separatist aftermath of de Gaulle's *Vive Le Quebec Libre* speech.

Once events *have* magnetised external allies into an arena, the task of displacing them again may be all but insuperable. I suggest that the experience of Cyprus and Lebanon proves that there are only two ways of doing it. A society which is divided by a force field is perpetually in peril of some group starting something into which all other internal and external allies are drawn. A consociation can only work on one of two conditions. Either fortunate conjunctions of circumstance paralyse any possible external intervention, allowing internal forces to devise a consociation and therefore to agree that keeping external forces at a distance is the foundation of national co-existence. Or external allies must make an arrangement amongst themselves to guarantee an internal tranquillity, to create procedures governing their own interventions so that their relations with each other cannot be dictated by internal confrontationists hoping to force the external powers to break their agreements with each other. Northern Ireland's chances of developing the Anglo-Irish Agreement into the second of these approaches depend on both the British and Irish governments; and the realisation upon the part of those within Northern Ireland that the development of such a joint sovereignty arrangement is what stands between Northern Ireland and Cyprus and Lebanon.

In Cyprus and in Lebanon during the 1960s and 70s, external powers were magnetised inwards in support of contending blocs. In the Cyprus case, both Greece and Turkey actively supported Cypriot paramilitary organisations and were prepared, if they could not reach an agreed solution for Cyprus, to go to war with each other over it. Turkey wanted to partition the island (*taskim*) and Greece wanted to absorb it into her own territory (*enosis*). They agreed with each other only with difficulty to make Cyprus independent and but for US and UN forces acting as a brake, the arrangement would probably have fallen to pieces in 1963 when internal forces, relying upon metropolitan backing, created collisions within the bicommunal constitution. In Lebanon the exclusion of external powers by internal agreement worked in a manner of speaking until conflict between the Maronites and the Moslem/Left over the status of Palestinians in the country acted as a magnet to Syrian and Israeli interventions. These two countries at war with each other are highly unlikely to avoid generating proxy wars on Lebanese soil with Lebanese lives and slogans, although Syria has attempted when conditions have permitted it to act as an arbiter.

Long before France took control of Lebanon and Syria after the First World War, it had been acting as a protector of the largest of the Christian groups, the Maronites, against the Druze with whom they co-existed in Mount Lebanon.[6] The partition that created present-day Lebanon in 1920 absorbed not only Mount Lebanon but the coastal towns and a further zone including larger numbers of the Sunni (the main denomination of Islam and the majority of the population of present-day Syria) and Shi'ite, so that the entity contained a 55 per cent Christian majority in 1930. The occupation of France during the Second World War created an opportunity for a section of the Maronite leadership to co-operate with Sunni Moslems to bring about independence on multicommunal principles in 1943–6. The 'National Pact' provided that Christians would eschew dependence on France and the west to support themselves while the Moslems would eschew any effort to mobilise pan-Arab support against Christians. The public appointments were to be distributed on a sectarian basis, the religious authorities retained a high degree of civil power over their own people diluting the state's sovereignty claims, and the Maronite president (elected by the chamber of deputies) was to select a Sunni Moslem prime minister. So long as the greater part of the society was under the control of local landowning notables with a high degree of local authority, even the sectarian potential for division was blurred by alignments of particular personalities often cutting across sectarian lines. And so it remained until the rise of Nasser and Arab nationalism threatened the hold of landed and merchant oligarchs throughout the Arab world. In 1958 Syria joined

Egypt in the United Arab Republic. The president of Lebanon, Chamoun, seeking to secure himself a second term of office and siding openly with the west in obvious contravention of the National Pact—called in the US Marines to prop himself up against Moslem and Druze insurgents. The system might have collapsed but the commander of the army, General Fa'ud Shihab, refused to use the army on Chamoun's behalf. Subsequently he was himself elected president. The insurrection, despite its popular character, was actually kept more or less under control of traditional landed and merchant leaders and sectarian alignments were again cross-cut by personality differences. The future Maronite president (1970–76) Suleman Franjiya, by no stretch of the imagination a liberal, supported the insurgents because of personal opposition to Chamoun. Shihab made Rashid Karami, the leader of the insurrection in Tripoli, prime minister; both Pierre Gemayel, the leader of the only organised popular party, the Maronite Phalange, and Kamal Joumblatt, a Druze landlord who also had socialist following in the towns, were brought into the government.

Shihabism provided Lebanon with the closest approximation it ever got to democratization and an internal equilibrium of the sects. Although much of its efforts at social reform were thwarted by elite opponents who resented Shihab's efforts to promote popular forces in opposition to themselves, he managed to restore the balance of the National Pact by friendship with Nasser and with Gaullist France (at that time considered acceptably neutral). Internally the Civil War of 1958 exposed problems of order. The various Sunni militias and that of the Phalange had exposed the impossibility of securing any state monopoly on the use of force. Shihab tried to build up the Moslem recruitment to the army which was heavily Maronite at the top levels—and the Deuxieme Bureau (military intelligence) kept the various gangs in order. In other words, before the state could achieve an approximation to a monopoly on the use of force, it had first of all to admit that effectively it hadn't got one. But success in this kind of venture critically depended—as indeed the whole basis of Lebanese independence had depended—upon avoiding some external issue polarising people internally

over the use of state force (as Chamoun had nearly done in
1958).

The growing importance of the Palestinian refugee question
and the decline of Shihabism are interconnected. The Shihabist apparatus, which became a focal point of mutually
opposed criticism partly on account of the actions of the
Deuxieme Bureau and partly on account of its own graft, was
none the less something of a sectarian middle ground in
Lebanese politics, even if a rather selective and undemocratic
one (excluding for example the Shi'ites). After the 1967
Arab-Israeli war and more particularly after their expulsion
from Jordan by King Hussein in 1970, the Palestinian liberation movements adopted a higher profile in Lebanon. While
the Moslems and the emerging Lebanese left were critical of
the efforts of the Deuxieme Bureau to control them, Maronites
saw them not only as a potential ally of the left but also a likely
means of involving Lebanon in confrontation with Israel. On
this question Shihabism was attacked from both ends (the
more so after the 1969 Cairo Agreement gave Palestinian
groups freedom of organisation in Lebanon). It was also
attacked on civil liberties grounds. Some opponents of Shihabism saw it as socially too radical and others saw it as too
conservative.

In 1970 Franjiya was elected president by a cluster of
opponents of Shihabism from every conceivable angle—some
who favoured a heavier line against Palestinians and others
who overtly supported Palestinians. While he governed with a
strong representative Sunni prime minister Saib Salam, the
impending dangers were manageable. But the contradictory
basis of his support was dramatically exposed after an Israeli
raid on Palestinian targets in Lebanon. Salam's demand for
the sacking of the army commander was refused and thereafter Franjiya appointed less representative Moslem prime
ministers to concentrate powers in his own hands. The
fulfilment of the one common objective of his 1970 supporters, the dismantling of Shihabist influence in the army and its
Deuxieme Bureau, led in practice to an ever-increasing weight
of Franjiya's Maronite supporters, making it an even less
credible mediator between contending factions. After the 1973
Arab-Israel war, as the more conservative Arab states were

making steps toward a US-sponsored settlement with Israel, the radical Palestinians in Lebanon—backed by Syria which opposed the settlement—became a growing obstacle to the Arab-Israeli peace process. But the choice between exerting some kind of control over Palestinians in Lebanon or allowing them to draw Lebanon into more direct conflict with Israel was not a question free of other implications for Lebanon. With the army now backing a much more plainly Maronite supremacist position, attitudes toward the Palestinians involved a choice for or against Maronite dominance. The Moslems and the left saw the Palestinians as allies in an effort to secure an overhaul of the National Pact and a non-confessional system which would reflect the reality that there was no longer a Christian majority. The Maronite militias hoped that by confronting the Palestinians and provoking them into action, they could magnetise the Lebanese Army into alliance with themselves.

When the Lebanese civil war broke out in 1975, Syria initially facilitated Palestinian action and became engaged in securing a revision of the National Pact to create a more equal sectarian balance. But the Maronites' efforts to magnetise the Lebanese army into confrontations against Palestinians and the left helped bring about the disintegration of the army, which a coup by a Shihabist officer (who charged Franjiya with replacing Shihabist officers by Maronite partisans) did not manage to halt. At this point, the Druze leader Joumblatt escalated the conflict to defeat on the Maronites, whose earlier actions in uprooting Moslem and Palestinian enclaves in 'their' areas hinted at partitionist intent or at least the use of a partition threat to strengthen their negotiating hand. The Syrians, securing US, French and Soviet sanction, began to intervene to prevent Joumblatt's victory. President Assad hoped that doing this would prevent the Maronites from being tempted to call for support from Western or Israeli sources and enable him to arbitrate between them and the Lebanese Left and PLO. Anyway to have expected that Israel would simply tolerate a victory by Joumblatt and the Palestinians—creating a state which became fully committed to the radical Palestinian opposition to Israel—would have been absurd, even if Syria had not had its own reasons for wanting to prevent this happening. The Syrian intervention became acceptable as mediatory because the Maronite bloc saw it as a shield against defeat and the only power under whose authority the National Pact could be revised and the results made to stick. While some Maronites and Moslem leaders came round to accepting the inevitability of a Syrian mediated arrangement of this kind, other Maronites began to look toward Israel as an external ally, a move which tended to realign Syria again with the Palestinians and the left. Lebanese politics today must be among the most complicated of any subjects because the pursuit of the impossible objectives leads to recrimination and fragmentation. Different parts of the small territory are under the control of different militias and armies, each in need of external backing against threats posed by others. The state or any other common authority barely exists so war is an endemic condition. So precarious are truces that factional splinters can break them and set off chains of disturbance without responsibility being clearly attributable. And so long as Syria and Israel are at war it seems inconceivable that Israel would ever allow Syria to orchestrate an overall peace (even if there were not legions of other enemies of Syria that might help internal elements to disrupt it).

On the problems of maintaining ceasefires, Owen observes that 'both sides contain small radical groups, or simple *agents provocateurs*, who have their own special interest in breaking ceasefires and keeping things hot. In addition, the major militias tend to hold the other side responsible for attacks on its own civilians, often exercising a sort of mutual blackmail . . ..'[7]

Britain had prised Cyprus away from the Ottoman Empire in 1878 in circumstances where British rule seemed a lesser evil to the 80 per cent Greek population of the island only forty miles from the Turkish coast.[8] Until the 1930s Greek and Turkish populations in other areas of contention were moved about in millions. Thereafter the post-imperial Kemalist regime in Turkey made no dispute when Greece was given the Dodecanese islands off the Turkish coast forfeited by Italy at the end of the Second World War. And until Britain applied pressure to Turkey to declare its interest in Cyprus in 1954–5, it took the line that Cyprus was under British rule and there was therefore no Cyprus question. Britain's mischievous use of the Turkish minority (18 per cent) to thwart Greek demands for *enosis* is undisputable. But the idea that Turkey would simply have allowed *enosis* to happen assumes that Turkish national irredentism would have behaved in a manner totally different from Greek national irredentism. The only Greek organisation in Cyprus that took Turkish fears into serious account was the Communist Party AKEL which the Greek and Turkish governments, the United States and Britain and the internal paramilitary organisations (the Greek EOKA and Turkish TMT) all viewed with hostility. After the United States took over from Britain the task of propping up the Greek regime against the communist insurgents in 1947, the right in Greece and Cyprus took up the *enosis* question in earnest—thereby proving their independence of British backing. When Britain dug its heels in against Archbishop Makarios' demands in 1954, the Greek government and Makarios gave the go-ahead to the EOKA campaign launched by the extreme anti-communist George Grivas. AKEL, whose position moved away from *enosis* towards independence, had opposed the use of violence against the British partly for fear of the effects of a violent campaign on Greek-Turkish Cypriot relations. EOKA's campaign ran straight into the British snare. When Britain recruited Turks into the police, EOKA killed Turkish policemen. When Turkish *agents provocateurs* of TMT raised the demand for partition (*taskim*) with the backing of the Turkish government, the rioting in 1958 enabled them to force Turks into enclaves with ample assistance of the fear of Greek reprisalism. These enclaves in the five major towns were recognised by the British as separate municipalities. Cypriot independence was eventually worked out largely by the Greek and Turkish governments to balance their contending interests and to avoid direct conflict between themselves—but it did very little to oblige them to co-operate to make Cyprus workable. Instead it left their internal allies on Cyprus in a position to act upon the assumption that in a crisis (which they might precipitate without metropolitan approval) metropolitan backing would be forthcoming. And worse than that, it created the temptation to use Cyprus as a proxy battleground between them when eventually President

Makarios was attempting to accommodate the Turkish Cypriots and to repudiate metropolitan interference after 1967. It may be that once the enclaving and territorial separation intensified in 1963 the brittle arrangement only worked because the UN forces helped to regulate relations between Turkish enclaves and the areas outside them—and the United States repeatedly vetoed Turkish invasions to turn the enclaving structure into a real partition.

The 1960 constitution of Cyprus, which Britain, Greece, Turkey and Cyprus undertook to uphold under the Treaty of Guarantee, entrenched Turkish veto powers and encouraged them to use one set of entrenched powers to bargain on other issues. Thus their budget veto was used as a lever in disputes over the 70/30 ratio of public offices and to secure the permanent establishment of the separate Turkish municipalities. And although the Treaty of Alliance provided for Greece and Turkey to station troops on the island to train a Cypriot army, disputes about how to organise such an army led to a decision by default not to have one at all. Before 1963 the Turks stuck to the letter of the constitution in the expectation of mainland support. Hoping to break the Turkish veto powers in 1963, Makarios decided to abrogate the constitution without securing advance Greek government backing which would have been denied had he asked. Instead, he relied upon mainland backing after the event. So the rioting and consolidation of Turkish enclaves in 1963 brought mainland backing not to restore the constitution (effectively broken) but to check each other. Just how little control the Greek government had over its own forces and the ad hoc Greek national guard and just how unreassuring that might have been to the Turks is suggested by the choice of Grivas (of all people) to re-assert overall control over all Greek forces on Cyprus. Only the sheer strategic realities—Turkey could send aircraft over Cyprus that Greece could not—prevented Grivas from knocking out the coastal enclave at Kokkina. In 1967 after the Greek military coup—which may have found US support partly on account of its desire to cool off the Cyprus question—Makarios attempted to make Cypriot independence a reality and authorised intercommunal talks in the hope of regularising the relations between the Turkish enclaves and the rest of the island. But at this stage the lack of an armed force that could defuse the dangers of confrontationism became severely dehabilitating. His neutralism, dependence on AKEL's support, and criticism of the Greek Junta encouraged the latter to stimulate into action EOKA B, a group of hard-line *enosists*. While EOKA B (which could raise about 5 per cent of the Greek/Cypriot vote) was intent on *enosis*, their sponsors in Greece were intent upon spiking Makarios, and the US may have seen a gift horse pretext for allowing a Turkish invasion to occur in which partition would settle the Cypriot rivalry between NATO powers and Makarios' neutralism in one fell swoop. The EOKA B coup against Makarios in 1974 openly flouted the Cypriot constitution and the provisions against *enosis* and was followed by a Turkish invasion and partition which the United States navy did not prevent as they had prevented all previous ones. A coup to bring about *enosis* had the effect of making *enosis* conclusively impossible.

When blocs collide in civil wars in which neither can inflict defeat upon the other, they are reduced to gambling (the extreme and one-sided version of which is demonstrated by the OAS) to secure a favourable alignment of external forces. Each tries to secure a maximum input from supposed allies and to minimise the input on behalf of its opponents. But being somewhat evenly balanced external forces have a disproportionate influence over the outcome. Apparently very minor changes in the stances of external forces loom into the most enormous considerations. The nature of the condition is described in the story told by Lina Tabarra toward the end of her book *Survival in Beirut*. 'We've won the elections,' she announces in excitement in the salon of Raymond Edde, the one major Maronite leader in Lebanon who refused to form a militia and thus remained a viable interlocuteur between contending factions. But she is not talking of the Lebanese elections, rather the American defeat of Ford by Carter. The reasoning behind her joy was that this meant the exit of Henry Kissinger and his supposed or proposed partition plan for Lebanon. But as she says herself, 'The news of Carter's victory seems to me to call for a real celebration. I'm overlooking the fact that the plan, *if there ever was a plan*, has been realised to all intents and purposes by this time [Nov. 1976].'[9] (My italics).

Even if partitionist *intent* is much more clearly visible on one side than the other, the effect spreads because everyone's power depends on their hold on a piece of territory. As the state collapses, no unarmed element any longer has any space in which it can operate politically. The Turkish Cypriots, for example, might have been content with the 1960 constitution if their separate municipalities had been accorded a very high level of autonomy. The enclaving effect in 1963 more or less withdrew them from Cyprus, but the overwhelming area of the country remained much as it had been because the 80 per cent Greek majority were under no compelling pressure to reciprocate. In Lebanon, by contrast, the construction of the Maronite enclaves from East Beirut northwards along the coast and the Syrian and Israeli occupations forced their opponents to follow suit to preserve bases of their own. Partitionist pressures rise as the threat relationships generalise themselves and the state's authority collapses so that there are no 'neutral' spaces in which political indifference, neutrality, liberality and so on are any longer possible. Even committed trans-sectarian organisations like the Syrian Social National Party have to create pockets of space in multiconfessional areas in order that they should not otherwise disintegrate, and they only survive through external support and a degree of toleration from other forces.

It may seem at first sight as though there is something very unintelligent about political leadership that leads to these kinds of fixes. Retrospective histories tend to have an 'if only . . .' quality about them. But such an impression would be completely erroneous. The Greek-Cypriot expectation of *enosis* was not obviously different from that of the Greeks on the Dodecanese. But they were provoked by British power in 1954 saying 'never' to the decolonisation of Cyprus. The Turks on Cyprus might by and large have allowed *enosis* to happen had it not been for the mainland Turkish backing of TMT, even if in many cases EOKA violence forced them to accept TMT protection in their enclaves. But the *enosis* ideal would never have been so compelling itself if it hadn't been massively echoed in metropolitan Greece. The 'fault', if it can be said to be one, was that the moment there was any question of Cyprus leaving British jurisdiction, it was a potential zone of national border antagonism between Greece and Turkey and any hostilities, whoever contributed to them, were in danger of letting loose representative violence. If British divide and rule tactics were so successful it was because there was a massive possibility for them there in the first place. And once flared, it generated real reasons for itself. The only way to prevent it from becoming a reality was to eschew any resort to force that might turn into Greek/Turkish force. And with metropolitan backing for both forms of paramilitarism, there was only one way to limit its spread and that wouldn't necessarily work; the mass communist party AKEL did its best to stay out of the violence, even to the point of not responding to attacks on it in kind. AKEL's refusal may have provided Makarios with the only really strong lever he had to rein in EOKA, when it got out of hand, with the argument that it was important not to sow division amongst Greeks. And AKEL's support for the independence formula may have helped Makarios eventually settle for it.

The passive influence of AKEL must have had an enormous if unquantifiable effect in preventing the dangers of representative violence from getting out of hand in predominantly Greek areas. Yet AKEL was every bit as richly provoked by British power on Cyprus as anyone. The point is that in the middle of a force field the most 'effective' people seem to be those most actively engaged in stirring it up. To be 'effective' becomes the same thing as being violent. Yet if the force field is tending to undermine the only thing that really matters— the capacity of internal peoples not to be magnetised into an intrinsically antagonised alignment with external blocs—the only way to protect the assets of co-existence is to be 'ineffective'. Being more accurate, all efforts to be 'effective' have to be restrained, by respect for transcendental values in ways 'they' can recognise as an intended basis for reconciliation and not in the abstract formulae which postpone reconciliation until after victory. If that means nothing else then at minimum it means not physically threatening them. And in these situations, breaking up the only existing secular authority that stands between the representative violence of 'them' and 'us', is threatening. All that is redeeming seems 'ineffective' and everyone who insists upon being 'effective' is in danger of becoming an agent of partitionism whether they intend it or not. Once external allies have been magnetised into alliance with internal antagonists, everything is in the lap of the gods. Arbitrating powers only appear by accident. In Cyprus the USA had a paramount interest in preventing war between NATO powers (but only in preventing the partition of Cyprus insofar as that might have started one: once partition seemed a way of reducing that risk it became acceptable). In Lebanon, Syria suddenly turned into an arbitrator when it did its unexpected (but given US, France, Soviet and Israeli interests, predictable) reversal on the Lebanon left.

Once degeneration into territorial breakdown has occurred, it is exceedingly difficult to restore any kind of peaceful co-existence between territorial fragments. The breakdown itself exposes the collapse of the original objectives of conflict and largely destroys the entity for which the contest took place in the beginning: the state apparatus. When there are no neutral areas where people can communicate under the presumed protection of state authority there is no state. Even somewhat repressive states tend to preserve spaces for equal citizenship which disappear under these circumstances. The territorial enclaves become *de facto* states. But if anyone tries to recognise this fact as a starting point for rebuilding they are liable to be accused of treason. Ceasefires which they organise can be disrupted with great ease because even the slightest shocks rapidly escalate through the unchecked operation of representative violence. Small groups can create actions that rapidly involve bigger groups and external allies at different stages of the 'reprisal' process.

Leaders who compromise have to be exceedingly careful to show that they are not in fact compromising but recognising 'reality'. The fate of President Makarios at the hands of EOKA B or the recent coup that displaced Mr Hotebika from the leadership of the Maronite Lebanese forces after he attempted to put a signature to a deal with Shi'ite and Druze forces in Lebanon suggest the impossible nature of these pressures. The partitionist outcomes then scarcely need a master plan. So long as the external powers that have been magnetised are not able or willing themselves to guarantee a settlement involving the internal parties, no internal parties can ever make peace, because everyone knows that little disturbances can become big ones. The closest approach to peace is an unspoken recognition that only when the number of interfaces between antagonists has been reduced to the simplest possible line—and internal chaos is left to generate it perhaps—can the external powers be sure that any further infractions can be prevented by each other and that therefore all further infractions are threats of real war. The fewer and more impregnable the interfaces the less are the possibilities for small groups to detonate hostilities.

The escape from all of this is external powers who are themselves committed to preserving peace and can rely on a large part of the internal population who want the same thing. In this way the risks of representative violence set in motion by armed elements can be contained. Boring and unexciting as this conclusion must be, it is what stands between Northern Ireland and the fate of Cyprus or Lebanon. No one should deceive themselves into imagining that there are higher levels of natural tolerance between Catholics and Protestants in Northern Ireland than between Greeks and Turks on Cyprus or the various sects in Lebanon. In all three societies there is plenty of evidence that so long as the threat of physical force crises can be kept at a distance, people can co-operate and live together. Nor should they imagine that there is anything intrinsically more sophisticated about their politicians or paramilitary leaders than those in Lebanon and Cyprus. Several of the 1975–6 Lebanese civil war lords had in fact co-operated very well with each other in power-sharing of sorts under Shihab. And just at this moment, Northern Ireland might be in a much healthier state if there was a body like AKEL with 30 to 40 per cent of the popular vote. Politically speaking, there is just one asset which these places had not got: the determination of the British and Irish governments to co-operate together. Lebanese Shihabism had to hang on popular electoral legitimacy. All the Anglo-Irish co-operation requires is compliance.

To rehearse what happened to Lebanon: President Franjiya was elected by a coalition of opposites which for diametrically antagonistic reasons opposed the rough and ready efforts of the Shihabist system to keep order. The Anglo-Irish Agreement is under much the same kind of pressure. Under Franjiya the state reverted more and more towards supporting Maronites, and Maronite militias increasingly started trying to shape the response of the army towards the Palestinians. Vigilance and rebellion look like opposites while there is a state for the former to hijack and the latter to oppose. Take away the state and the solid foundation of their differences collapses, leaving only the antagonism that has been endlessly recreated by the asymmetrical relationship of the state to both blocs. When the state has collapsed and territorialism is completed, all talk of equity is moonshine because everything is subdivided into territorial boxes and 'issues' are only auxiliary justifications for antagonism. Everything is in danger of becoming totally simple and at the same time— insofar as politics attempts to solve the then insoluble— enormously complex.

If there was ever any serious chance of avoiding partitions, it was in spite of all confrontationist politics and because of the mass of people who could see intuitively where they led. There are legions of people who are content not to be seen as 'effective' or powerful—and legions who know that effectiveness towards a particular end must be governed by the framework of order within which that end is to be realised. It is the faith that order will be restored in spite of chaos and not through it that keeps them sane—and keeps away the temptation to be 'effective'. Perhaps there are many of us to whom this comes too effortlessly, and who if we open our mouths or pick up a pen are in danger of hypocritically underestimating the force of the reasons for violence. But then no such faith is possible in the first place if we do not know that we are all hypocrites and that it may be only a mercy that we are placed in a situation where we can recognise it without enormous cost to ourselves. And none of us can be innocent of a violence that is everywhere. Only repentance for it and witness to faith in the unity of human kind in any way tends to belittle its coercive pressures. I couldn't have written these lines from any other experience than that of meeting many who in their lives refused the siren call of effectiveness, did not embrace reasons for violence with which they were amply provoked, and who practise their faith by living risks in order that that part of humanity they come into communication with shall be one. Such a world is divided by violence and force fields, except there is living faith that it is not. Where force fields have uprooted all authority that enables people to live in security under its sign, there may be no political way or too many apparently contradictory ways of expressing this faith. It is 'reduced' to what it really is, which is example, stripped of secure rationalisations and certainties about its 'effectiveness'. Politics can teach little that this light does not already teach.

When Christ went to Jerusalem, the greetings to the Messiah who came to deliver 'now' were evidently political. When he charged the Pharisees—who attempted to preserve the integrity of Jewish institutions and religion in accommodation with Roman rule—with hypocrisy, many a Zealot revolutionary must have thought they heard their leader. And no doubt Judas thought he was only forcing a reluctant revolutionary leader to act when he betrayed him. But charged with calling himself the Messiah, he simply did not answer the battery of political questions put to him, though an unequivocal answer one way or the other might have aligned him with either Zealots or Jewish rulers. And his defenders were reduced to pleading his good works in his defence. So the alliance of revolutionaries and accommodators called for a political amnesty for the revolutionary Barabbas. History—the story of 'effectiveness'—would certainly have forgotten Christ and his message were it not for the Resurrection. The miracle of the Resurrection makes visible to us, who live in the world of 'effectiveness', that which is 'not effective'. But then the blindness of our worship of effectiveness plays its last trick. Christ risen from the dead becomes a subject of 'debate' about whether he was mega-effective, a spiritual superpower or a fraud (according to ideological disposition). The 'debate' destroys the miracle and allows us to forget that we are tempted to worship the 'effective'. So long as we are trapped in this worship we shall not see Christ's disciples, whether they be Christian or non-Christian.

Notes and References

The bibliography includes all sources referred to in the text which are listed under particular authors. In the notes below, sources are listed with full reference only where they do *not* appear in the bibliography. Normally a source is identified by the author's surname. Where two or more authors with the same surname are listed in the bibliography, the initials of the author referred to are also given in the notes. Where there are two or more items listed in the bibliography by the same author, an italic (*a, b, c,*) is given corresponding to the bibliographic reference.

Multiple quotations from the same author within one paragraph are page referenced in a consolidated footnote in the order in which they are referred to in the paragraph. To reduce the density of notes some references within single paragraphs have been consolidated into single footnotes, wherever I judge (and hope) that the result is not confusing. I have tried to avoid referring to my forthcoming *Origins of National Conflict in the Province of Ulster 1848–1886,* as it is not in print and all the other references are in print. Where this has not been possible I have referred to it as Wright, F. (d).

Chapter 1 (pp. 1–27)
1. Mason, Vol 1 on Errigal Keroge parish, Vol 3 on Clonmaney parish; Edwards, R.D., 227–31; Slaski, 21; Taylor, 27.
2. Crawford, (*b*); Wall; Hagen, (*b*) 20; Henderson, 93–8; Kula, 48–9.
3. Hagen,(*a*).
4. Jaszi, 66; Macartney, 50; Wandycz, 68–71, 129–30.
5. Hagen, (*b*) 25.
6. Gellner, (*a*) and (*b*). David Miller's analysis of the origins of Ulster Unionism utilises Gellner's work also, but he pays little attention to the educational aspect of Gellner's theory. This is, I think, crucial to an understanding of the appeal of Irish

nationalism to Catholics within the north of Ireland. However, Gellner's approach needs to be modified in order to make it relevant to situations in which language is not the mark of division between nationality groups.

7. Beckett, 295–305; Holmes, F., 47–76; Mason, Vol 2 on Glenavy and Tullyrusk parishes; Mason, Vol 3 on Killelagh parish; Akenson, (*a*) 90.
8. Akenson, (*a*) 117–22.
9. Holmes, F. 95–109.
10. Wright, (*d*).
11. Wandycz, 131–41; Eyck, 268–87
12. Marx, 221–2 and 233.
13. Seaton-Watson, 212–13.
14. Wandycz, 149; Wright,(*d*).
15. Taylor, 173.
16. Bowen, 85.
17. Wandycz, 229.
18. Cullen, 20, 26–8; Crawford, (*a*) 194; Macaffe and Morgan, 46–64; Dickson, 4, 13 n, 21, 35; Crawford, (*c*) and Trainor, 88; Jones, 22, 23 and 43.
19. Walker, M., 55, 79; Henderson; Wandycz, 71.
20. Darby,(*a*); Darby, (*b*) and Morris; Wright, F., (*c*).
21. Crawford, (*c*) and Trainor drew attention to the Armagh situation in the 1780–1800 period for which Byrne is the main primary source; the most illuminating work is Miller, (*a*), but see also Gibbon; Stewart,(*b*); Miller,(*b*); Wright,(*c*).
22. Senior; Broeker.
23. Bowen, 176; Broeker, 35–8, 167 and 211–27; Senior.
24. The following seven pages are largely based on Wright, F., (*d*), but see Boyd, A; Budge and O'Leary; Patterson (*b*); Gibbon; Miller, (*b*); Cooke; Stewart, (*b*); Buckland, (*a*); Buckland, (*b*). The concept of communal deterrence is developed by Esman.
25. Girard, (*a*) 13–25, quotations from 15–16.
26. Girard, (*a*) 145–9; 174–5.
27. Girard, (*a*) 49, 54, 67, 78, 79, 82.
28. Hobbes.
29. Sorel, 92 and 80–4.
30. Girard, (*a*) 24–25.
31. Arendt, Ch. 4 and p. 36.
32. Arendt, 155, 223, 243.

Chapter 2 (pp. 28–54)

1. Wiskemann, 58; Gibbon; Hagen, (*b*); Wright, (*d*).
The strongest opponents of exclusive dealing were sections of

long established merchant and business strata, who faced this kind of development as a straightforward threat to their potential markets. In Ulster the pre-1868 liberals depended heavily upon such elements; their importance shrank politically as the franchise was extended and as Catholics shifted towards a more self-organised and ultimately nationalist politics. In Prussian Poland this kind of politics survived longer. The urban Jewish population included the most deeply entrenched section of the upper middle classes. Not only did the Prussian three class franchise magnify their importance above their numbers, but being vulnerable to anti-semitic boycotts by both Germans and Poles, they were consistent standard bearers of progressive liberalism. In the end they (like the Ulster Liberals) found themselves forced to choose electoral alliance with the German blocs against militant Polish nationalism. (See Hagen (*b*) 299–303, 155 and 116).

2. Wiskemann, 38–9, 54; Wright, F., (*c*); Budge and O'Leary, 94; Murdzek, 9.
3. This section depends upon Whiteside; Taylor; Macartney; Wiskemann; Seaton-Watson; Jaszi; Garver; Bruegel; Pauley. Whiteside, 31 makes a brief but explicit comparison between the politics of Germans in Bohemia and Protestants in Ireland.
4. Taylor, 166–8; Macartney, 179.
5. Garver, 112–16.
6. Whiteside, 77, 181.
7. Hitler, 10, 85, 100.
8. Garver, 81–2, 146–56; Wiskemann, 58.
9. Whiteside, 160–87 and 221.
10. Wiskemann, 67; Seaton-Watson, 245.
11. Bruegel, 6–9.
12. Pauley, 24–9; Wiskemann, 99, 102–4, 171.
13. This section depends upon Wandycz; Hagen (*a*) and (*b*); Murdzek; Blanke; Eley; Tims; Koehl.
14. The more I read about Bismark's concerns, the less clear I am about the motives he may or may not have had. For present purposes they are not important. What matters is that the Kulturkampf had irreversible effects in the Polish east.
15. Clapham, 291.
16. The importance of the local German pressures in the east was clearly greater than the doubtful diplomatic intentions in the direction of Russia. See Blanke.
17. Hagen,(*b*) 172–3. Tims, 66.
18. Murdzek, 28; Tims, 162–7; 169 n and 186 n; Eley, 333–48, Hagen, (*b*) 274–5.

19. Murdzek, 23; Tims, 136; Polonsky, 54–61; Wandycz, 285–95, 321, 326.
20. Mansergh, 274–5.
21. Walker, B; Bew, (a) and Wright; Wright, (c).
22. Lyons, 141–57.
23. For the following pages, Bew, (a) and Wright; Kirkpatrick; Cooke; Gibbon; Buckland (a) and (b); Patterson (b); Boyd, A.
24. Boyd, A., 161 and 171–3.
25. Mansergh, Ch. 2 and Ch. 4.
26. Halévy, Vol 5. 93–110; Gilbert Ch. 2.
27. Halévy Vol. 6. 58–73.
28. The story of the 1912–14 period in Ulster is told in Stewart (a).
29. Seaton-Watson, 234.
30. Wiskemann, 77; Lyons, 378–9; Wandycz, 344.
31. Mansergh, 278.

Chapter 3 (pp. 55–74)

1. Emmanuel.
2. This section depends upon Abun-Nasr; Ageron; Confer; Brogan; Laffont.
3. Abun-Nasr, 256.
4. Ageron, 76, 34.
5. Ageron, 77; Laffont, 260–1; Ageron, 86.
6. Confer, 82; Gordon, D., (a) 17.
7. Arendt, 89–120; Brogan, 329–87.
8. Laffont, 262–74.
9. Confer, 31–44.
10. Moore, B., 508.
11. This section on the pre-civil war period is drawn largely from Potter.
12. Mills, 16–25.
13. Starobin, 202–14; Wade, 336-8; Phillips, 275–6; Genovese, 225–34.
14. Shugg, 76-96.
15. Jones, 117–21.
16. Franklin,(a).
17. DuBois, (a) 17–31; Jones, 168–9; Shugg 198–9; Curry.
18. Coulter, 29; Wharton, 59; Stampp, 126–31; Coulter, 110.
19. Coulter, notwithstanding paragraph one of p. 111, see paragraph two of p. 111 and p. 164; Davis and Gardner, 296–7.
20. Singletary, 5.
21. Singletary, 29.
22. Degler; Stampp, 165. Also on these southern white republicans or 'scalawags' as they are sometimes known, Donald; Trelease; Ellen.

23. DuBois (*a*), Asa Gordon, Ch. 3; Wharton.
24. Woodward, (*a*) and (*b*).
25. Mississippi is chosen for illustration because: the evidence for the existence of some such arrangement in the Delta and river counties is well documented; taking account of Trelease's emphasis on the numerical importance of lower class white republicans, his figures for such people in Mississippi are not large; subsequent studies of the Deep South in the 1930s referred to in Chapter Six were done in Mississippi.
26. Wharton, 64, 95, 169; Harris, W.C., 375–8.
27. Harris, W.C., 383–4; Wharton.
28. Wharton, 203; Holmes, W; Gardner and Davis, 393.
29. Garner, Ch. 8 and Ch. 11; Wharton Ch. 13.
30. Harris, W.C., 634.
31. Singletary, 81–99.
32. Harris, W.C., 638.
33. Hackney, 25; Howard 167; Kousser.
34. Holmes, W; Hackney, 112–4; Howard, 204–5; Foner, 114–19; Key; Kousser.
35. Degler, 293–9 and 353–67; Dittmer, 96–8.
36. Rabinowitz, 315 and 332–9.
37. Meier, 125; DuBois,(*b*) 128–9; Harlan, Vol I, especially Ch. II.
38. Dittmer, 163–80.

Chapter 4 (pp. 75–85)
1. Wiskemann, 69.
2. Geschwender's work about Detroit explores the way in which Henry Ford sought black labour, how the UAW responded and the impact of that response on Henry Ford etc. Had I read this work earlier I would have incorporated its insights here.
3. For an example of the kind of debates of this period see Tych on the debate on the Polish question at the Socialist International Congress of 1896.
4. A spectacular case of this kind was that of the Tashkent Bolsheviks after 1918. Russian Central Asia was virtually cut off from Bolshevik controlled areas for some years and the Great Russian settlers of this area seem to have set themselves up as Bolsheviks, preferring to maintain links with Moscow, notwithstanding their exceedingly dubious commitment to socialist politics, rather than be submerged under Islamic separatisms. Until Moscow was able to impose any direct control, these Tashkent Bolsheviks contrived to antagonise relationships with the Islamic populations so much that the central committee issued a warning that Turkestan could not be allowed to become a "Russian Ulster", a national minority counting on support from the centre. E.H. Carr, 334–43; Alleg, (*b*); Rywkin.

5. Bew, (a) and Wright.
6. Patterson, (a) and (b); Gray; Pauley; for a statement of the position of the Independent Orange Order in its early stages see Braithwaite and Crawford.
7. Boyle, J.W; Edwards, O.D. Ch. 4.
8. Patterson, (a); Patterson, (b) 51, 57–8, 147.
9. Garver, 241–2, 245–57, 281–3. Wiskemann, 51.
10. Jaszi, 177–84.
11. Patterson, (b) 121–2.
12. Bauer, (a) 127–8, 57–8, 98–100.
13. Bruegel, 16–37.
14. Watt, 396–401; Morrow, 67–74 (especially fn 1, p. 71); Andrezejewski; Von Reikhoff, 66.
15. Farrell, (a); Farrell, (b); Buckland, (c).
16. Patterson, (b) 115–42.

Chapter 5 (pp. 86–111)

1. Moore, B. My presentation of Moore is necessarily brief and therefore somewhat over-simplified. In the French case, for example, he concludes that the middle peasantry were the arbitrating force, essential to the revolution, and also the brake upon its radicalism. Thus a bourgeoisie did not make the revolution so much as inherit it. In the English case, landlords, despite their continued power in the 19th century, are shown to have acquired bourgeois political and economic traits, the former by setting a precedent for executing kings and the latter by expelling people from their domains and using their lands to graze sheep. My simplified presentation is designed to emphasise the lack of any such break in the case of the German Reich of Bismark and the Junkers.
2. Arendt, 123–57; Moore, B., 508.
3. Lyttelton, 93.
4. Bauer, (b) 169. I should stress that I am placing much more weight upon this aspect than Bauer did. But as he subsequently says that 'Fascism has shown the capitalist class of *all* countries that a *resolute minority of daring mercenaries* can deprive a whole people of its freedom . . . and establish a capitalist—militarist dictatorship' (my emphasis) (p. 183), the interesting question is why such mercenaries were unable to do it everywhere.
5. Smith, D.M., (Italy); Shoup, (Serbia); Adler 132.
6. Waite. Although the line of argument here follows Waite, emphasising the role of frontier conflicts and the destabilising effects of paramilitarism generated by them, the general presentation of the Weimar Republic here rests on Bracher;

Turner; Abraham. Convenient diagramatic presentation of the intricacies of parliamentary representation can be found in Kinder and Hilgemann, 148, 150, 192.

7. Bessell, 6.
8. Hertzmann; Wheeler-Bennett, 60–1; Wright, J.R.C., 72; Bessell, 67.
9. Gerschenkron, 143–6; Wunderlich, 353.
10. Von Riekhoff; Ossietzky, 118.
11. Ledeen, 19. The account below rests primarily upon Ledeen; Smith; Lyttelton; Nolte; Zivojinovic; Singleton, F.
12. On Mussolini's lack of enthusiasm for frontier irredentism in the early phases of the Fascist movement. Lyttelton, 90. My use of Ledeen's work on D'Annunzio in Fiume requires some explanation. For Ledeen the Fiume revolt was directed against the old order in Western Europe and its essence was 'the liberation of the human personality' or 'radicalisation of the masses' (preface p. x.). That it could become such a creative enterprise was surely because it disappointed precisely those ultra-nationalist tendencies it initially attracted but then left to follow other more frankly brutal directions. It is clear that Fiume might have been made a base for escalated antagonism between Italians and Croats (see Zivojinovic, Ledeen, 146–7), that some were encouraging D'Annunzio to use it as a launching pad for enterprises like those the Facists did eventually conduct in Venezia—Giulia against Slovenes. The restraints applied to anti-Semitism, anti-Croatian expulsionism etc., made all the positive features of Fiume stand out in sharper relief, but they also made it of declining importance for the subsequent development of Fascism.

As to whether D'Annunzio had serious prospects of using Fiume as a base from which to encourage and assist Croatian insurrection against Serb dominance of Yugoslavia, without that hope the whole Fiume enterprise would appear to have become purposeless (p. 184). Perhaps the sheer fantasy of this exercise was also what made Fiume relatively harmless. Although Croats who disliked incorporation into Yugoslavia may have found some common purpose with Italians against the dominant Versailles powers (Maček mentions Italian good offices in conveying Croatian interests to the peace conference), the proposed Italian zone on the Adriatic coast included a large slice of the Croatian ethnic territory. The mysterious Dr Frank who needed *12 million lira at once but did not need arms* for his 'insurrection' (p. 182) does sound like the double dealer that Nitti reckoned him to be.

13. Smith, 48–9.
14. Brogan, 556.
15. Confer, 72.
16. Brogan, 616–22.
17. Mansergh, 280–1.
18. Farrell (*b*), Ch. 2; Buckland, (*c*) 181; 184. The importance of the distinction between legal and illegal forces in ethnic frontier contest is that legality ensures some kind of restraint. For example a 'Notice to "B" men' quoted by W. Clark, p. 70, explicitly links good behaviour (meaning restraint against reprisalism) with the need 'to keep the English people with us' (meaning the backing of the British government). Clearly this argument for restraint would have been useless if the British government had not appeared to be behind them. An organisation that is simultaneously engaged in ethnic conflict and in attacking its own national government for betrayal or treason undermines all institutional restraints upon national egoism.
19. Farrell, (*b*) Ch. 3; Barker, 102–10; Waite; Bessell; Nolte; Ledeen.
20. Buckland, (*c*) 184.
21. Cell, 180 and 190. But see also Ch. 6 below.
22. Merkl, 115 and 474.
23. Pauley.
24. Hitler, 246, 598, 591, 593, 108.
25. Merkl, 33.
26. Smith, 64.
27. Hitler, 53.
28. Bessell, 83–5.
29. Abraham, 202.
30. Broszat,(*a*) especially 124–9.
31. Wiskemann, 197.
32. Barker, 188–92; Pauley, 83–100, 131–2.
33. Wiskemann, 199–200. Bruegel, 79–85, 103–9, 123–8, 143–53.
34. Bruegel, 301.
35. Polonsky; Von Riekhoff; Bessell, Ch. 4.
36. Von Riekhoff, 355–64.
37. Bessell, 130.
38. Polonsky, 463–6.
39. Broszat, (*b*); Höhne, 269–97.
40. Storry, Ch. 7.

Chapter 6 (pp. 112–163)
1. Rose, (*a*) 465; Williams, (*a*) 135; Key, 9.
2. Calculated from Key, p. 7. On a restricted definition of the Deep

South—areas with black majorities—its 'centre of gravity' would have been in Mississippi and South Carolina, where 36.6% and 20.2% of whites lived in black majority counties (in no other state was the figure higher than 12%). A more conventional definition of the Deep South, Mississippi, South Carolina, Alabama, Louisiana, and Georgia, would include the states in which at least half the white population lived in counties with 30% black populations or more.

3. Miller, (*b*); Wright, F. (*a*; Muse, 19–25; Jacques Roseau in the ITV Channel Four series on the Algerian War, Nov. 1984.
4. Farrell, (*a*) 83–6; Buckland (*c*) 221–46.
5. Buckland, (*c*) 20.
6. Ardrey, 118, 257, 311, 362, 266.
7. West, 476.
8. Ardrey, 305, 379.
9. Ardrey, 258, 262, 257.
10. Hitler, 126–8; Ardrey, 127.
11. Hitler, 103.
12. The idea of internal and external mediation of desire was developed by Girard in the context of literary criticism: Girard, (*b*) 9–17, 42, 58.
13. King, 148.
14. Gordon, (*b*) 28.
15. Amin, 70–1; Alleg, (*a*).
16. Memmi, 11; Berque, 332.
17. Benatia, 21–3.
18. Berque, 310–11.
19. Ageron, 123–64; Benatia, 21.
20. Ath-Messaoued and Gillette, 30, 118; Abun-Nasr, 319–21; Ageron, 163–4.
21. Lottman, 156.
22. Bourdieu, 58–62.
23. Fanon, 39, 30, 47. Bourdieu, 58.
24. Fanon, 42, 43, 35.
25. Fanon, 69, 116, 31.
26. Sartre's preface to Fanon, 20–1, 24–6. Camus, 120.
27. Cell, 165–7; Ball 7 and 19.
28. Edmonds, 174, 190–1, 199.
29. Edmonds, 161–3, 133, 143, 164, 148; Degler, 362.
30. Cox, 559; Muse, 29.
31. Dollard, 147–65; Davis and Gardner, 24–44, 37–8, Powdermaker, Ch. 17.
32. Cleaver, 212.
33. Davis and Gardner, Ch. 18; Cell, 162.

34. Davis and Gardner, 462, 426–7, 468–74.
35. Ball, 30.
36. Cox, 561.
37. Powdermaker, 52–5, 330–4; Cox 561–4; Davis and Gardner, 50–7.
38. Cell, 178–80.
39. Cox, 444; Dollard, 155.
40. Ball, 200.
41. Thrasher and Wise.
42. Howard, 275–94; Fenton and Vines.
43. Davis and Gardner, 418–20; Dunbar 64–5.
44. King 42–9, 54.
45. King, 34.
46. Forman, 514; Fanon, 31; Cleaver, 45.
47. Brady, 16.
48. West, 85–8, 102; Babic.
49. Compton, 91.
50. Farrell, (a) 88, 197.
51. Wright, (a) 241.
52. Clark, W., 12, 32, 51–3.
53. Isles and Cuthbert, 52—62.
54. Wright, (d); Bew, (a) and Wright; Kennedy and Olleranshaw.
55. From the 1871 Census for the county borough of Belfast.
56. Hepburn, (a) and Collins; Aunger.
57. Hepburn, (b); Akenson, (b) 44–5; Buckland,(c) 247–65; Farrell, (a) 101.
58. Bew, (b), Gibbon and Patterson, 75–101.
59. Akenson, (b) 177–88.
60. Farrell, (a) 90.
61. Isles and Cuthbert, 58.
62. Farrell, (a) 139–42.
63. Chafe, see more extensively in Chapter seven.
64. Wright, (a); Shea, 113.
65. Wright, (a); Robinson, 27.
66. Harris, R., 171–81, 146–7, 198–200, 186, 194–5.
67. Wright, (c).
68. Wright, (d).
69. Harris, R., 172, 185.
70. Quoted in Lyons, 334.
71. Boyd, R.
72. O'Neill, 116.
73. Shea, 135, 141–3; Brady, 12.
74. Rose, (a) 272; Moxon-Browne, 75; Nelson, S. (a) 155–87; Nelson, S. (b) 67–75.

75. Fennell. It should be noted that both Rose (*a*) p. 208 in 1968 and Moxon-Browne p. 6 in 1978 found 15% of Catholics describing themselves as British.
76. Barritt and Carter 120–4; Curran 4–11.
77. Tone, 341–66. His later more overtly separatist writings were written at some distance from the northern situation and, unlike the 'Argument on behalf of the Catholics', there is no reason to suppose that their sentiments were representative.
78. The point I am driving at here is that while some minorities from each bloc show signs of separating themselves from its mainstream and attempting to articulate positions that cut across the religio-national division, exceedingly few actually go to the point of endorsing the mainstream of the other bloc. Thus, for example 15% of Catholics gave their national identity as British (Rose 1968; Moxon-Browne 1978) but only 5% supported the Unionist party in 1968—and 20% of Protestants gave their national identity as Irish (in 1978 reduced to 8%) but less than ½% voted for the Nationalists in 1968 or for the SDLP or other nationalist parties in 1978. What is interesting about the middle ground is that it is there, but it is exceedingly hard pressed to do more than provide cement for compromises made between elements in the main line blocs. The present-day Alliance party and the pre-1969 Labour party contained within them substantial diversity of opinion (see Rose; and Moxon-Browne).

    By contrast with another ethnic frontier conflict situation— that of the Slovenes in Austrian Southern Carinthia, where some German organisations talk a territorialist language not unlike that of Orangeism—the degree of polarisation is very high. The ratio of Slovenian nationalists to speakers of the Slovene (or Windisch) language appears to be around one to five (Barker 227–8), whereas the ratio of Irish nationalists to non–nationalist Catholics is nearly the reverse of that.
79. West, 788, 797–8.
80. Muse, 127.

Chapter 7 (pp. 164–216)
1. Oates, 82.
2. Oates, 281.
3. Brink and Harris, 74.
4. Brink and Harris, 116.
5. Key; Leuchtenburg; Bass and De Vries, 369–91; Moore, J. (*a*); Moore, J. (*b*); Hunter.
6. Billington; Smyth; Burns; Wilkeson; Kelleher. In the Gaines

case (Kelleher) instead of requiring integration on the grounds that there was no separate facility, the Supreme Court created the precedent from which the subsequent school desegregation cases followed. It declared a separate law school that was established unequal to its white equivalent.

7. Bass and De Vries, 137; Muse, 12.
8. e.g. quotation from *Greensboro Daily News* in Chafe 55.
9. Tindal, 403, 431; Street, Ch. 4.
10. Key, 329–344.
11. Foner, 275–92; Kirkendall, 68–80; Geschwender, 47–53; Caute.
12. Pritchett.
13. Bartley.
14. Raines, Ch. 1; King, 65–6.
15. Oates, 188–201; Raines, 361–6, 425–31; Schlesinger, Ch. 35 and 36.
16. Garrow; Raines, Ch. 4
17. Forman; Carmichael and Hamilton; Carson; Raines.
18. Bass and De Vries, Ch. 4 (Alabama), Ch. 9 (Mississippi).
19. Brink and Harris, 138–53.
20. Key, 206. On Virginia and North Carolina, I have depended heavily on Key; Bass and De Vries; Muse (for Virginia); and Chafe (for North Carolina).
21. Muse, quotations from 8, 33 and 48–9.
22. Muse, 103.
23. Chafe, 73, 90, 97.
    I should make it clear that the word 'pre-empt' that I have used creates an ambiguity which is not in Chafe. Chafe takes the view that Hodges virtually invented the white backlash threat as a way of putting the brakes upon serious desegregation in 1955–59. My reasons for being reluctant to accept this argument whole-heartedly are explained in the next paragraph of the text.
24. Carlson, 69.
25. Chafe, 96, 146, 212–18.
26. Key, 229.
27. Cleaver, 82–4.
28. Chafe, 239; Taeuber.
29. Kerner.
30. Geschwender, 72.
31. Nelson, H; Cleaver, 93.
32. This account depends on Chafe and Myerson. The opinion survey is from Carlson, 96–8.
33. Carmichael and Hamilton, 53, 81.
34. Farrell, (a) Ch. 8; Sean Cronin, *Irish Times*, 28 May, 1984.
35. Lawrence, Ch. 3 and 5; Wilson, 140.

36. Gallagher, T., 26–7. On the PTA, Scorer and Hewitt.
37. Gallagher, T., Scott, 11, 14, 26.
The declining significance of Irish identities in Britain is not particularly exceptional. Wrzesiński shows that while German-Polish identity questions retained vitality near the border in the 1920s, they lost much of their significance in urban areas of the west of Germany where bilingual Poles joined (for example) the German communist party.
38. Boserup; O'Brien, 137–52.
39. Wilson, 349–50.
40. Isles and Cuthbert; Bew (*b*), Gibbon and Patterson, 152–3; *Northern Ireland Progress,* Jan 1968.
41. *Reports of the NI Housing Trust* 1963–64, 1964–65. *Regional Statistics,* No. 12, 1976 (HMSO).
42. *Ulster Business Journal,* 1975 Vol 2. No. 6/7 June/July and No. 9 September, *Ulster Year Books,* 1975 and 1965.
43. Oliver, 89; Faulkner, 57; O'Dowd, Rolston, Tomlinson, 108–9.
44. Rose, (*a*) 289; O'Dowd *et al,* 57; Aunger.
45. Derived from Tables of Religion, *NI Census,* 1971 and *UK Labour Statistics,* 1971. The manufacturing sector accounted for 30 per cent of Protestant male and 19 per cent of Catholic male employment. Above average hourly wage rates and high percentages of Catholics in the workforce coincided most strikingly in only two large sectors—24 per cent Catholic in man-made fibres and 32 per cent in rubber and tyres (both with hourly wage rates between 75p and 80p compared to an average of 66p; base percentage of Catholics in census, 27.5 per cent). Both of these were post-war developments that were strongly attracted by grants—being highly capital intensive—rather than by a search for already established labour skills. The long established engineering and shipbuilding industries remained overwhelmingly Protestant.
46. Darby, (*c*) and Murray; Wright, F. (*a*) 273–4.
47. Curran, 27–53; White, 38–9; Osborne, (*a*).
48. *Campaign for Social Justice.*
49. McCann, 23.
50. McCann, 46–7; O'Neill, 48.
51. McCann, 49.
52. Gallagher, E. and Worrall, 31–8; Boyd, A., 179–82.
53. Arthur; *The Cameron Report*; Curran; Devlin; Edwards, O; Farrell, (*a*); Faulkner; Hastings; Insight; McCann; McKeown, C; O'Neill; Riddell; *The Scarman Report*; Wallace; White.
54. Farrell, (*a*) 249.
55. Wallace, 53.

304 *Northern Ireland: a comparative analysis*

56. This point is made in a critical way by Brian Faulkner (49–52). Faulkner argued that either the government should have stood firm or that it should have recommended one-man-one-vote on its own initiative. Though he supported the second option, it seems more than probable that the effect of his resignation was to increase rather than decrease the ease with which this measure secured acceptance.
57. O'Neill 121–2; Wallace, 60; for election results. *The Times*, 26 and 27 February, 1969.
58. Boyle (*a*), Hadden and Hillyard, 14–15.
59. Wilson, 844–5; Wallace 36–8.
60. Wallace, 65. These may have referred to the 'IRA' bombs which were actually planted by extreme loyalists.
61. White; Cameron.
62. Scarman, 67.
63. Scarman, 131; Wallace, 7.
64. Poole, (*a*).
65. O'Brien, 247–58.
66. Boal, (*a*) 274.
67. Poole, (*b*) 300–1; Darby, (*b*) and Morris; Boal, (*a*) 266; Gallagher, E. and Worrall, 50.
68. Birrell *et al*; *NIHE Belfast Household Survey*, 1978; Singleton, D. 178–94.
69. *NIHE Household Survey.*
70. Table 15.9, *Regional Statistics, 1975*, 203; Quigley.
71. White, 95; McCann, 82–3; Hastings 145.
72. Gallagher, E and Worrall, 38, 72–3.
73. Rose, (*a*), 179–202.
74. Harding.
75. Franklin, (*b*) 494; Sowell, 228–9; Zashin, 243.
76. B.J. Widick in Holli (ed.).
77. Carmichael and Hamilton, 145.
78. Hamilton, 122; Zashin, 248–50.
79. Chafe, 346; Weinberg, 134; *Financial Times*, 20 May, 21 May, 1980.
80. Ansbro, 218; Cleaver, 95.

Chapter 8 (pp. 217–265)
1. Pearson, 91.
2. Paxton, 34–7. Article 6.
3. The material on the 4th Republic is drawn primarily from Williams (*a*); Claudin, 336–41, on the Communist party; Hartley, 95–144 on early Gaullism. It should be noticed that until the Communist party left office in 1947 it was much less enthusiastic for decolonisation than it became thereafter.

4. It hardly needs to be pointed out that the focus of this chapter is on French reactions to the FLN rising rather than the rising itself. My main sources are Horne; Behr; Clark, M; Abun-Nasr; Williams,(*b*). On Nasser, see Stephens. Also very useful was the ITV Channel 4 five-part series on the Algerian War in November 1984.

5. Williams, (*b*) Ch. 7; Hartley, 147-57.

6. Laffont, 452.

7. Clark, M., 394.

8. Pickles, 64.

9. Clark, M., 453; McKeown, M.

10. McKittrick. A British army officer estimates that half the serving officers (presumably excluding those in the locally recruited Ulster Defence Regiment) favour a military withdrawal.

11. Williams, (*b*) Ch. 10.

12. David McKittrick, 15 May 1984, *Irish Times*. 'Executive was doomed before the strike even began' said a retired British General.

13. Moxon-Browne, 26–8.

14. Wilson, 872.

15. Murray; Asmal; *New Ireland Forum Report* appendix, on 'the costs of violence arising from the Northern Ireland Crisis since 1969'. Dublin 1984. In each case the sources appear to be the Irish Information Partnership and McKeown, M.

16. Moxon-Browne, 6.

17. Nelson, S., 104.

18. Gallagher, E. and Worrall, 75.

19. *Irish Times*, 28 January 1971. During a debate of no-confidence in the government's law and order policies, Boal rejected internment as it 'broke a fundamental of natural justice'. He only suggested that if it was used by the then Unionist government, they would probably intern 50 per cent each of Protestants and Catholics. Other Paisley supporters elevated this tail of Boal's argument to the level of the central argument. Those who stuck with Paisley in this period when his anti-internment policy was less than popular felt vindicated when Whitelaw did eventually intern Loyalists. But by then Paisley was no longer attempting to pursue the path charted out by Boal.

20. Osborne, (*b*).

21. Boal, (*b*) and Douglas, 342; O'Dowd *et al*; or as Richard Rose puts it (Rose,(*a*) 98) 'No economic plan could be without implications for Protestant-Catholic relations'.

22. Faulkner, 206–25; White, 140–56.

23. White, 157.
24. Faulkner himself (262–3) takes the view that stronger action at the beginning might have worked. He records asking the secretary of state Merlyn Rees to instruct the security forces to enforce the law on the first days of the strike. But that was very far from giving Rees the kind of commitment to stay in office at all hazards which would have made the vigorous use of the security forces against the strike an intelligible strategy. See also David McKittrick (reference in note 12).
25. Nelson, S. (*b*) 155–60.
26. Osborne, (*b*).
27. Rose, (*b*) 45–52; Moxon-Browne, 114-16.
28. For the story of the Peace People, see Ciaran McKeown *The Price of Peace.*
29. Boyle, (*b*) Hadden and Hillyard.
30. Moxon-Browne, 58.
31. Moxon-Browne, 75.
32. *New Ireland Forum Report,* Dublin 1984; *Irish Times,* 4 May 1984 'Haughey says media stress on differences "uncalled for" '. *Irish Times,* 22 May 1984. MRBI/*Irish Times* opinion poll.
33. *Irish Times,* 9 April 1984. Alliance Party Conference Report. *Irish Times,* 3 May 1984, 22.
34. *Irish Times,* 7 July 1984 'The Way Forward'; Moxon-Browne, 111.
35. *Derry Journal,* 22 May 1984.
36. The Anglo-Irish Agreement.
37. De Gaulle, 44–51.
38. De Gaulle, 96–7, 114, 123; Ageron, 251.
39. Hartley, 157–93; Pickles; Horne.
40. Williams, (*b*) 177; on the efforts of OAS sympathisers including Poujard to build links to the peasant disturbances, see Wright, G. 162–72, 244–6.
41. Aziz.
42. Benatia, 25–8.
43. Gordon, (*b*) 27.
44. Vitalis Cros in ITV Channel 4 series on the Algerian War. Nov 1984.
45. Taillefer; Laffont, 493–512; Hennisart.
46. Laffont, 507.
47. For examples (i) 2 May 1984, *Irish Times.* David McKittrick on allegations about SAS operations in the Irish Republic in the mid-1970s. (ii) 21 May 1984, *Irish Times.* Report of a border incursion on 19 May 1984 followed by a British government apology. (iii) 6 and 9 April 1984 *Irish Times.* Reports relating to

the trial of a police officer for murder, arising out of incidents on 12 December 1982. The officer's evidence revealed that he was part of an uncover surveillance team that had followed suspected terrorists into the Republic. This and other cases in which there was strong suggestion of deliberate shooting of unarmed persons by the security forces became the subject of an investigation by the Manchester Deputy Chief Constable John Stalker. The circumstances of his removal from the inquiry before it had finished its work remain shrouded in some mystery which may yet prove to be scandal.

48. Laffont, 493.
49. The usual remark to make about British opinions on Northern Ireland is that they show a definite lack of commitment to keeping it. Metropolitan Britains have little sympathy with 'Loyalists' who frustrate what appear to be well-meaning attempts by British governments to find 'solutions'. Thus Mori polls in 1980 and 1984 showed that 50% (1980) and 45% (1984) would vote in a referendum to end N.I.'s membership of the U.K. If any serious effort was made to do this, then the more important figure would be the 29% (1980) and 39% (1984) in favour of retaining N.I. within the U.K.

Chapter 9 (pp. 266–290)
1. Major Denoix de Saint-Marc, one of the leading figures in the 'Generals' revolt' against De Gaulle in 1961, interviewed in Channel 4 series on the Algerian War.
2. Ottaway, D and M.
3. Shoup; Singleton F; Clissold.
4. Fanon, 77–9 and 51.
5. Lijphart, 172.
6. This section on Lebanon is based upon: Salibi; Gordon D.C., (c); Deeb; McDowall; Owen; Tabarra; Hudson.
7. Owen, 944.
8. This section on Cyprus is based upon: Kyle; Souter; Attalides; Panteli.
9. Tabarra, 171.

Bibliography

Abraham, David, *The Collapse of the Weimar Republic. Political Economy and Crisis* (Princeton 1981)

Abun-Nasr, Jamil M., *A History of the Maghreb* (Cambridge 1971)

Adler, Max, 'The Ideology of the World War', pp. 125–35 in Tom Bottomore and Patrick Goode (eds.) *Austro-Marxism* (Oxford 1978)

Ageron, Charles Robert, *'L'Algérie algérienne' de Napoléon III à de Gaulle* (Paris 1980)

a Akenson, Donald H., *The Irish Education Experiment. The National System of Education in the 19th Century* (London and Toronto 1970)

b Akenson, Donald H., *Education and Enmity. The Control of Schooling in Northern Ireland* (New York and Newton Abbot, 1973)

a Alleg, Henri, 'Algeria', in *Political Violence in Comparative Perspective* edited by John Darby, A.C. Hepburn and N. Dodge (Belfast 1987)

b Alleg, Henri, *Etoile Rouge et Croissant Vert. L'Orient Sovietique* (Paris 1983)

Amin, Samir, *The Maghreb in the Modern World* (Harmondsworth 1970)

Andrezejewski, Marek, 'Poland vis-à-vis Gdansk Social Democrats 1918–39', *Acta Poloniae Historica*, No. 38, 1978, 131–46.

Ansbro, John J., *Martin Luther King Jr. The Making of a Mind* (Orbis 1982)

Ardrey, Robert, *The Territorial Imperative* (London 1972)

Arendt, Hannah, *The Origins of Totalitarianism* (London 1967)

Arthur, Paul, *Government and Politics of Northern Ireland* (London and New York 1984)

Asmal, Kadar (chairman), *Shoot to Kill? International Lawyers' Inquiry into the Lethal Use of Firearms by the Security Forces in Northern Ireland* (Cork and Dublin 1985)

Ath-Messaoued, Malek and Alain Gillette, *L'immigration algérienne en France* (Paris 1976)

Attalides, Michael A., *Cyprus: Nationalism and International Politics* (Edinburgh 1979)

Auger, E.A., 'Religion and Class: an Analysis of 1971 Census Data.' Ch. 2 in R.J. Cormack and R.D. Osborne (eds.) *Religion, Education and Employment* (Belfast 1983)

Aziz, Philippe, 'L'Algérie Francaise n'etait pas un utopie—une interview du colonel Antoine Argoud.' *Histoire pour Tous*, Sept./Oct. 1977, 91–3

Babic, Ivan, 'Military History of Croatia'. Ch. 4 in Francis H. Eterovich and Christopher Spalatin (eds.), *Croatia Land, People and Culture* Vol 1 (Toronto 1964)

Ball, William Watts, *The Editor and the Republic,* edited by Anthony Harrigan (Chapel Hill 1954)

Barker, Thomas, *The Slovene Minority in Carinthia* (Boulder & New York 1984)

Barritt, Denis P. and Charles F. Carter, *The Northern Ireland Problem* (London, New York and Toronto 1962)

Bartley, Numan V., *The rise of Massive Resistance* (Baton Rouge 1969)

Bass, Jack and Walter De Vries, *The Transformation of Southern Politics. Social Change and Political Consequence since 1945* (New York and Scarborough, Ontario 1977)

a Bauer, Otto, *The Austrian Revolution* (London 1925)

b Bauer, Otto, 'Fascism', pp. 167–86 in Tom Bottomore and Patrick Goode (eds.) *Austro-Marxism* (Oxford 1978)

Beckett, J.C., *The Making of Modern Ireland* (London 1972)

Behr, Edward, *The Algerian Problem* (London 1961)

Benatia, Farouk, *L'appropriation de L'espace à Alger après 1962* (Algiers 1978)

Berque, Jacques, *French North Africa. The Maghreb between two World Wars* (London 1967)

Bessel, Richard, *Political Violence and the Rise of Nazism. The Storm Troopers in Eastern Germany 1925–1934.* (New Haven and London 1984)

a Bew, Paul and Frank Wright, 'The Agrarian Opposition in Ulster Politics 1848–1887' in Samuel Clark and James S. Donnelly Jr (eds.) *Irish Peasants. Violence and Political Unrest 1780–1914* (Madison 1983)

b Bew, Paul, Peter Gibbon and Henry Patterson, *The State in Northern Ireland* (Manchester 1979)

Billington, Monroe, 'Civil Rights, Truman and the South', *Journal of Negro History,* 1973, 127

Birrell, W.D., P.A.R. Hillyard, A.S. Murie and D.J.D. Roche, *Housing in Northern Ireland* (London 1971)

Blanke, Richard, 'Bismark and the Prussian Polish Policies of 1886'. *Journal of Modern History,* June 1973, No. 2

a Boal, Fredrick, 'Segregation and Mixing: Space and Residence in Belfast'. Ch.10 in Fredrick Boal and J. Neville Douglas (eds.), *Integration and Division. Geographical Perspectives on the Northern Ireland Problem* (London and NY 1982)

b Boal, Fred and J. Neville Douglas (eds.), *Integration and Division. Geographical Perspectives on the Northern Ireland Problem*. Overview in Ch. 13 (London and NY 1982)

Bonacich, Edna, 'A Theory of Ethnic Antagonism: the Split Labour Market', *American Sociological Review.*

Boserup, Anders, *Who is the Principal Enemy? Contradictions and Struggles in Northern Ireland* (London 1972)

Bourdieu, Pierre, *Algeria 1960* (Cambridge 1979)

Bowen, Desmond, *The Protestant Crusade in Ireland* (Dublin and Montreal 1978)

Boyd, Andrew, *Holy War in Belfast* (Tralee 1969)

Boyd, Robin, 'Northern Protestants by Themselves', 20 March 1986, *Irish Times*

Boyle, J.W., 'The Belfast Protestant Association and the Independent Orange Order', *Irish Historical Studies* XIII (1962–63)

a Boyle, Kevin, Tom Hadden and Paddy Hillyard, *Law and State. The Case of Northern Ireland* (London 1975)

b Boyle, Kevin, Tom Hadden and Paddy Hillyard, *Ten Years on in Northern Ireland. The Legal Control of Political Violence* (London 1980)

Bracher, Karl D., *The German Dictatorship. The Origins, Structure and Effects of National Socialism* (Harmondsworth 1971)

Brady, Seamus, *Arms and the Men. Ireland in Turmoil* (Bray 1971)

Braithwaite, Richard and Lindsay Crawford, *Orangeism—its History and Progress—a Plea for First Principles* (Belfast 1904)

Brink, William and Louis Harris, *The Negro Revolution* (New York 1963)

Broeker, Galen, *Rural Disorder and Police Reform in Ireland 1812–36* (London and Toronto 1970)

Brogan, Denis W., *The Development of Modern France 1870–1939* (London 1967)

a Broszat, Martin, *The Hitler State* (London and New York 1981)

b Broszat, Martin, *Nationalsozialistische Polenpolitik* (1939–45) (Frankfurt (M) 1965)

Bruegel, J.W., *Czechoslovakia before Munich* (Cambridge 1973)

a Buckland, Patrick, *Irish Unionism. A Documentary History 1885–1923* (Belfast 1973)

b Buckland, Patrick, *Ulster Unionism and the Origins of Northern Ireland 1886–1922* (Dublin and New York 1973)

c Buckland, Patrick, *The Factory of Grievances. Devolved Government in Northern Ireland 1921–1939* (Dublin and New York 1979)

Budge, Ian and Cornelius O'Leary, *Belfast. Approach to Crisis* (London 1973)

Burns III, Augustus, 'Graduate Education for Blacks in North Carolina 1930–51', *Journal of Southern History* 1980, 195

Byrne, J., *An Impartial Account of the Late Disturbances in County Armagh 1784–1791* (Public Record Office of Northern Ireland)

The Cameron Report. Disturbances in Northern Ireland HMSO Cmd 532 (Belfast 1969)

The Campaign for Social Justice in Northern Ireland. Londonderry. One Man, One Vote (Dungannon 1965)

Camus, Albert, *Resistance, Rebellion and Death* (New York 1974)

Carlson, Jody, *George Wallace and the Politics of Powerlessness* (New Brunswick 1981)

Carmichael, Stokely and Charles V. Hamilton, *Black Power* (London 1968)

Carr, E.H., *The Bolshevik Revolution 1917–1923* Vol I. (Harmondsworth 1966)

Carson, Clayborne, *In Struggle: SNCC and the Black Awakening of the 1960s* (Cambridge, Mass and London 1981)

Caute, David, *The Great Fear. The anti-Communist Purge under Truman and Eisenhower* (London 1978)

Cell, John W., *The Highest Stage of White Supremacy. The Origins of Segregation in South Africa and the American South* (Cambridge 1982)

Chafe, William H., *Civilities and Civil Rights. Greensboro, North Carolina and the Black Struggle for Freedom* (New York and Oxford 1980)

Clapham, J.H., *Economic Development of France and Germany 1815–1914* (Cambridge 1961)

Clark, Kenneth B., *The Civil Rights Movement. Momentum and Organization* (Daedelus 1965) 239.

Clark, Michael K., *Algeria in Turmoil. A History of the Rebellion* (New York 1959)

Clark, Wallace, *Guns in Ulster (Belfast 1967)*

Claudin, Fernando, *The Communist Movement. From Comintern to Cominform* (Harmondsworth 1975)

Cleaver, Eldridge, *Post-prison Writings and Speeches,* edited by Robert Scheer (London 1972)

Clissold, Stephen, 'Croat Separatism: Nationalism, Dissidence and Terrorism', *Conflict Studies,* No. 103 (London 1979)

Compton, Paul, 'The Demographic Dimension of Integration and Division in Northern Ireland', Ch. 4 in Fredrick Boal and J. Neville Douglas, *Integration and Division* (London and New York 1983)

Confer, Vincent, *France and Algeria. The Problem of Civil and Political Reform, 1870–1920* (New York 1966)

Cooke, A.B., 'A Conservative Party Leader in Ulster: Sir Stafford

Northcote's Diary of a Visit to the Province in October 1883', in *Proceedings of the Royal Irish Academy* 75, sec. C, No. 4, 1975.

Coulter, E. Merton, *The South during Reconstruction, 1865–1977* (Baton Rouge 1947)

Cox, Oliver C., *Caste, Class and Race* (New York and London 1970)

a Crawford, W.H., 'The Influence of the Landlord in Ulster' in L.M. Cullen and T.C. Smout, *Comparative Aspects of Scottish and Irish Economic and Social History, 1600–1900* (Edinburgh 1978)

b Crawford, W.H., 'The Rise of the Irish Linen Industry', Chapter 2 in L.M. Cullen (ed.) *Formation of the Irish Economy*, (Cork 1969)

c Crawford, W.H. and B. Trainor, *Aspects of Irish Social History 1750–1800* (Belfast 1969)

Crowe, Charles, 'Tom Watson, Populists and Blacks reconsidered', *Journal of Negro History*, 1970, 99

Cullen, L.M., *An Economic History of Ireland since 1660* (London 1972)

Curran, Frank, *Derry. Countdown to Disaster.* (Dublin 1986)

Curry, Richard, *Radicalism, Racism and Party Alignment. The border States During Reconstruction* (Baltimore and London 1969)

a Darby, John, *Intimidation and the Control of Conflict in Northern Ireland* (Dublin 1986)

b Darby, John and Geoffrey Morris, *Intimidation in Housing* (Belfast 1974)

c Darby, John and D. Murray, 'The Londonderry and Strabane Study: Out and Down in Derry and Strabane', ch. 8 (ii) in R.J. Cormack and R.D. Osborne (eds.), *Religion, Education and Employment* (Belfast 1983)

Davis, Allison, B. Burleigh and Mary Gardner, *Deep South: A Social Anthropological Study of Caste and Class* (Chicago and London 1941)

Deeb, Marius, *The Lebanese Civil War* (New York 1980)

De Gaulle, Charles, *Memoirs of Hope. Renewal 1958–62. Endeavour 1962–* (London 1971)

Degler, Carl, *The Other South* (New York 1974)

Devlin, Bernadette, *The Price of my Soul* (London 1969)

Dickson, R.J. *Ulster Emigration to Colonial America 1718–1775* (Belfast 1976)

Dittmer, John, *Black Georgia in the Progressive Era 1900–1920* (Urbana, Chicago and London 1980)

Dollard, John, *Caste and Class in a Southern Town* (New York 1957)

Donald, David, 'The Scalawag in Mississippi Reconstruction' in Edwin Rozwenc (ed.) *Reconstruction in the South* (Lexington, Toronto and London 1972)

a DuBois, W.E.B., *Black Reconstruction in America* (New York 1962) *b* DuBois, W.E.B., *WEB DuBois Speaks*, edited by Philip S. Foner, 2 Vols (New York 1962)

Dunbar, Tony, *Our Land Too* (New York 1969)

Edmonds, Helen, *The Negro and Fusion Politics in North Carolina* (Chapel Hill 1951)

Edwards, Owen Dudley, *The Sins of our Fathers* (Dublin 1970)

Edwards, Ruth Dudley, *An Atlas of Irish History* (London 1973)

Eley, Geoff, *Reshaping the German Right. Radical Nationalism and Political Change after Bismark* (New Haven and London 1980)

Ellen, Warren, 'Who were the Scalawags?' *Journal of Southern History*, 1972, 217–40.

Emerson, Rupert and Martin Kilson, *The American Dilemma in a Changing World. The Rise of Africa and the American Negro* (Daedelus 1965)

Emmanuel, Arghiri, *Unequal Exchange: A Study of the Imperialism of Trade* (London 1972)

Esman, M.J. 'Malaysia: Communal Co-Existence and Mutual Deterrence', 227–43 in E.Q. Campbell (ed.), *Racial Tensions and National Identity* (Nashville 1972)

Eyck, Frank, *The Frankfurt Parliament 1848–9* (London 1968)

Fanon, Frantz, *The Wretched of the Earth* (Harmondsworth 1967)

a Farrell, Michael, *Northern Ireland. The Orange State* (London 1976)

b Farrell, Michael, *Arming the Protestants* (Dingle 1983)

Faulkner, Brian, *Memoirs of a Statesman,* edited by John Houston (London 1978)

Fennell, Desmond, 'The Northern Catholic, An Inquiry', (*Irish Times* 5 and 10 May 1958)

Fenton, John and Kenneth Vines, 'Negro Registration in Louisiana', in August Meier and Elliott Rudwick, (eds.), *The Making of Black America*, Vol II: *The Black Community in Modern America* (New York 1976)

Foner, Philip S., *Organized Labour and the Black Worker* (New York 1976)

Forman, James, *The Making of Black Revolutionaries: a Personal Account* (New York 1973)

a Franklin, John H., 'The Militant South', p. 250–61, in Allen Weinstein and Frank Otto Gatell (eds.), *American Negro Slavery* (London & Toronto 1973)

b Franklin, John H., *From Slavery to Freedom: a History of Negro Americans* (New York 1980)

Gallagher, Tom, 'Scottish Catholics and the British Left 1918–1936', *The Innes Review*, Vol 34 No. 1. Spring 1983

Gallagher, Eric R.D. and Stanley S. Worrall, *Christians in Ulster 1968–70* (Oxford, New York, Toronto and Melbourne 1982)

Garner, James W., *Reconstruction in Mississippi* (Baton Rouge 1968)

Garrow, David G., *Protest at Selma. Martin Luther King Jr and the Voting Rights Act 1965* (London and New Haven 1978)

Garver, Bruce M., *The Young Czech party 1874–1901 and the Emergence of a Multiparty System* (London and New Haven 1978)

a Gellner, Ernest, *Thought and Change* (London 1964)

b Gellner, Ernest, *Nations and Nationalism* (Oxford 1983)

Genovese, Eugene D., *The Political Economy of Slavery* (New York 1967)

Gerschenkron, Alexander, *Bread and Democracy in Germany* (New York 1966)

Geschwender, James A., *Class, Race and Worker Insurgency. The League of Revolutionary Black Workers* (Cambridge 1977)

Gibbon, Peter, *The Origins of Ulster Unionism* (Manchester 1975)

Gilbert, Martin, *The European Powers 1900–1945* (London 1970)

a Girard, René, *Violence and the Sacred* (Baltimore and London 1981)

b Girard, René, *Deceit, Desire and the Novel* (Baltimore and London 1976)

c Girard, René, *To Double Business Bound. Essays on Literature, Mimesis and Anthropology* (Baltimore and London 1978)

Gordon, Asa, *Sketches of Negro Life and History in South Carolina* (Columbia, SC, 1971)

a Gordon, David C., *The Passing of French Algeria* (London 1966)

b Gordon David C., *North Africa's French Legacy* (Cambridge, Mass. 1962)

c Gordon, David C., *Lebanon. The Fragmented Nation* (London 1980)

Gray, John, *City in Revolt: James Larkin and the Belfast Dock Strike of 1907* (Belfast 1985)

Hackney, Sheldon, *Populism to Progressivism in Alabama* (Princeton 1969)

a Hagen, William W., 'National Solidarity and Organic Work in Prussian Poland 1815–1914', *Journal of Modern History*, Vol 4. No. 1 1972, 38–64

b Hagen, William W., *Germans, Poles and Jews. The Nationality Conflict in the Prussian East 1772–1914.* (Chicago & London 1980)

Halévy, Elie, *A History of the English People in the 19th Century*, Six Vols (London 1961)

Hamilton, Edward K., 'On Non-Constitutional Management of a Constitutional Problem', in Stephen R Grubard (ed.) *A New America?* (New York 1978)

Harding, Vincent, 'History: White, Negro and Black', *Southern Exposure* Vol. 1 Nos. 3 and 4, 1974.

Harlan, Louis and Booker T. Washington, *The Wizard of Tuskegee*, Two Vols (New York & London 1972 and 1983)

Harris, Rosemary, *Prejudice and Tolerance in Ulster* , (Manchester 1975)

Harris, W.C., *The Day of the Carpetbagger. Republican Reconstruction in Mississippi* (Baton Rouge & London 1979)

Hartley, Anthony, *Gaullism. The Rise and Fall of a Political Movement* (London 1972)

Hastings, Max, *Ulster 1969. The Fight for Civil Rights in Northern Ireland* (London 1978)

Henderson, W.D., *Studies in the Economic Policy of Frederick the Great* (London 1963)

Henissart, Paul, *Wolves in the City. The Death of French Algeria* (London 1963)

a Hepburn, A.C., and B. Collins, 'Industrial Society. The Structure of Belfast in 1901', in Peter Roebuck (ed.), *Plantation to Partition* (Belfast 1981)

b Hepburn, A.C., 'Employment and Religion in Belfast 1901–1951', in R.J. Cormack and R.D. Osborne (eds.), *Religion, Education and Employment*, (Belfast 1983)

Hertzman, Louis, D.N.V.P., *Right-wing Opposition in the Weimar Republic 1918–24.* (Lincoln, Neb. 1963)

Hezlet, Sir Arthur, *The 'B' Specials* (London 1972)

Hitler, Adolf, *Mein Kampf,* introduced by David C. Watt (London 1974)

Hobbes, Thomas, *Leviathan* (1651), (Cambridge 1935)

Höhne, Heinz, *The Order of the Death's Head. The Story of Hitler's S.S.* (London 1972)

Holli, Melvin G., (ed.) *Detroit* (1978)

Holmes, R. Findley, *Henry Cooke.* (Belfast and Ottawa 1981)

Holmes, William F., 'Whitecapping. Agrarian Violence in Mississippi', *Journal of Southern History* 1969, 165

Horne, Alastair, *A Savage War of Peace, Algeria 1954–62* (London and Basingstoke 1977)

Howard, Perry H., *Political Tendencies in Louisiana* (Baton Rouge 1971)

Hudson, Michael C., *The Precarious Republic. Political Modernization in Lebanon* (New York 1968)

Hunter, Robert, 'Virginia', in J. Braeman, R. Bremner and D. Brody (eds.) *The New Deal,* Vol II (Columbus 1975)

Insight Team, *Sunday Times on Ulster* (Harmondsworth 1972)

Isles, K.S. and Norman Cuthbert, *An Economic Survey of Northern Ireland* (Belfast 1957)

Jaszi, Oscar, *The Dissolution of the Hapsburg Monarchy* (Chicago and London 1971)

Jones, Maldwyn Allen, *American Immigration* (Chicago and London 1960)

Joumblatt, Kamal, *I Speak for Lebanon* (London 1982)

Kelleher, David, 'The Gaines Case. The Demise of Separate but Equal', *Journal of Negro History*, 1971, 262

Kennedy, Liam and Philip Olleranshaw, (eds.), *An Economic History of Ulster 1820–1940* (Manchester 1985)

The Kerner Commission, *Report of the National Advisory Commission on Civil Disorders* (New York 1968)

Key, V.O., *Southern Politics in State and Nation* (New York 1949)

Kinder, Hermann and Werner Hilgemann, *The Penguin Atlas of World History*, Vol 2, (Harmondsworth 1978)

King, Martin Luther, Jr., *Strength to Love* (Glasgow 1980)

Kirkendall, Richard S., *A Global Power. America since the Age of Roosevelt* (New York 1973)

Kirkpatrick, R.W., 'Origins and Development of the Land War in mid-Ulster 1879–1885', p. 201–35 in F.S.L. Lyons and R.A.J. Hawkins (eds.), *Ireland Under the Union*, (Oxford 1980)

Koehl, Robert L., 'Colonialism inside Germany 1886–1918', *Journal of Modern History*, 1953, No. 3

Kousser, J. Morgan, *The Shaping of Southern Politics. Suffrage Restriction and the Establishment of the One-Party South 1880–1910* (New Haven & London 1974)

Kula, Witold, *An Economic Theory of the Feudal System. Toward a Model of the Polish Economy 1500–1800* (London 1976)

Kyle, Keith, *Cyprus. Minority Rights Group Report No. 30* (London 1984)

Laffont, Pierre, *Histoire de la France en Algérie* (Paris 1980)

Lawrence, R.J., *The Government of Northern Ireland* (Oxford 1965)

Ledeen, Michael A., *The First Duce. D'Annunzio at Fiume* (London and Baltimore 1977)

Leuchtenburg, W.E., *Franklin Roosevelt and the New Deal* (New York 1963)

Lever, Évelyne, 'L'OAS et les Pieds-Noirs', *L'Histoire* No. 43, March 1982

Lijphart, Arend, 'Consociation: the Model and its Application in Divided Societies', Ch. 6 in *Political Cooperation in Divided Societies*, edited by D. Rea (Dublin 1982)

Lottman, Herbert R., *Albert Camus. A Biography* (London 1979)

Lyons, F.S.L., *Ireland since the Famine* (London 1971)

Lyttelton, Adrian, 'Italian Fascism' in Walter Laquer (ed.) *Fascism* (Harmondsworth 1979)

Macartney C.A., *The House of Austria 1790–1918* (Edinburgh 1978)

Macaffe, W. and V. Morgan, 'Population in Ulster 1660–1760', in P. Roebuck (ed.), *Plantation to Partition* (Belfast 1981)

Maček V., *In the Struggle for Freedom* (London 1957)

Mason, W.S., *A Statistical Account or Parochial Survey of Ireland*, Three Vols (Dublin 1814, 1816 and 1819).

Mansergh, Nicholas, *The Irish Question 1840–1921* (London 1965)

Marx, Karl, *The Revolutions of 1848*, edited by David Fernbach (London 1973)

McAllister, Ian, *The Northern Ireland Social Democratic and Labour Party—Political Opposition in a Divided Society* (London and Basingstoke 1977)

McCann, Eamonn, *War and an Irish Town* (London 1980)

McDowall, David, *Lebanon. A Conflict of Minorities*. Minority Rights Group Report No. 61 (London 1983)

McKeown, Ciaran, *The Passion of Peace* (Belfast 1984)

McKeown, Michael, 'A register of Northern Ireland's Casualties 1969–80', *Cranebag*, 1980

McKittrick, David, Interview with former British officer in Northern Ireland urging withdrawal, *Irish Times* 8 March 1984

McMillen, Neil R., 'Black Enfranchisement in Mississippi. Federal Enforcement and Black Protest in the 1960s', *Journal of Southern History*, 1977, 349

Meier, August, 'Toward a reinterpretation of Booker T. Washington', in August Meier and Elliot Rudwick, *The Black Community in Modern America*, (New York 1976)

Memmi, Albert, *The Colonizer and the Colonized*, (London 1974)

Merkl, Peter H., *Political Violence under the Swastika. 581 Early Nazis* (Princeton and London 1975)

a Miller, David, 'The Armagh Troubles 1784–1795'. p. 155–91 in Samuel Clark and James S. Donnelly Jr., *Irish Peasants, Violence and Political Unrest 1780–1914* (Madison 1983)

b Miller, David, *Queen's Rebels: Ulster Loyalism in Historical Perspective* (Dublin and New York 1978)

Moore, Barrington, Jr., *Social Origins of Dictatorship and Democracy* (Harmondsworth 1977)

a Moore, John R., 'Louisiana', in J. Braeman, R. Bremner and D. Brody, *The New Deal*, Vol II (Columbus 1975)

b Moore, John R., 'The Conservative Coalition in the US Senate 1942–5', *Journal of Southern History* 1967, 368

Morrow, Ian F., *The Peace Settlement in the German Polish Borderlands*, (London 1936)

Mosse, George L., *Nazism. An Interview with Michael A. Ledeen*, (Oxford 1978)

Moxon-Browne, Edward, *Nation Class and Creed in Northern Ireland* (Aldershot 1983)

Murdzek, Benjamin P., *Emigration in Polish Socio-Political Thought* (New York 1977)

Murray, Russell, 'Political Violence in Northern Ireland 1969–1977', Ch. 12 in Fredrick Boal and J. Neville Douglas, *Integration and Division* (London and New York 1983)

Myerson, Michael, *Nothing could be Finer* (New York 1978)

Nathan, Richard P., 'The Reagan Presidency in Domestic Affairs', Ch. 3 in Frederick I. Greenstein (ed.), *The Reagan Presidency. An Early Assessment,* (Baltimore and London 1983)

Nelson, Harold A., 'The Defenders—a Case Study of an Informal Police Organization', in Antony Platt and Lynn Cooper, *Policing America* (Englewood Cliffs, NJ 1970)

a Nelson, Sarah, 'Protestant ideology considered', *British Sociology Yearbook,* No. 2 (London 1975)

b Nelson, Sarah, *Ulster's Uncertain Defenders. Protestant Political, Paramilitary and Community Groups and the Northern Ireland Conflict* (Belfast 1984)

Nolte, Ernst, *Three Faces of Fascism* (New York 1969)

Oates, Stephen B., *Let the Trumpet Sound. The Life of Martin Luther King Jr.* (New York 1982)

O'Brien, Conor Cruise, *States of Ireland* (London 1972)

O'Dowd, Liam, Bill Rolston, and Mike Tomlinson, *Between Civil Rights and Civil War* (London 1980)

Oliver, John A., *Working at Stormont* (Dublin 1978)

O'Neill, Terence, *Autobiography* (London 1972)

a Osborne, Robert D., 'The Lockwood Report and the Location of Second University in Northern Ireland', p. 167–77 in Fredrick Boal and J. Neville Douglas (eds.), *Integration and Division* (London and New York 1982)

b Osborne, Robert D., 'Voting Behaviour in Northern Ireland 1921–1977', Ch. 6, p. 137–66 in Fredrick Boal and J. Neville Douglas *Integration and Division* (London & New York 1982)

Ottaway, David and Marina, *Algeria. The Politics of a Socialist Revolution* (Berkeley and Los Angeles 1970)

Owen, Roger, 'The Lebanese Crisis: Fragmentation or Reconciliation', *Third World Quarterly,* Vol 6. No. 4, 1984, 934–49.

Panteli, Stavros, *A New History of Cyprus, from Earliest Times to the Present Day* (London and the Hague 1984)

a Patterson, Henry, 'Independent Orangeism and Class Conflict in Edwardian Belfast', *Proc. Royal Irish Academy*, Vol. 80, sec. C, No. 4, 1980.

b Patterson, Henry, *Class Conflict and Sectarianism* (Belfast 1980)

Pauley, Bruce F., *Hitler and the Forgotten Nazis. A History of Austrian National Socialism* (London and Basingstoke 1981)

Paxton, John, (ed.), *The Statesman's Year Book 1974/5* (London and Basingstoke 1974)

Pearson, Raymond, *National Minorities in Eastern Europe 1848–1945* (London and Basingstoke 1983)

Phillips, Ulrich B., *The Slave Economy of the Old South,* edited by Eugene D. Genovese, (Baton Rouge 1968)

Pickles, Dorothy, *Algeria and France* (London 1963)

Polonsky, Antony, *Politics in Independent Poland* (Oxford 1972)

a Poole, Michael A., 'Religious Displacement in the Summer of 1969', *Fortnight* 1971. *The Scarman Report*, 245–9.

b Poole, Michael A., 'Religious Residential Segregation in Urban Northern Ireland', Ch. 11 in Fredrick Boal and J. Neville Douglas, *Integration and Division* (London and New York 1982)

Potter, David M., *The Impending Crisis 1848–1861* (New York 1976)

Powdermaker, Hortense, *After Freedom. A Cultural Study in the Deep South* (New York 1969)

Pritchett, C.H., *Congress versus the Supreme Court 1957–60* (Minneapolis 1961)

Quigley, W.G.H. *et al.*, *Economic and Industrial Strategy for Northern Ireland*, H.M.S.O. (Belfast 1976)

Rabinowitz, Howard, *Race Relations in the Urban South 1865–1890* (New York 1978)

Raines, Howell, *My Soul is Rested. The Story of the Civil Rights Movement in the Deep South* (New York 1983)

Riddell, Patrick, *Fire over Ulster* (London 1970)

Robinson, Peter D., *The North Answers Back* (Belfast 1969)

a Rose, Richard, *Governing without Consensus* (London 1971)

b Rose, Richard, *Northern Ireland. A Time of Choice* (London and Washington 1976).

Rywkin, Michael, *Moscow's Muslim Challenge. Soviet Central Asia* (London 1982)

Salibi, Kamal S., *Crossroads to Civil War. Lebanon 1958–76* (London 1976)

The Scarman Report. Violence and Civil Disturbances in Northern Ireland in 1969, HMSO Cmd 566 (Belfast 1972)

Scorer, Catherine and Patricia Hewitt, *The Prevention of Terrorism Act. The Case for Repeal*, NCCL (London 1981)

Schlesinger, Arthur M. Jr., *A Thousand Days. John. F. Kennedy in the White House (London 1965)*

Scott, George, *The R.C.s. a Report on Roman Catholics in Britain Today* (London 1967)

Seaton–Watson, R.W., *A History of the Czechs and Slovaks* (London, New York and Melbourne 1943)

Senior, Hereward, *Orangeism in Ireland and Britain 1795–1836* (London and Toronto 1966)

Shea, Patrick, *Voices and the Sound of Drums. An Irish Autobiography* (Belfast 1981)

Shoup, Paul, *Communism and the Yugoslav National Question* (London 1971)

Shugg, Roger, *Origins of Class Struggle in Louisiana* (Baton Rouge 1968)

Singletary, Otis, *Negro Militia and Reconstruction* (New York, Toronto, London 1963)

Singleton, Dale, 'Poleglass. A Study of Division', p. 178–94 in Fredrick Boal and J. Neville Douglas (eds.), *Integration and Division* (New York and London 1982)

Singleton, Fred., *A Short History of the Yugoslav Peoples* (Cambridge 1985)

Slaski, Kazimierz, 'Ethnic Changes in Western Pomerania', *Acta Polaniae Historica*, Vol 7, 1962, 7–27.

Smith, Denis Mack, *Mussolini*, (London 1981)

Smyth, Calvin, 'Arkansas Reaction to Smith v. Allwright', *Journal of Negro History*, 1982, 10.

Sorel, Georges, *Reflections on Violence* (New York 1961)

Souter, David, 'An Island Apart. A Review of the Cyprus Problem'. *Third World Quarterly*, Vol 6. No. 3. 1984

Sowell, Thomas, 'Ethnicity in a Changing America', in Stephen R. Grubard (ed.), *A New America?* (New York 1978)

Stampp, Kenneth, *The Era of Reconstruction, 1865–77* (New York 1978)

Starobin, Robert S., *Industrial Slavery in the Old South* (London, Oxford, New York 1975)

Stephens, Robert, *Nasser. A Political Biography* (Harmondsworth 1971)

a Stewart, A.T.Q., *The Ulster Crisis* (London 1967)

b Stewart, A.T.Q., *The Narrow Ground. Aspects of Ulster 1609–1969* (London 1977)

Storry, Richard, *A History of Modern Japan* (Harmondsworth 1982)

Street, James H., *The New Revolution in the Cotton Economy. Mechanization and its Consequences* (Chapel Hill 1957)

Tabbara, Lina Mikdadi, *Survival in Beirut. A Diary of Civil War.* (London 1979)

Taeuber, Karl, E. and A., 'The Negro as an Immigrant Group', Ch. 9 in Ceri Peach (ed.) *Urban Social Segregation* (London and New York 1975)

Taillefer, Andre, 'L.OAS face aux Musulmans', *Histoire Pour Tous*, Sept/Oct 1977, 127–32

Taylor, A.J.P., *The Hapsburg Monarchy 1801–1918* (London 1985)

Thornton III, J. Mills, *Politics and Power in a Slave Society. Alabama 1800–1860* (Baton Rouge 1978)

Thrasher, Sue and Leah Wise, 'The Southern Tenant Farmers Union'. *Southern Exposure*, Vol 1. Nos. 3 and 4, 1974.

Tims, R.W., *Germanizing Prussian Poland* (New York 1941)

Tindal, George B., *The Emergence of the New South 1913–1945* (Baton Rouge 1967)

Tone, Theobald Wolfe, '*An argument on behalf of the Catholics of Ireland*

(1791)', in the *Life of T.W. Tone,* by himself and his son in two volumes, Vol 1 (Washington 1826)

Trelease, Allen, 'Who were the Scalawags?', *Journal of Southern History*, 1963, 445–68

Turner, Henry A. Jr., *Stresemann and the Politics of the Weimar Republic* (Princeton 1965)

Tych, Feliks, 'The Polish Question at the International Socialist Congress in London in 1896. A Contribution to the History of the Second International', *Acta Poloniae Historica*, No. 46, 1982, 97–140

Von Ossietzky, Carl, *The Stolen Republic* (Berlin 1971)

Von Riekhoff, Harald, *German-Polish Relations 1918–1933* (Baltimore and London 1971)

Wade, Richard C., 'Slavery in the Southern Cities', p. 328–41 in Allen Weinstein and Frank Otto Gatell (eds.), *American Negro Slavery* (London & Toronto 1973)

Waite, R.G.L., *Vanguard of Nazism. The Free Corps Movement in Post-War Germany 1918–1923* (Cambridge, Mass 1952)

Walker, Brian M., *Parliamentary Election Results in Ireland 1801–1922* (Dublin 1978)

Walker, Mack, *Germany and the Emigration 1816–1885* (Cambridge, Mass 1964)

Wall, Maureen, 'Catholics in Economic life', in L.M. Cullen (ed.) *Formation of the Irish Economy* (Cork 1969)

Wallace, Martin, *Drums and Guns. Revolution in Ulster* (London, Dublin and Melbourne 1970)

Wandycz, Piotr S., *The Lands of Partitioned Poland 1795–1918* (Seattle 1974)

Watt, Richard M., *The Kings Depart. The German Revolution and the Treaty of Versailles 1918–19* (1973)

West, Rebecca, *Black Lamb and Grey Falcon* (London 1982)

Weinberg, Louise, 'A New Judicial Federalism?', in Stephen Grubard (ed.) *A New America?* 129–41

Wharton, Vernon Lane, *The Negro in Mississippi, 1865–1890* (New York 1965)

Wheeler-Bennett, John W., *The German Army in Politics 1918–45* (London and Basingstoke 1980)

White, Barry, *John Hume. Statesman of the Troubles* (Belfast 1984)

Whiteside, Andrew G., *The Socialism of Fools. George Ritter Von Schönerer and Austrian Pan Germanism* (Berkeley 1975)

Whyte, John H., 'Is Research on the Northern Ireland Problem Worthwhile?' Inaugural lecture as Professor of Irish politics at Queen's University of Belfast, Jan. 1983

Wilkeson, Doxey. A., 'The Negro School Movement in Virginia', p. 259–73 in August Meier and Elliott Rudwick, *The Black Community in Modern America* (New York 1976) *a* Williams, Philip M., *Crisis and Compromise. Politics in the Fourth Republic* (New York 1966)

b Williams, Philip M., *Wars, Plots and Scandals in Postwar France* (Cambridge 1970)

Wilson, Harold, *The Labour Government 1964–1970* (Harmondsworth 1971)

Wiskemann, Elizabeth, *Czechs and Germans* (London, New York, Toronto 1938)

Wolters, Raymond, *Negroes and the Great Depression. The Problem of Economic Recovery* (Westport, Conn 1970)

a Woodward, C. Van, *Origins of the New South. 1877–1913* (Baton Rouge 1951)

b Woodward, C. Van, *The Strange Career of Jim Crow* (New York 1974)

a Wright, Frank, 'Protestant Ideology and Politics in Ulster', *European Journal of Sociology*, No. 14, 1972, 213–80

b Wright, Frank, 'The Ulster Spectrum' in David Carlton and Carlo Schaerf (eds.), *Contemporary Terror* (London & Basingstoke 1981)

c Wright, Frank, 'Communal Deterrence and National Identity in 19th Century Ulster', in *Political Violence in Comparative Perspective*, edited by John Darby, A.C. Hepburn and N. Dodge (Belfast 1987)

Wright, Gordon, *Rural Revolution in France. The Peasantry in the Twentieth Century* (Stanford and London 1968)

Wright, J.R.C., *'Above Parties'. The Political Attitudes of the German Protestant Church Leadership 1918–1933* (Oxford 1974)

Wrzesińki Wojciech, 'The Union of Poles in Germany and its Attitude toward Problems of Consciousness of Nationality, (1922–39)', *Acta Poloniae Historica*, 1969, No. 20, 52–74.

Wunderlich, Frieda, *Farm Labour in Germany* (Princeton 1961)

Zashin, Elliot, 'The Progress of Black Americans in Civil Rights', the past two decades assessed in Stephen R. Grubard (ed.), *A New America?* (New York 1978)

Zieliński, Henryk, 'The Social and Political Background of the Silesian Uprisings', *Acta Poloniae Historica*, 1972, No. 26, 73–108

Zivojinovic, Dragan R., *America, Italy and the Birth of Yugoslavia. 1917–1919* (New York and Boulder 1975)

Index